Machiavelli's Secret

Machiavelli's Secret

The Soul of the Statesman

RAYMOND ANGELO BELLIOTTI

Published by State University of New York Press, Albany

© 2015 State University of New York

All rights reserved

Printed in the United States of America

No part of this book may be used or reproduced in any manner whatsoever without written permission. No part of this book may be stored in a retrieval system or transmitted in any form or by any means including electronic, electrostatic, magnetic tape, mechanical, photocopying, recording, or otherwise without the prior permission in writing of the publisher.

For information, contact State University of New York Press, Albany, NY
www.sunypress.edu

Production, Eileen Nizer
Marketing, Michael Campochiaro

Library of Congress Cataloging-in-Publication Data

Belliotti, Raymond A.
  Machiavelli's secret : the soul of the statesman / Raymond Angelo Belliotti.
    pages cm
  Includes bibliographical references and index.
  ISBN 978-1-4384-5721-5 (hc : alk. paper)—978-1-4384-5720-8 (pb : alk. paper) 978-1-4384-5722-2 (e-book)   1. Machiavelli, Niccolò, 1469-1527—Ethics. 2. Statesmen—Psychology. I. Title.

JC143.M4B387 2015
172—dc23   2014034925

10 9 8 7 6 5 4 3 2 1

To Marcia, Angelo, and Vittoria

Chi pecora si fa, il lupo se la mangia

[Those who make themselves sheep, the wolf devours]

Contents

Preface		ix
Acknowledgments		xi
Introduction		1
Chapter 1	The Value of Patriotism	5
Chapter 2	Religion and Morality	49
Chapter 3	The Problem of Dirty Hands	83
Chapter 4	The Soul of the Statesman	131
Appendix A	Texts and Their Abbreviations	165
Appendix B	Machiavelli's Life and Times	169
Appendix C	Case Studies—Heroes and Villains	179
Notes		197
Bibliography		205
About the Author		213
Index		215

Preface

I have taught courses that include sections on Machiavelli's thought for almost four decades. One day, however, a student walked into my office and asked several unusual questions: "Does Machiavelli ever talk about the workings of the ruler's mind—his inner life, the turmoil and torment of dealing in the international sphere, and the emotional reactions he might have to difficult choices he makes while choosing to advance the interests of some of his subjects over others? What is the effect of being a Machiavellian ruler on the ruler himself?"

Although I had read most of Machiavelli's work, as well as numerous books and articles comprising the secondary literature, I had not thought deeply—well, I had not thought at all—about the questions my student posed. In addition, I had just completed a book on Dante and moral philosophy in which I discussed, among other things, the poet's view that vice was its own punishment and virtue its own reward. Dante, following Plato, chronicled the effects that performing certain actions have on the character, psyche, or soul of perpetrators. Accordingly, even if Machiavelli never explicitly discussed such issues in his writings, the questions my student lodged were highly relevant to a host of other matters: What are the emotional burdens of a Machiavellian ruler? Why would a ruler choose to bear such burdens? What reasoning would guide such a ruler in making his political choices and crafting his actions? What is the likelihood that a Machiavellian ruler could retain his soul given the paradoxical and extensive demands upon his psyche?

Such is the genesis of this work: a few questions asked by a curious undergraduate who wondered more about the emotional and mental well-being of a Machiavellian ruler than about the supposed principles of statecraft underwriting Machiavelli's political philosophy.

Acknowledgments

Numerous people contributed to this work directly or indirectly. As always, my family comes first. My wife, Marcia, provided immeasurable emotional support and critical commentary as I undertook this project. Eighteenth-century Italian playwright Carlo Goldoni wrote, "*Muore per meta chi lascia un' immagine di se stesso nei figi*" [He only half dies who leaves an image of himself in his sons]. I am fortunate to have spawned and raised a son, Angelo, who extravagantly exceeds my image in every important way. I am blessed twice by having also a daughter, Vittoria, whose unwavering sense of justice, boundless capability to love, and intense family pride are prized by all who know her. As ever, that this book will long outlive its author and my words will be available to torment my children when I am no longer here warms my spirit.

Thanks to Michael Rinella, acquisitions editor, for his faith in this project and his diligence in shepherding it through the production process. Ryan Morris deserves special praise for her superb copyediting of the text. Finally, thanks to Joanne Foeller, an expert of book formatting who corrected my numerous errors and prepared the final manuscript with unmatched efficiency and grace.

I also thank Lexington Books for their permission to reprint and adapt material from my *Niccolò Machiavelli: The Laughing Lion and the Strutting Fox* (Lanham, MD: Lexington Books, 2009).

Introduction

That Niccolò Machiavelli was one of the first major political thinkers to describe the problem of dirty hands is well-recognized. The paradox of dirty hands seemingly rests on two convictions: categorical moral prohibitions are sometimes appropriately transgressed or overridden in political and in everyday contexts, and a good person will feel and be guilty from having broken those prohibitions, while a politician embodying the excellences of his office will understand the necessity of sometimes doing so. Military and political leaders, acting on our behalf and in our name, sometimes act in ways that are incontestably condemned by the imperatives of impersonal morality, but under certain circumstances such acts prevent great harms or achieve great goods for limited constituencies to whom these agents owe special duties. In politics and elsewhere, we sense at times that a particular action is the best course to pursue, but that the efforts of our leaders nevertheless involve using means that are typically wrong, perhaps even horrifying. Statesmen must often transgress clear, paramount moral principles, and the demands of their positions rightly require them to do so. The paradox of being *morally required* by the special duties grounded in personal relationships to *violate moral standards* arising from impersonal morality seems irresolvable and deeply unsatisfying. This work grapples with and aspires to unravel the paradox of dirty hands.

Machiavelli insists that statesmen must "learn how not to be good"; that the best of them "love their countries more than their souls"; and that they "must risk their souls" in the course of executing their duties to constituents. But what is the appropriate reaction of an agent who uses "evil well"? What sort of inner life does such a person experience and endure? Machiavelli never seems to explicitly analyze or even sketch an answer to such questions. Michael Walzer undoubtedly expresses the conventional view of scholars familiar with Machiavelli's work:

> [Machiavelli] does not specify the state of mind appropriate to a man with dirty hands. A Machiavellian hero has no inwardness. What he thinks of himself we don't know. I would guess, along with most other readers of Machiavelli, that he basks in his glory. But then it is difficult to account for the strength of his original reluctance to learn how not to be good. In any case, he is the sort of man who is unlikely to keep a diary and so we cannot find out what he thinks. Yet we do want to know him; above all, we want a record of his anguish.[1]

Although Walzer's remarks undoubtedly express the conventional view of most readers of Machiavelli, the thesis of this work is that even though Machiavelli did not *explicitly* address the issue of the internal condition of statesmen, he left numerous clues in his writings that allow us to piece together the puzzle. Machiavelli's secret is that the condition of the soul of his ideal statesman is implicit in his work if only we will attend carefully to the clues he left us. The Machiavellian hero most certainly has "inwardness," and he is surely deeply affected by the evil means he must sometimes employ. This work aspires to reveal Machiavelli's clues, craft them into a coherent whole, and thereby describe and later evaluate the inwardness and even the possibility of Machiavelli's ideal statesman.

In chapter 1, "The Value of Patriotism," I state, explain, and analyze Machiavelli's highest value: patriotism. Machiavelli was convinced that patriotism was both intrinsically and instrumentally valuable. Love of and service to country vivified the human spirit, nurtured civic *virtù*, sustained a robust personal identity, and permitted human beings to pursue a deserved glory that generated a trace of immortality. I also introduce two case studies of historical leaders who thought they were using evil well in service of patriotic ends: Prime Minister Churchill and his alleged actions regarding the German bombing of Coventry, England, and President Reagan during the Iran-Contra affair.

In chapter 2, "Religion and Morality," I explain Machiavelli's complex understanding of the value and uses of religion for sound government. Machiavelli interprets God and salutary religion in accord with his patriotic and political values. I also analyze Machiavelli's view of morality. Traditional understandings of Machiavelli conclude that he separated the political from the moral realm, or that he aspired to privilege a pagan morality over a Christian morality, or that he sought to introduce an entirely new moral code. I argue that all such renderings are mistaken. Another popular view is that Machiavelli subscribed to the proposition that "the ends justify the means."

I demonstrate why that view is wrong and that Machiavelli, instead, endorsed the position that "a few ends partially excuse some typically horrifying means." Finally, I explain the crucial differences between the popular view and what Machiavelli genuinely held.

In chapter 3, "The Problem of Dirty Hands," I confront the problem of dirty hands and the solutions mainstream morality offers. I describe Machiavelli as a type of moral deontologist who concludes that statesmen who dirty their hands while discharging the duties of their offices thereby stain their souls. Although such political leaders do the right thing, all factors considered, they remain partially responsible for violating categorical moral principles. Unlike consequentialist thinkers, who fully exonerate agents who do the right thing, all factors considered, Machiavelli concludes that transgressing categorical moral principles leaves an immoral remainder. In addition, I explain how and why some excuses can only partially exonerate agents who dirty their hands. Finally, I analyze a case study in dirty hands: President Truman's decision to drop atomic bombs on Japan during World War II. I then return to the cases of Churchill and Coventry and the Iran-Contra affair and speculate as to Machiavelli's assessments of those actions. Finally, I examine Machiavelli's evaluations of a host of historical military and political leaders. In so doing, I begin to accumulate the clues that allow readers to fully understand the inner life of Machiavelli's ideal political statesman.

In chapter 4, "The Soul of the Statesman," I put the pieces of the puzzle together and describe the inner life of a Machiavellian statesman. I address the question of why a statesman should worry about losing his or her soul. Finally, I explain the critique of Machiavelli lodged by his contemporary and friend Francesco Guicciardini and conclude the work by summarizing Machiavelli's legacy.

The theses I advance in this work concerning the problem of dirty hands and the internal condition of Machiavellian statesmen are not necessarily committed to any of the following propositions:

- Machiavelli explicitly pondered the inner life of his ideal statesman, came to the conclusions I here advance, but suppressed

the information in the interests of intentional obscurantism or because of some other motivation.
- Machiavelli conceived his thoughts in ways that prefigured the history of moral theorizing: the disputes between teleology and deontology, consequentialism and absolutism, and collectivism and individualism.
- One of Machiavelli's primary concerns was arriving at philosophical truths. Another of his primary concerns was delving into the inner lives of political agents.
- My interpretation of Machiavelli reflects his original intentions and the plain meaning of his texts. Thus, the interpretation reveals Machiavelli's actual thinking about the matters discussed.
- What I call "Machiavelli's secret" reflects precisely what Machiavelli thought about the inner lives of statesmen and what he intentionally concealed. What I call "clues" are hints that Machiavelli intentionally left in order that clever readers of his work could unravel his secret.

On the contrary, the clues Machiavelli left are simply his core principles of effective political action and his observations about what is at stake when rulers act in service of the common good of their nations. I advance theses that constitute an interpretation of Machiavelli's writings. As such, I take what strike me as core Machiavellian principles and place them in the context of modern moral theory. Moreover, I draw out the implications of these principles for the inner lives of Machiavellian statesmen. That is, I ask and answer questions such as: "What is Machiavelli logically and normatively committed to regarding the problem of dirty hands and the internal condition of statesmen given his views on X, Y, and Z?" "What would be the nature of the inner life of a Machiavellian statesman given how that person is supposed to conduct himself?" Finally, I strive to advance the interpretation that coherently fits the greater part of Machiavelli's work. In sum, I aspire to cast light on an often neglected part of the Machiavellian picture, the internal condition of his ideal statesman, by extrapolating from well-explored Machiavellian themes. These implications and extrapolations constitute Machiavelli's secret. Accordingly, even if Machiavelli never actually ruminated about the inner life of his ideal statesman, we can reasonably portray the nature of that life from Machiavelli's descriptions of and prescriptions about effective political action.

1

The Value of Patriotism

The problem of dirty hands centers on how military and political leaders must often transgress clear, paramount moral principles and are rightly required to do so by the demands of their positions. The paradox of being morally required by the special duties grounded in personal relationships to violate moral standards arising from impersonal morality seems irresolvable and deeply unsatisfying. Identifying Machiavelli's highest value is critical to understanding the role of his rulers and statesmen, and constitutes the first clue in piecing together the evidence about the relationship between what such rulers and statesmen must do in fulfilling their political duties and how those actions register, if at all, changes in their souls or characters.

In my view, Machiavelli's highest value is patriotism. On several occasions he testifies that he loves his city more than his soul or that he admires those who do likewise:

> I love my native city more than my own soul. (Ltr. 331: 4/16/27)

> [So] much more did those citizens then [Florentines who united other regions and waged the War of the Eight Saints against Pope Gregory XI and his oppressive legate circa 1375] esteem their fatherland than their souls. (FH III 7)

> I am very certain that he [Cosimo Rucellai] would cheerfully have sacrificed all he had in the world, and even life itself, for his friends and that there was no enterprise, however difficult and dangerous, which he would not have undertaken for the good of his country. (AW I 7)

Machiavelli's commitment to public service, his ardor for his country, his conviction that political activity animated his soul, and his willingness to sacrifice for the public good resonate throughout his life and saturate his private correspondence:

> There is my desire that these Medici princes should begin to engage my services, even if they should start out by having me roll along a stone. . . . Whoever has been honest and faithful [especially in public service] . . . as I have, is unable to change his nature. (Ltr. 224: 12/10/13)

> Never did I disappoint that republic [Florence] whenever I was able to help her out—if not with deeds, then with words; if not with words, then with signs—I have no intention of disappointing her now. (Ltr. 270: 5/17/21)

The Final Chapter

Beyond his testimony that he loves his city more than his soul, the final chapter of *The Prince* provides Machiavelli's most eloquent expression of patriotism. He crafts the first twenty-five chapters of *The Prince* straightforwardly. Machiavelli's prose is lean, concise, and articulate, but without rhetorical flourish. He derives his conclusions supposedly from historical examples and his diplomatic experiences. He does not mourn over the supposed baseness of human beings or the series of zero-sum contests that presumably constitute international affairs. He accepts the world as it is and hopes to compile a manual for successful rule in that world. Machiavelli is understated and matter-of-fact throughout the bulk of the work.

But in the final chapter of *The Prince*, "Exhortation to Seize Italy and Free Her from the Barbarians," Machiavelli shifts rhetorical gears abruptly. He trumpets passionately that the time is ripe for a prince to unite regional forces and evict foreign dominators out of Italy once and forever. Citing the historical examples of Moses, Cyrus, and Theseus, Machiavelli points out that Italy is more enslaved than the Hebrews, more oppressed than the Persians, and more defenseless than the Athenians. Italy lacks leadership. But within grave adversity lies glorious opportunity. Once before a prince (Cesare Borgia? Pope Alexander VI? Francesco Sforza of Milan? Pope Julius II? Machiavelli himself?) had emerged who might serve as the instrument for Italian redemption, but *Fortuna* cruelly cast him aside. But now Divinity and the Church favor the Medici family: "God has already shown his hand. The sea has been divided; a cloud has escorted you on your journey; water has flowed out of the rock; manna has fallen from on high. Everything has conspired to make you great" (P 26).

Others have failed through inadequate methods and strategies, but the Medici can succeed. New methods and means are available. (Translated: Machiavelli has sketched the way and is, of course, currently between jobs and available for hire.) Italians have proved themselves cleverer, stronger, and quicker than foreigners in individual duels. Their armies have disappointed only because of inadequate leadership: too many self-styled chiefs, too few disciplined followers. No leader bearing *grandezza d'animo* [noble soul] has manifested the blessed union of *Fortuna* and *virtù* within his spirit. But now opportunity must not be permitted to evaporate. Italy awaits a redeemer: "No words can describe the appetite for revenge, the resolute determination, the spirit of self-sacrifice, the tears of emotion that would greet him. . . . What Italian would refuse to pledge him allegiance? Everyone is sick of being pushed around by the barbarians. Your family must commit itself to this enterprise" (P 26).

Unquestionably, the emotional final chapter of *The Prince* diverges sharply with the prose and texture of the rest of the text. This and other interpretive riddles are thought by some scholars to be resolved by understanding Machiavelli as a fervent Italian patriot who aspires to unveil a blueprint for Italian unification. This reading of Machiavelli gained momentum in the mid- to late nineteenth century, during and after the period of the Italian *Risorgimento*. In that vein, Pasquale Villari (1827–1917) wrote: "Machiavelli proceeds to draw his conclusions, then at last the practical side and real aim of [*The Prince*] are clearly seen. It is a question of achieving the unity of his Italian motherland and of delivering it from foreign rule. This was certainly the holiest of objects."[1] Francesco De Sanctis (1817–1883) adds: "Let us therefore be proud of our Machiavelli . . . the bells are ringing throughout the land announcing the entry of the Italians into Rome. The temporal power is falling. The shout arises, 'Long live Italian unity!' 'Glory to Machiavelli.'"[2]

On this view, *The Prince* is precisely what it presents itself to be: a manual for princely success. But that success is qualified. The new ruler should use his power to reform a corrupt, weak state as preparation for the emergence or return of a healthy, expansionist republic. The manipulative, conniving, forceful measures of the prince—exercising the subtle wiles of the fox and the frightening domination of the lion—are the prerequisites for the vigorous republic Machiavelli mythologizes in *The Discourses* and his other writings. Moreover, the prince's overarching goal is to make himself, or at least render the scope of his authority, obsolete. *The Prince*, then, is the beginning but not the end of Machiavelli's heroic account of political triumph.

According to the Machiavelli-as-patriot interpretation, *The Prince* is a manual for unification in an unsettled context. Once the monarch attains national unity, promotes the common good, and nurtures a strong national character, his power should be dispersed. Once the conditions required for a sound republic are in the place, the advice of *The Discourses* should prevail. Many supposed differences between *The Prince* and *The Discourses* can be reconciled once we understand that *The Prince* was written as a battle plan for one situation, reforming a corrupt state and unifying Italy, while *The Discourses* was a general account of Machiavelli's political philosophy and showed his appreciation for popular forms of government in those countries enjoying favorable conditions.

In Machiavelli's judgment, the five loose-knit regions of Italy were in a dire predicament in the early sixteenth century. They could either remain disunified and provide easy targets for invading barbarians, or they could follow the leadership of a strong man, rise above factional bickering, and unite for the greater good: Either continued victimization or unification. In *The Prince*, Machiavelli argues that the regionalized people of Italy were generally corrupt—they lacked civic *virtù*—so the monarch would sometimes be forced to use fraud and coercion to unify the nation, invigorate citizens, and fend off external aggressors.

Sounds peculiar, does it not? The cure for corruptness is fraud and coercion? What Machiavelli meant was that the prince, while governing, should not always abide by the standards of conventional private morality. If certain inherently evil practices had to be used, they should be thought of as "evil well-used" because they flow from necessity: external forces, antecedent events, and compelling circumstances. Necessity will often compel rulers to commit deeds that violate paramount principles of impersonal morality: cruelty, deceit, and promise-breaking are often preferable, politically, to liberality, mercy, honesty, and promise-keeping. The purpose, though, of the prince's strategies is unequivocal: He maximizes his prospects of earning enduring glory by imposing order and security, and beginning the reformation of his corrupt citizens and subjects.

Machiavelli was convinced that only an absolute monarch can transform a corrupt society. In his judgment, civic *virtù* in Italy had disintegrated, which made a popular republic impossible. *Virtù* could only be spawned through proper laws, training, and education. The corrupt, fragmented state cannot rehabilitate itself. Instead, a powerful political officer must mold it by crafting a pure social foundation based on strong arms and sound laws. The strong nation-state prevents foreign intrusions, and eventually helps citizens rise above selfish individualism, establishes communal bonds, increases the material and spiritual quality of life, and thereby cultivates personal and national *virtù*.

In *The Discourses* and in his other writings, Machiavelli praises republicanism. Only the supreme importance of achieving national unity underwrites the prince and his actions. Once this goal is attained and the nation solidified, the scope of the prince's power are contracted and a mixed government arises. Having guided the newly created nation-state from conditions of weakness to a condition of strength, the prince has made autocracy obsolete. *Virtù* is then best secured through republicanism. A Machiavellian republic has a system of checks and balances much like those that existed among the consuls, senate, and plebeians in the ancient Roman republic.

This interpretation can muster considerable textual support. First, Machiavelli consistently argues, beyond what he says in *The Prince*, that the military and political *virtù* of a single leader is crucial for founding a new regime or reforming a corrupt state (D I 9, 17, 18; D III 1). Machiavelli recurrently affirms his conviction that an autocratic leader, who often employs force and fraud to secure his ends, is a critical stage in the development of a healthy state. Romulus seizes power through aggression, but thereafter cedes authority to the people and the senate in order to facilitate republican rule.

Second, this interpretation makes sense of the emotional final chapter of *The Prince*. The stirring call to arms is nothing more than a summary of the main point of the work: to rally support for the unification and redemption of Italy. The earlier chapters of the book were the methods required to begin reforming a corrupt, newly conquered territory. The final chapter passionately expresses the overarching purpose of that yearning.

Third, this view reconciles Machiavelli's fascination with the principalities in *The Prince* with his undeniable preference for republicanism elsewhere. *The Prince* is a necessary stage of development for new or corrupt territories not yet prepared for self-government. Moreover, advocates of this view can point to textual support in *The Discourses* for Machiavelli's position that although republican rule is generally best, not all states have the prerequisites in place for self-government (D I 55).

Fourth, this interpretation underscores why a republic should, when propitious, replace a principality. Republics are more flexible than principalities, more able to adapt to changing circumstances, better equipped to conquer new territories, and, thus, more likely to endure (D I 29; D II 2, 4, 6, 9, 21; D III 9, 28). Given Machiavelli's overall political philosophy, concluding that a principality is sometimes a required stage in the process of building a forceful republic is reasonable.

Fifth, this view can account for Machiavelli's desire to seek employment with the Medici even though he was part of the former republican government of Florence. After that regime was ousted, he was suspected of participating in an anti-Medici conspiracy and was tortured thereafter. Machiavelli's job search is not crass opportunism; instead, he sought political office in order to help a new prince sow the cultural seeds that would eventually be reaped as the prerequisites for a return to republicanism. Hopefully, Italian liberation would also result. Machiavelli, then, writes *The Prince* as one more instance of his relentless public service and devotion to his country.

Sixth, in addition to the final chapter of *The Prince*, advocates of this interpretation can point to textual evidence in *The Discourses* that Machiavelli aspired to a united Italy. There he indicts the Roman Catholic Church as the perpetrator which has thwarted Italian solidarity: "No geographical region has ever been unified or happy if it has not been brought under the political control of a single republic or ruler, as has happened in France and Spain. And the only reason why Italy has not been unified as they have been, the only reason why she does not have a republic or a prince who has been able to acquire control of the whole territory, is the existence of the church" (D I 12).

The Machiavelli-as-patriot interpretation of *The Prince*, though, faces several significant objections. The most daunting is the problem of the transition. Surely Machiavelli did not suppose that a prince, after acquiring new territories and painstakingly crafting the civic *virtù* of the populace through strong arms, sound laws, and robust religion, would quietly release his power in deference to republican rule? The more reasonable dynamic is that such a prince would luxuriate in his power and privilege and, if anything, would strive for more of the same. The prince's quest, after all, begins in private ambition coupled with the recognition that tyranny does not issue in enduring glory. He must facilitate the common good and promote civic *virtù* in order to develop a healthy, expansionist regime able to compete vigorously in international military and political affairs. If he efficiently and effectively advanced these goals, would he not reason that he deserved to be honored and obeyed, not shunted aside for an experiment in self-government?

One response by advocates of the Machiavelli-as-patriot interpretation is that Machiavelli did expect the transition to go smoothly and cited history in support of that possibility. For example, he praises Romulus for establishing a senate and yielding most of his power to it, reserving only the authority to command the army after war had been declared and of convening the senate itself (D I 9). Here Machiavelli expresses his preference for a powerful prince to cede absolute control in deference to the common good. Still, for a powerful prince who gains power through force and guile, and thereby rises to prominence to willingly yield that power is highly unlikely. Why would Machiavelli entertain even the possibility of such a transition? One possibility is that he is convinced that this is what is required for a unified Italy that endures and his patriotism clouds his reasoning into hoping that Romulus types will be more common than we might suspect. Machiavelli, despite his reputation in some circles, is not a dispassionate, clear-headed realist. Instead, his patriotism often trumps his vision of reality and of the possible. This response is plausible as it underscores Machiavelli's romanticism.

If so, Machiavelli would be neither the first nor final thinker to yearn for one great man to accomplish so much or to fantasize about a smooth transition from one type of state to another radically different one. For example, in *The Statesman*, Plato describes ruling as a directive science, the ability to weave the elements of the state into a just proportion. These exemplars should rule based on their ability to nurture the souls of citizens. An ideal statesman is above the law because his wisdom is superior to the justice arising from best crafted laws. Laws are general and impersonal and will often disappoint in particular cases because they cannot adequately take into account variations of character and circumstance. The ideal statesman has only one absolute imperative: do what is wise and virtuous. Thus, he should be able to ignore or alter the law as appropriate. As always, Plato insists that the uninformed mass of people in a democracy cannot attain the expertise required for wise rule (S 292e). But the number of genuine statesmen possessing such a talent is meager, perhaps only one or two in the world (S 293a-e). Even in his most realistic rendering of politics, Plato does not entirely cast aside his longing for one great man to redeem a state.

In addition, well after Machiavelli wrote, Marxists scripted a political transition beginning with the overthrow of capitalism to a relatively strong central government to the withering away of the state under communism. They, too, brushed aside the conventional wisdom that power tends to solidify and expand rather than relinquish its own prerogatives.

Perhaps a better response on the problem of the transition from monarchy to republicanism is available to Machiavelli: For a corrupt, impotent territory to blossom into a robust state with the prerequisites for a successful, expansionist republic would take a generation or more. All princes are mortal. The bane of good government has been hereditary rule. History attests that the death of an exemplary leader is too often followed by the inept bungling of his vainglorious, feckless son (D I 2, 19). A ruler who seizes power violently should rule prudently and virtuously thereafter, and transfer authority to the masses as soon as practicable instead of retaining authority and later bequeathing it to his heirs.

Accordingly, the transition from autocratic princely control to a self-governing republic might be gradual in certain situations. Throughout the prince's lifetime the prerequisites of republican rule are nurtured through strong arms, sound laws, robust religion, and promotion of civic *virtù*. Near or at the prince's death, transfer of power from the executive office to the senate and the people should take place proportionate to the state's readiness for self-government. The process could continue until a full-fledged republic is in place. The animating impulse for the transition, as always, is self-interest. The glory of the prince is amplified by the process, and a republic is more flexible, more likely to expand, and more enduring than a principality. Both the people and the prince thereby gain by an orderly transition. The prince, especially, should understand all this given the cornerstone of his endeavors is securing power to attain enduring glory. Near death, his earthly power is about to vanish, but his quest for lasting glory is still negotiable.

My response on behalf of the Machiavelli-as-patriot interpretation offers a plausible chance that the transition from principality to republic can occur. Ancient Rome, Machiavelli's favorite historical launching pad, made the transition. Why not sixteenth-century Florence or Rome? Machiavelli does, however, place enormous importance on the value military and political leaders bestow on their historical legacies. Is the quest for enduring glory—which certainly animates Machiavelli's labors—truly paramount for men who embody military and political *virtù*?

For Machiavelli, the answer is a resounding "yes." He places little or no stock in an afterlife and the promise of eternal bliss. Men embodying *grandezza d'animo* understand that crafting a legacy of deserved, enduring glory is the only certain way of denying the Grim Reaper total victory. By lingering in the hearts and souls of future generations, by inspiring those who follow to grander deeds than they might otherwise aspire to, and to thereby continue to serve the highest values of patriotism and political excellence, the greatest among us can extend their biographical lives honorably. No human can overcome biological mortality, but some military and political exemplars—as well as founders of salutary religions, estimable literary figures, and those who register excellence in their chosen fields—can transcend their deaths. Future generations will celebrate their accomplishments, seek to emulate their methods, and benefit from their examples. Death must extinguish all human beings, but it cannot always quash the most important values or the ongoing influence of the greatest among us. If personal immortality is unavailable to us, as Machiavelli strongly suspects, then our last best hope is to craft our lives and sculpt our souls in ways that maximize our prospects for attaining deserved, enduring glory. If Machiavelli is correct, this must be enough, for this is all finite human beings can realize.

Nevertheless, a critic might raise a second objection: the problem of the transition is secondary to the difficulty of unification. The entrenched tradition of preserving the independent power of individual regions in Italy was too strong to sustain even a dream of permanent unification. The self-interest of regional power brokers and the self-image of vested aristocrats depended on their influence within their domains. Italian unification entailed that regional prerogatives would yield to national priorities. Suppose Machiavelli himself had to choose between either a united Italy headed by, say, Rome or the status quo with a strong, independent Florence? Would "his country" not be deemed Florence?

Conversely, the trajectory of Machiavellian politics is toward a united Italy. Suppose Florence or Rome, through the Medici power connection, became strong enough to begin acquiring new territories. Every robust principality or republic has expansionist aspirations, according to Machiavelli (P 3; D II 2, 4, 6, 9; D II 21). Where are the most likely prospects for expansion? Where did the Ancient Romans first expand? Not in South Africa, China, or the East Indies. Not in France or Spain, at least not in the beginning. The vital expansionist state would, almost necessarily, start in Italy by bringing less powerful regions under its domain. Perhaps after initial successes brought larger, stronger armies with more experience and confidence, even those ubiquitous Spaniards could be dislodged from the Kingdom of Naples.

Granted, huge differences separate (1) the regions of Italy uniting voluntarily and freely in common cause, and forming a nation-state once and forever from (2) one strong region emerging and conquering the other areas. In both cases the peninsula would be under one centralized government, but the tone and tempo would be much different.

My point, though, is that the debate about what type of unified Italy, if any, Machiavelli imagined should be informed by his general political principles. From his vantage point the most glorious climax would be a united Italy, led by Florence with Machiavelli as chief *consigliere*, which could begin expanding beyond Italy. The next best choice would be a united Italy, led by Rome with Machiavelli as chief *consigliere*. In any case, with or without Florence, Rome, or Machiavelli, the logic of Machiavelli's political principles implied that a united Italy was the natural result of the emergence of a strong principality or republic on the peninsula. Contemporary political conditions, regional traditions, and a hostile Church protective of its own privileges notwithstanding, a version of Italian unification would eventually transpire. That the blessed event would not occur until more than 340 years after Machiavelli's death attests to the might of *Fortuna*, the power of regional identification, and the recalcitrance of the Church.

My view, then, is that Machiavelli is committed to a transition from princely to republican rule because the bulk of his writings—virtually everything other than *The Prince* celebrates republicanism as the superior form of government. Those who conclude otherwise must take *The Prince* as Machiavelli's foundational text and his other writings as either pure dissimilitude or expressing views other than his own. In addition, I am convinced Machiavelli harbored vague but genuine hopes for Italian unification. In retrospect those aspirations seem unrealistic, but I do not perceive Machiavelli as a hard-headed realist. Also, the notion that Machiavelli wrote even *The Prince* only in order to celebrate the ongoing power of a self-serving ruler lacks merit. Even in that book Machiavelli distinguishes evil well-used from evil ill-used; castigates certain rulers for their excesses; advises leaders on how to attain the enduring glory of a heroic, political exemplar as opposed to the infamy of a tyrant; and calls on a champion to unite Italy for the good of all.

In any case, readers need not subscribe to my analyses of the interpretive problems surrounding Machiavelli's writings to agree that Machiavelli's highest value is patriotism, which is the point I wish to establish in this chapter. The objections I raised against and tried to answer on behalf of the Machiavelli-as-patriot interpretation of *The Prince* center on whether Machiavelli's apparent account of the transition from a monarchy to a republic is plausible, whether Italian unification was possible in the historical context within which Machiavelli wrote, and whether the quest for enduring glory was sufficient motivation for a prince to prefigure republicanism. If readers conclude that the problem of transition was not insurmountable and that unification was possible at the time that Machiavelli wrote, then they will judge that Machiavelli was a patriot who rendered timely advice in *The Prince*. If readers conclude that the problem of transition was insuperable or that the possibilities of unification were nil, then they will conclude that either Machiavelli did write the work as an expression of patriotic zeal but he was deluded, or that he wrote *The Prince* for reasons other than to ignite nationalistic fervor.

Only those in this final group raise a problem for the major theses about Machiavellian leaders and the condition of their souls that follow in this work. But the problem is minor and easily quarantined. Those readers of Machiavelli who (wrongly in my view) take *The Prince* to be the foundational work that expresses the Florentine's deepest preferences for monarchy, who deny that Machiavelli would urge a transition from a monarchy to a republic, who reject the proposition that princes would be motivated by a quest for enduring glory, and who insist that a Machiavellian prince secures power only or primarily for purposes of self-aggrandizement that conflict with nurturing the common good can consider what I say about the soul of Machiavellian statesmen to pertain only to republican leaders and not to Machiavellian princes as these critics conceive them to be.

But I am not aware of any scholar who calls Machiavelli's own patriotism into question. Thus, one could deny that the Machiavelli-as-patriot interpretation of *The Prince* is persuasive, but accept the conventional view that Machiavelli was a fervent patriot.

The fundamental question, then, is why Machiavelli embraced patriotism as his highest value. My answer is that Machiavelli concluded that patriotism was both intrinsically and instrumentally valuable because of the need to develop civic *virtù*, the nature of the world, the requirements of personal identity, the importance of personal security, and the nature of the quest for deserved glory.

The Need to Develop Civic *Virtù*

According to Machiavelli, human beings are naturally evil and will follow wicked impulses whenever possible (D I 3, 4, 5, 29; D II 13, D III 6). Some men can conceal their nature for a specified time, but their wantonness will eventually emerge. Only necessity—in the form of sound laws, good habits, and external conditions—makes men good. Necessity forces human beings to respond intelligently to external conditions and to rise above their inherent selfishness. Machiavelli consistently judged that human nature was so inclined toward evil that people were turned to the good only by necessity (D I 3). Also, necessity often demands action that reason would oppose (D I 6).

Machiavelli does not stray from his cold portrayal of unchanging human nature. The only hope for civilized arrangements is coercion, either explicit or subtle: by external conditions; the force of strong arms, which is the prerequisite for good laws; the reinforcing powers of religion and education; and the internalization of values that are first viewed as impositions, then accepted as legitimate boundaries of action. All these mechanisms lead to good habits where actions conducive to a healthy republic become, literally, a second nature. Only in this fashion, through discipline grounded ultimately in military might, does depraved human nature blossom into a national character embodying civic *virtù*.

For any such transformation to happen, human beings must have capabilities for altruism or, at least, enlightened self-interest. Machiavelli never highlights those capabilities. Surely, they are not created *ex nihilo*. But instead of seeing human beings as complex organisms of diverse potentials, some good and some bad, Machiavelli insists that fundamentally we are wicked. This jaundiced view of human nature fuels his corollary belief that the overall amounts of good and bad, and *virtù* and corruption in the world are constant; only their distributions in particular countries and peoples change (D II pref.). Together with the inherent scarcity of natural resources, these two convictions lead Machiavelli to the dreary conclusion that international affairs are a series of zero-sum contests: my country's advance is made at your country's expense.

The rule that men act appropriately only from necessity has a few exceptions: those with glistening military and political *virtù*—such as founders or reformers of territories—embody the resources of will, passion, and ambition required to pursue magnificent military and political enterprises. They are able to distinguish pursuing power for narrow ambition from striving for enduring glory. Such men, graced with *grandezza d'animo*, become, with a measure of compatible *fortuna*, legends (D I 9).

Founders and reformers introduce new policies, laws, and social patterns. Most important, they transform citizens through a necessity whose ballast is strong arms, compelling laws, and vigorous religion. In this manner, men of political and military *virtù* bend evilly inclined human beings toward the common good. Founders and reformers, with their unwavering eye on enduring glory, aspire to create a political order that endures beyond their lifetimes and that energizes civic *virtù* among the people. Unlike tyrannies that neither transform citizens in salutary ways nor endure for a significant period, praiseworthy principalities and republics are self-consciously redemptive (P 8; D I 10). Paradoxically, the quest for enduring glory and national salvation blends uneasily with the brutal, ruthless measures Machiavelli warmly endorses. Moreover, men graced with moral *virtù* do not typically resort to the cruelties required to found and reform worthy social orders; nor do they yearn to be political saviors. Evil men, on the other hand, are unlikely to covert corruption into civic *virtù* (D I 18, 26). From the outset, the emergence of an ideal Machiavellian statesman is problematic.

The rare founder or reformer Machiavelli venerates is a good, strong man with exceptional charisma. He must inspire his subjects by the manner in which he lives and the aplomb with which he wields military and political authority (D III 1). Most strikingly, he must brandish evil well even though he is not initially inclined to do so. He must knowingly dirty his hands in service to his own enduring glory and the common good. That several of Machiavelli's exemplars are mythological figures should not surprise.

The Role of *Virtù*

Few words in a political text have generated as much controversy as Machiavelli's use of the term "*virtù*." Typically translators caution readers not to associate the term with moral virtue. That warning, though, is misleading because at times Machiavelli does speak of moral *virtù*. This, however, is not the primary way he uses the term. *Virtù* has been, more or less accurately, translated as efficiency, skill, strength, excellence, discipline, manliness, admirable qualities, ability, virtue, effectiveness, will power, exceptional qualities, vigor, greatness, courage, intelligence, and a host of related attributes.

Machiavelli's rendering of *virtù* is complicated because he readily includes three sometimes conflicting qualities into the general understanding of that term: (1) discharging excellently one's functions, whatever they may be; (2) demonstrating virility through exercising power, autonomy, and resoluteness; and (3) practicing moral rectitude as understood by conventional morality grounded in Christianity. Accordingly, those who seek to interpret *virtù* univocally foster ambiguity and confusion. To remedy that potential problem, I prefer to discuss five senses of the term that reflect to varying degrees the three qualities contained in the general understanding of it: military *virtù*, political *virtù*, civic *virtù*, moral *virtù*, and artistic *virtù*.

Consider the English word "good." We are familiar with good people, good books, good knives, good cooks, good sex, good cars, good presentations, good times, good athletes, good singers, good teachers, and the like. "Good" sometimes but not always connotes "moral rectitude." At other times, "good" describes a person, event, or object that performs its function well. The word "excellent" does the same. In ordinary discourse we are rarely confused because context determines the meaning of such words. For example, we do not scratch our heads in puzzlement over how a car can manifest moral goodness. We understand, instead, that a good car is a vehicle that rarely breaks down, runs smoothly, and is easy to maintain.

A critic might object: "If Machiavelli intended *virtù* to connote different qualities for politicians, militarists, artists, and the like, why did he not use a different term for each or at least different modifiers to highlight such differences?" My response is how could *virtù* not connote different qualities in different contexts? The most general meaning of the term is virtue, understood as excellence in discharging one's functions. Are not the virtues of an excellent artist different from those of an excellent politician, an excellent teacher, an excellent warrior, and the like? But why did he not use different modifiers to distinguish civic *virtù* from military *virtù* from artistic *virtù*, and so on? Classical writers were rarely that precise. For example, most of the Socratic paradoxes arise from Plato's use of the same term ("knowledge") in different senses or contexts: deep theoretical understanding of the Forms; truths generated from philosophical dialectic; wisdom arising from divine inspiration; and knowing-that and knowing-how gained from worldly experiences. Machiavelli recognizes various types of excellences appropriate to different roles and uses the same general term for them. This is typical of classical writers who were much less precise than contemporary analytic philosophers. (That Machiavelli was often imprecise in this sense is also attested to by the dozens of radically different interpretations of the meaning of his work that have emerged throughout the centuries. For an example of how loosely Machiavelli used the term *virtù*, review what he says about Agathocles of Sicily in *The Prince*.)

Accordingly, for Machiavelli, *virtù* connotes an excellence relevant to a person's function. Human beings inhabit a world of scarce resources and keen competition that coalesces uncomfortably with our bottomless ambitions and passions. Worse, we are susceptible to the whims of *Fortuna*, which often conspire against our best-devised stratagems. Only people embodying *virtù* are able to cope with *Fortuna*, confront adversity with renewed purpose, imagine and pursue grand deeds, and maintain their resolve and passion in a relentlessly competitive world.

Fortuna always affects human actions by limiting possibilities and foiling the most assiduous calculations. But human free will and *virtù* retain vibrancy and permit us the agency to conceive and assess our deeds regardless of the constraints of necessity and the machinations of *Fortuna*. Still, the presence of necessity and *Fortuna*, along with the behavior of other human beings and the nature of the world, often render strict compliance with morality impossible. At most, however, the presence of necessity and *Fortuna* generate only partial excuses for human action. We remain largely responsible for our deeds. As such, *virtù* and necessity are codependent. Where necessity constrains possibilities and thereby narrows the range of human choice, *virtù* becomes paramount in making the proper decision and choosing the best alternative. The power of necessity, then, tills the fertile soil for the testing of human *virtù*.

Specifically, Machiavelli refers to military *virtù*, political *virtù*, civic *virtù*, moral *virtù*, and artistic *virtù* (P 7, 8, 12, 14, 15, 19, 21,

25, 26).³ The qualities of excellence defining each type will differ. Military commanders require discipline, bravery, single-mindedness, drive, skill, energy, knowledge, and the boldness to ignore conventional morality when necessary. Political leaders need many of the same qualities, but also a special shrewdness and prudence in dealing with foreign threats and internal plots. The attributes of the lion, in order to frighten wolves, and the fox, in order to evade traps, are crucial (P 18). Civic *virtù* is the hallmark of a sound republic. Citizens, initially motivated by self-interest and personal aggrandizement, are shaped by good laws, strong arms, and sound education into serving the common good of an expansionist state. By moral *virtù*, Machiavelli means exercising the values of conventional, impersonal morality. Artistic *virtù* defines excellence in literature and the arts. The greatest men—those able to found, reform, preserve, and expand healthy political units—must exude military and political *virtù*. Such leaders must effectively measure the prevailing situation; reflect on the available choices, priorities, and probable consequences; and act decisively and successfully. Citizens in a healthy political unit must exhibit civic and moral *virtù* if the unit is to continue to flourish.

Clearly for Machiavelli the most important forms are military and political *virtù*. A sound political unit, grounded in good laws and strong arms, is a prerequisite for the rigorous education needed to promote civic and moral *virtù*. The opposite of *virtù* is corruption. Corruption for Machiavelli is weakness: *ozio* [sloth or idleness], civic and moral decay, lack of discipline, softness, timidity, muted will, resignation, inability to compete, hesitancy, indecisiveness, an *animo effeminato* [effeminate soul].

Much ink has been exhausted discussing Machiavelli's description of the notorious Agathocles of Sicily, King of Syracuse. Within the space of a few sentences, Machiavelli seems to contradict his own words:

> One ought not, of course, to call it *virtù* to massacre one's fellow citizens, to betray one's friends, to break one's word, to be without mercy and without religion. By such means one can acquire power but not glory. If one considers the *virtù* Agathocles demonstrated in braving and facing down danger, and the strength of character he showed . . . then there seems to be no reason why he should be judged less admirable than any of the finest generals. But on the other hand, his inhuman cruelty and brutality . . . mean it would

be wrong to praise him as one of the finest of men . . . one can attribute neither to fortune nor to *virtù* his accomplishments, which owed nothing to either. (P 8)

At first blush, the paragraph seems rife with contradictions. Did Agathocles embody and exercise *virtù* or not? But these contradictions can be dissolved by distinguishing the various types of *virtù* Machiavelli invokes. I interpret the passage as attributing military *virtù* to Agathocles, in response to his undeniable courage and resolve in rising up through the military ranks and seizing power. He lacked, however, political *virtù* because he misused power and meted out gratuitous cruelties. Also, he was without civic and moral *virtù*. Agathocles exercised military *virtù* through which he seized power, but we should not attribute his transient success to luck or to political *virtù* or to moral *virtù*. As an aside, Machiavelli claims that the "finest of men" are not inhumanely cruel and that acquiring power is not enough to merit glory. He preserves a distinction between tyrants and princes. A concern for enduring glory should inform a ruler's deeds. Such glory must be deserved and cannot be grounded in misuse of authority or needless cruelties. Enduring, deserved glory embodies a normative dimension that distinguishes it from mere notoriety:

> And though able, to their perpetual honor, to set up a republic or a kingdom, [infamous and detestable men] turn to a tyranny. Nor do they realize how much fame, how much glory, how much honor, security, quiet, along with satisfaction of mind, they abandon by this decision and into what great infamy, censure, blame, peril, and disquiet they run. . . .
>
> Truly if a prince is seeking glory in the world, he should wish to possess a corrupt city, not to ruin it wholly like Caesar but to reform it like Romulus. Truly the heavens cannot give a great opportunity for glory, nor can men desire a greater. (D I 10)

In contrast to my interpretation of Machiavelli on Agathocles, Harvey Mansfield argues that "Agathocles has *virtù* but cannot be said to have *virtù*. It is not enough to say that [Machiavelli] uses the word in different 'senses'; he uses it in two contradictory senses as to whether it includes or excludes evil deeds. What could be more clear, more essential, and more inconsistent than that?"[4]

Mansfield's outrage misses the mark. Surely moral *virtù* almost always excludes evil deeds (although extreme cases require choices between degrees of evil or demand evil well-used). Just as surely, military and political *virtù* include "evil well-used" (P 8). At times, military and political leaders must transgress categorical moral principles in order to advance their highest goals: founding, reforming, preserving, and expanding a worthy state. In the following chapters these distinctions become clearer. That one form of *virtù* aspires to exclude evil deeds but other forms of *virtù* include evil well-used is no more a contradiction than saying that while a good knife cuts sharply a good doctor heals cuts is a contradiction.

The more troubling aspect of the chapter arrives later when Machiavelli, after earlier stigmatizing the excessiveness of Agathocles's methods, includes Agathocles among those who used evil well: "Those who use cruelty well may indeed find both God and their subjects are prepared to let bygones be bygones, as was the case with Agathocles" (P 8). One possibility is that Machiavelli takes Agathocles to have used evil well in military matters, but to have used evil wrongly in political matters. Beginning from humble origins, Agathocles rose to military power and displayed *virtù* in so doing, which required evil well-used. His political career, however, was marred by excesses, cruelties, and betrayals that Machiavelli derides. In short, Agathocles was a political destroyer of his city, a tyrant. That Agathocles was ruthless in obtaining military power does not faze Machiavelli; that Agathocles was excessively cruel once he had political power—that he acted as a tyrant instead of a Machiavellian ruler—merits condemnation. Agathocles, lacking prudence, represents ravenous ambition untempered by an understanding of what constitutes enduring glory.

The question arises whether the freedom and well-being of the citizens in a republic are merely means to the fundamental purposes of the state: the enduring glory of military and political leaders, and the historical grandeur of the nation. Because the common good and individual liberty are requirements for the enduring glory of leaders and the lasting stature of the nation, I conclude their relationship is tighter than that between an end and a means. Part of the definition of the enduring glory of leaders and national grandeur is the extent to which they facilitate the common good and nurture civic *virtù*. This is the case regardless of the conscious intentions upon which the leaders acted. Political leaders must renounce the selfish motivations of tyrants and act from enlightened self-interest, which benefits their citizens and subjects.

The ends of the state are the personal glory of the prince and the enhanced well-being of the citizens (P 26). Machiavelli is clear in *The Prince* and even more emphatically in *The Discourses* that these ends require territorial expansion (P 3, 7; D II 2, 4, 6, 9, 21). Numerous commentators have concluded that the well-being of citizens is only a means to the glory of the ruler, which is paramount; that the personal power of the prince, not the good of the state or the people, is the only true goal of a Machiavellian ruler.[5]

Such a reading is unfair. Rulers earn glory because they have founded, reformed, preserved, or expanded healthy states. A healthy state has strong arms, sound laws, and rigorous education. The state must expand because on Machiavelli's uncompromising worldview the only other choice is enslavement. True, rulers burn with *ambizione* [ambition] and unabashedly aspire to enduring glory, but such glory can be attained only by invigorating the state and enlarging the common good.

Does it follow that the well-being of citizens is only a regrettable, but required, means to what rulers really want? The connection between attaining glory and benefiting the people is too tight to separate neatly. The ruler's deepest aspiration springs, true enough, from self-interest. But he comes to understand that what is in his self-interest cannot be gained selfishly. If selfishness is ignoring the interests of others when one should not, then the ruler must shun it in order to satisfy his self-interest in enduring glory. That one cannot, in Machiavelli's view, attain glory selfishly speaks volumes. Achieving personal glory and advancing the common good are inextricably connected. From the standpoint of the people, the pursuit of glory by the statesman is inseparable from attaining the common good. None of this assumes that the leader has purely altruistic motives or even that his heart necessarily aches for the plight of his people. But a Machiavellian ruler must rise above selfishness, must recognize the inexorable connection between advancing the well-being of the people and attaining personal glory, and must, accordingly, cast aside all inclinations toward tyranny. Accordingly, the well-being of citizens is part of the *definition* of personal glory, rather than merely a means of attaining it.

Those who are tyrants come to power having already lost their souls. Concerned only with their own aggrandizement, tyrants ignore the common good and "do not even realize how much reputation, glory, honor, security, peace of mind, and satisfaction of spirit they are giving up" (D I 10). Tyrants mistakenly take one-person rule to be an end in itself instead of a means to facilitate collective well-being.

Machiavelli's invocation of glory strikes me as presupposing the audience of history. The masses are too easily fooled by results; they judge only by the outcomes of actions, much of which can hinge on the whims of *Fortuna*. Thus, the approbation of the masses is an unreliable measure of greatness. But the judgments of history, as defined by the more sophisticated evaluations of the learned that are detached from the immediacy of the moment, are more trustworthy. A more refined analysis than that offered by the impressionable masses is required to identify those exemplars who deserve enduring glory.

However, even the honorable pursuit of glory by those of *grandezza d'animo* is secondary to the value of patriotism: "When it is absolutely a question of the safety of one's country, there must be no consideration of just or unjust, of merciful or cruel, of praiseworthy or disgraceful; instead, setting aside every scruple, one must follow to the utmost any plan that will save her life and keep her liberty" (D III 41).

No political community, however, endures forever (D III 5). Decline and corruption are inevitable as nations become victims of their own success and fall prey to corruption. The lack of vigorous enemies, the seductive comforts of *ozio*, the caprices of *Fortuna*, and annoying class strife will conspire against permanent domination (D III 1). Nations, like all living organisms, are born to suffer and perish. But within the process lie possibilities for the only prize worth striving for: enduring glory, the recognition that certain individuals and political communities are more than a cut above the others. This, again, is the reward Machiavelli offers to those who heed his advice.

The Nature of the World

Machiavelli envisioned international affairs as grounded in a zero-sum context. He is convinced that the world is always in the same overall condition: the total amount of *virtù* and total amount of corruption is constant. What changes is the distribution of *virtù* and corruption in individual territories. He explains reallocations that have occurred throughout history and concludes that contemporary Italians and Greeks who admire the past and decry the present have a point. Their past was more glorious than their present. The masses generally lack civic *virtù* as they disrespect religion, law, and military service. Political leaders are even worse. They expect to be honored as divinities even though they are feckless commanders. Yes, the overall *virtù* in Italy and Greece has declined, but not the amount in the world. While contemporary Italians and Greeks compare unfavorably to the greatness of their ancestors, to conclude that the good old days as such were better on the whole than the present is an error: Only the distribution of *virtù* and corruption has changed (D II pref., 5; D III 43). "I judge that the world has always gone on in the same way and that there has been as much good as bad, but that this bad and this good have varied from land to land . . . but the world remained the same. There was only this difference, that whereas the world first placed excellence in Assyria, she later put it in Media, then in Persia, and finally it came to Italy and Rome" (D II pref.).

Human desires and appetites, left unfettered, are insatiable. We want more and more, but resources are limited by natural scarcity. Frustration and disappointment are the inevitable result (D II pref.; D III 21). Although Machiavelli does not draw out the implications, they are clear. One implication is that human desires cannot remain unfettered. Instead, they must be channeled into constructive outlets with possible fulfillments. Left to our natural inclinations we are doomed: the world will neither answer our implorations nor satisfy our expectations. The second implication is stark: The world is a competitive battleground for *virtù*. The success of one country must come at the expense of other countries. Activities such as pacifism weaken a country's military and civil order thereby inviting attack from stronger nations. Also, to remain regionally fragmented is to ensure limited success, vulnerability to the domination of others, and insufficient *virtù*. Either a strong nation-state must be formed or one region must be strong enough to conquer the others. Only then can the state become a successful player in world affairs. A country does not have a realistic option of withdrawing from the game. Even if it wants to retreat to peaceful self-sufficiency, other nations will not permit the choice (D III 2). Either the country gains respect through flexing its *virtù* or it will be humiliated and subjugated (D I 38; D II 13, 14, 15). Accordingly, world affairs are a series of zero-sum contests generated by the *ambizione* driving human nature, conditions of natural scarcity, and the constant total amount of overall *virtù*. Paradoxically, the entire zero-sum game is jeopardized when one nation becomes so dominate that others cannot effectively compete. Under such circumstances, the dominant nation tends toward corruption because of the lack of worthy enemies to test and sharpen its collective military and political *virtù* (AW II 77–81; D I 53).

Machiavelli's message is as cold as steel tempered too hard. The world is a competitive battleground. A nation's choices—unless it is astonishingly insignificant—are to expand or to be subjugated. The bluff, guile, courage, knowledge, and panache of a political leader must be backed by strong arms. Conditions of scarcity, the basic nature of human beings, the rush for glory by those with *grandezza d'animo*, and the relentless whims of *Fortuna* compel the need to triumph or to be destroyed. The call for enduring peace is a tinny hustle. A longstanding peace lures citizens into *ozio*—the indolent, soft, undisciplined, unworthy life—where leisure and the pursuit of luxury are paramount (D III 16). Whereas for Socrates the unexamined life is not worth living, for Machiavelli an unadventurous, unheroic scramble for *la dolce vita* is no life at all. *Ozio*, the lack of heroic action, and a deficiency of *virtù* lead to political ruin (D II 30).

Machiavelli's account prefigures Nietzsche's rendition of the will to power. For Machiavelli, *grandezza d'animo* is not fulfilled unless it confronts struggle, resistance, and opposition. Pursuing power, in the sense of increasing influence and strength, requires intentionally seeking and actually discovering obstacles to overcome. Indeed, *grandezza d'animo* is a will to the precise activity of struggling with and overcoming obstacles. Given the structure of the world and the nature of human beings, finding obstacles and encountering struggle is not difficult. Because suffering and pain attend the experience of such struggle, *grandezza d'animo* must desire suffering as a means to its own nourishment. The resulting paradox is that the fulfillment of *grandezza d'animo*—the overcoming of resistance—results in dissatisfaction as the struggle has (temporarily) concluded. *Grandezza d'animo* actually requires obstacles to the satisfaction of its specific desires because beyond specific desires, *grandezza d'animo* has a more fundamental desire to struggle with and overcome obstacles. In sum, *grandezza d'animo* deeply desires resistance to the satisfaction of its own specific first-order desires.

Accordingly, like Nietzsche's will to power, *grandezza d'animo* cannot embrace final serenity or permanent fulfillment. The satisfaction of one specific desire brings both fulfillment, a feeling of increased strength and influence, and dissatisfaction, as resistance has been overcome and is no longer present. Only endless striving and continual conquests fuel *grandezza d'animo*. Machiavelli, then, embraces the criterion of power: exertion, struggle, and suffering are at the core of overcoming obstacles; human beings experience, genuinely feel, and increase their power only through overcoming obstacles; and vigorous engagement in this process measures, amplifies, and refines *virtù*.

But why the overall amount of *virtù*, a standard of success for those with *grandezza d'animo*, must remain constant is a puzzle. Only if *virtù* is defined entirely by successful outcomes, by political and military wins as opposed to losses, can this be the case. Otherwise, even when one country wins and another loses, both could demonstrate *virtù*, although one may be superior to the other. This is a possibility that Machiavelli seems to allow because he generally disparages those who judge deeds only by their results instead of by their principles of action and quality of performance. He disapprovingly observes that the multitude is misled by appearances and outcomes (D III 35; D I 9; P 18). "As to the actions of all men and especially those of princes, against whom charges cannot be brought in court, everybody looks at their result. So if a prince succeeds in conquering and holding his state, his means are always judged honorable and everywhere praised, because the mob is always fascinated by appearances and by the outcome of an affair" (P 18).

Moreover, exercising *virtù* is no guarantee of success or glory (D III 30). Surely one man or an entire country can display admirable amounts of *virtù* but lose a military contest or political event through bad luck, unfavorable circumstances, or the greater *virtù* of the opponent. The result—a military or political loss—should not prove a lack of *virtù* as such. Boldness, energy, valor, and intelligence do not perish merely because they fail their purpose. If so, then the overall amount of *virtù* in the world could increase even though the sum total of military and political wins and losses remained constant. Machiavelli neither entertains nor resolves this puzzle.

We should pay heed that Machiavelli's "world" was limited: the five major regions of Italy, France, Spain, Turkey, Switzerland, and regions of Germany constituted his "international battleground." Obviously, communication, transportation, science, and technology were primitive. Wars, themselves, were mild affairs compared to the devastation of the world wars of the twentieth century and the current possibility of nuclear annihilation. In his *Florentine Histories*, Machiavelli presents a stirring account of the Battle of Anghiari in 1440 in which Florence preserved its domination in Tuscany. He notes that the fighting raged for about twenty-four hours with only one casualty: a soldier fell off his horse and was trampled to death (FH V 33).[6] Whether war would seem so necessary and heroic to him under conditions in the twenty-first century is doubtful.

For Machiavelli military conquest, especially when plausibly evaluated as the victory of heroic *virtù* over an irredeemably corrupt enemy, vivifies a nation. It presents opportunities for expression of the deepest human emotions, and, indeed, demands their revelation: unspeakable sadness and grief as loved ones perish; justified rage at the acts of the enemy and vows of vengeance; undeniable experiences of history-making, of leaving footprints as one participates courageously in a grand epic; intense spasms of self-esteem as precarious occasions to prove oneself to self and intimates have been encountered and surpassed; and soul-searing intimacy as collective efforts at rebuilding national infrastructure transform the world, as in one's youth, to a forum of seemingly infinite possibilities.

Of course, military defeat produces our deepest feelings of shame: a lingering sense of historical impoverishment; convictions of inferiority, betrayal, and divine abandonment; a profound understanding of failure. The world becomes, as in one's terminal moment, a place without hope, pity, or compassion.

That so many people who have encountered large-scale war describe that time as their defining moment, as the extended period when they felt most alive is unsurprising. Much was at risk. Apathy and collective narcolepsy were impossible. Prostrate, complacent faithlessness was not an available option. In war the price of humanness rises astronomically. We understand viscerally, and not merely rationally, the radical indeterminacy of life: the dread of cosmic exile, the longing for infinite redemption.

However, to urge a celebration of the wonders of war—especially given the horrifying scale of modern military conflicts—would be mindless. My point is only to understand that as the postmodern cultural smog descends upon us—as we mimic Sisyphus in our routinized life of technical adjustments, as lived experiences are replaced by ersatz images and representations, as the pleasures of manual labor and of the body are increasingly enjoyed vicariously, as the commodification of the world intensifies—our sense of wonder and of possibility, our opportunities for intense human emotion, our very humanness are in jeopardy.

Under such circumstances, the pathology of war, as the struggle for feeling writ large, is a pathetic reminder of our historical condition. Accordingly, the ultimate success of nonviolent resistance and pacifism as a way of life depends on massive numbers of socially organized people viscerally understanding them as necessary remedies for postmodern somnambulance and the remorseless savagery of a world eclipsed.

Machiavelli, though, insists the overall condition of the world remains the same. The contemporary concerns I identify are, for Machiavelli, merely the latest rendition of an endless song. He unsqueamishly steps where I evade: military and political success is required to energize a nation.

The Requirements of Personal Identity

Machiavelli does not renege on his gruff assessment of human nature. Left to our own devices we are nasty, brutish, and selfish. Only a strong state offers redemption. Only such a unit can exploit conditions of necessity to compel human beings toward civic and moral *virtù*. Inclination to a common good is unnatural for us. Patriotism and national character must be carefully promoted. Only they can elevate human beings from myopic focus on our greedy, grasping yearnings to a sense of common identity, shared good, and the importance of heroic deeds. For Machiavelli, only a healthy state can elevate human beings from their alienated, pathetic, natural impulses. True, he ignores the truths that cooperation, shared purposes, mutual aid, and the like must also be potentials within us. Otherwise, we would not even be susceptible to transformation. But his point, persuasive or not, is that such communal values would remain dormant but for the agency of a healthy, expansionist state.

For Machiavelli, a robust nation committed to advancing the common good is necessary for salutary personal identity. The prerequisites of the common good are freedom, equality under the law, a measure of free speech, and ability to participate in government. To serve the common good an action or policy must actually do good, must benefit the large majority of citizens, and be understood by those citizens as benefiting them. The most apparent actions serving the common good increase the prospects of the survival, order, and security of the state, all of which enhance the possibility that citizens will flourish. Only within the common good are individuals redeemed: elevated from the doom and gloom of unfettered *ambizione*, they gain wider identities, and realistic goals and projects. The common good is not universal. Its vitality depends on a secure, healthy expansionist republic that triumphs over foreigners. The common good is not merely an aggregation of individual interests, but the well-being of the whole that is more than just the sum of its parts. Order, stability, the rule of law, and wider sense of identity serve not only the republic itself but also the larger society (D I 2; D II 2; D III 22; FH IV 3–7; FH V 11, 32, 37). The ideals and social practices that human beings create are grounded in our natural needs and capabilities, and are tested by the results they produce in our lives.

Understanding the common good is akin to recognizing the transcendent dimension of any successful collection of people. For example, the greatness of an athletic team cannot be accurately known by totaling the positive attributes of each member. A great team is more than the sum of individual talents. The way players contribute to the team, how they meld together, whether they enhance or detract from the abilities of teammates, all affect the unit's success. The best five individual players do not always form the most successful basketball team. Republics are similar. The common good is more than the sum of individual interests and satisfactions. At its most splendid, the common good involves participating in a wider identity and pursuing important purposes that go beyond the self. The common good reinforces a sense of personal worth and contribution by connecting citizens to a cause greater than the interests of each person considered in isolation. Arthur Murphy describes the common good as "not what everybody wants when each is concerned to please [only] himself or all have been made submissive to the same mass pressures. It is the interest that can justify itself as public on terms of equity that apply to all, the terms of agreement that distinguish a community from a manipulated crowd."[7]

For Machiavelli, the distinction between a community and a manipulated crowd is less clear cut. In any event, he insists that only through communal attachments can human beings transform their inherently dismal natures into a magnificent national character. Alone we are decrepit, estranged, and selfish. Corruption involves selfishness, shortsightedness, indolence, and physical decay. The obsession with perceived past injustices and the desire for revenge—which is often antithetical to enduring glory—also characterize corrupt citizens. The laws and policies of a corrupt country struggle mightily and futilely to rewrite the past instead of focusing sharply on the present and future (FH III 5, 3; FH IV 14). Together we may become worthy of enduring glory. Recognizing our wider identities and feeling the bonds of communal projects nurture patriotism, which is critical in a republic. For Machiavelli, engaging in politics allows human beings to fully realize their higher potentials.

Machiavelli's understanding of how a strong republic advances the common good is reminiscent of a general aspect of the human condition. Many argue that existential tension is at the heart of human experience: our yearning for intimate connection with others and the recognition that others are necessary for our identity and freedom coalesce uneasily with the fear and anxiety we experience as others approach.[8] We simultaneously long for emotional attachment yet are horrified that our individuality may evaporate once we achieve it. This disharmony may never be fully reconciled once and forever, and so we find ourselves making uneasy compromises and adjustments during our life's journey as we oscillate along the continuum whose endpoints are radical individuality and thorough immersion in community, respectively. Individualism offers the prizes of feelings of specialness, empowerment, and uniqueness, but if exaggerated ends in estrangement, alienation, and crushing solitude. Community displays the awards of feelings of connection, enduring bonds, and invigorating intimacy; but, if distorted, degenerates into subservience, loss of identity, and suffocating conformity.

Human freedom for Machiavelli is not a libertarian paradise that sanctifies the (negative) liberties of atomistic individuals. Instead, the Florentine blesses the inescapable bonds we discover among fellow citizens that permit a wider identity that is necessary for nourishing civic *virtù* and for liberating people from their unnecessary domination by foreigners. Human freedom, in its fullest dimension, requires robust community, not arm's-length bargaining by unattached individuals. For Machiavelli, the individualistic contractualism at the heart of libertarianism presupposes a healthy government founded on thick, communal military and political principles.

Machiavelli tells us that as individuals we are doomed to act on the wicked, evil impulses of our natures. Only in community can the forces of necessity be brought to bear and energize the better angels of our being. Only a strong republic—based, as ever, on strong arms, sound laws, robust religion, and disciplined education—can generate the conditions that promote civic *virtù*: respect for the common good, and connection to a wider identity. Only in a strong republic is the common good the guiding principle of political action (D II 2). Machiavelli understood that a state founded on national unity has a greater chance to flourish than one harboring divergent languages, traditions, and laws (P 3). Principalities may be required in territories where the prerequisites of republican rule are absent; but the wise prince begins the process that anticipates republicanism in the next generation.

Machiavelli primarily champions the negative freedom of citizens—not only from the oppression of tyrants and foreigners, but also appreciates some positive freedoms—to propose new laws and to indict those who commit offenses against the liberty of the state (D I 18, 7; FH II 34). As with all positive personal values, appreciation of the common good is grounded in self-interest. Efforts on behalf of the common good maximize prospects for power, glory, security, and order. The common good, then, is tangible and material. Individuals find their fulfillment only within appropriate political communities, only in the common good. Without leaders, bristling with military and political *virtù*, the common good is elusive. If a political community lacks a sense of the common good—if it is corrupt—then strong princes are required to reform the situation. The foundation of the common good, as always, lies in self-interest: human beings are grateful to those who protect them and make their lives more secure and orderly. They understand that service to the common good advances their individual interests as well (D I 2; D II 24).

The Importance of Personal Security

Most strikingly, military strength is the prerequisite for human redemption. As individuals, we are nasty, brutish, and selfish. Only in a healthy, robust political community can civic and moral *virtù* sacrifice for the common good and identification with a wider identity and interests flourish. Such a political community is grounded in the order, stability, and security provided only by strong arms. Machiavelli anticipates the contemporary recruiting slogan of our armed forces—"Be All You Can Be."

Because military superiority is required for a healthy republic that promotes order, security, freedom, and civic *virtù*, military commanders are prime candidates for enduring glory (D II 27; D III 42, 45). Might may not make right in the deepest moral sense of that term, but might is a prerequisite for good government, which is the prerequisite for good laws and the other socializing influences that nurture the common good and instill civic *virtù* (D I 4, 19; D III 31, 33). Strikingly, given the nature of people, military strength is required to promote the conditions required for the flourishing of conventional morality. Without the order, discipline, and security fostered by military might, a healthy state cannot exist. Without a healthy state to direct the forces of necessity, human beings remain in their corrupt, wicked original position. Also, the founding of a fresh or the reforming of a corrupt state requires cruelties: evil well-used.

One side note: When Machiavelli first uses the phrase "evil well-used" he adds a qualifier: "*se del male è licito dire bene*" [if it is permissible to speak well about evil] (P8). This could be understood as Machiavelli wavering as to whether certain horrifying deeds can genuinely be referred to as evil well-used. But Machiavelli makes clear later in that chapter of *The Prince* that he endorses the locution. In fact, if Machiavelli did not accept it the entire problem of dirty hands evaporates. In my view, Machiavelli includes the conditional as a way of underscoring how his position strays from the pieties of the conventional classical understanding that rulers should do only good deeds.

As I will demonstrate later in this work, Machiavelli did not subscribe to the notion that good ends justify evil means. He does note that the masses judge actions only by their results (D III 35; D I 9; P 18). But he does not endorse this as normatively sound. Instead he merely describes what he takes to be the reality of public reaction: the masses are fascinated by appearances and successful outcomes.

Accordingly, initial acts of evil are required for moral *virtù* to have even an opportunity to be realized. These first deeds are whitewashed by the pious rhetoric that ensues and the judgments of the masses. In short, military *virtù* underwrites all the artistic, literary, musical, and other cultural achievements so cherished by civilized people (AW I 17–19).

The Quest for Deserved Glory

For Machiavelli, the highest ends of governments are expansion and glory; the highest end for human beings is enduring, deserved glory. Machiavelli's infrequently noted tragic view of life accepts that the only way to soften our mortality and finitude is to earn an enduring, honorable biographical life. Grand military and political projects in service to a healthy government are the typical routes to deserve such glory. Passionate, ambitious people hunger for recognition that endures beyond their lifetimes. This motivation, whether consciously felt or not, is critical to Machiavelli's political prescriptions.

Earlier I argued the plausibility of Machiavelli's position. I will now expand on that account. Machiavelli's *biological* life ended in

1527. The *autobiographical* life of Machiavelli—as measured by his exercises of freedom, his choices, and deeds—perished at the same time. (Although on occasion, a person's autobiographical life ends prior to his or her death. Consider the final eleven years of Nietzsche's life during which he endured a persistent catatonic state, or the life of a person in an irreversible coma who eventually perishes.) The *biographical* life of Machiavelli continues to this day and beyond. Moreover, certain of Machiavelli's interests—for example, suppose Machiavelli aspired to be remembered favorably by intellectuals centuries after his death and invested enough in that desire that it constituted one of his interests—may be fulfilled or thwarted *only* after Machiavelli's death. Machiavelli has died and remains dead. Lacking interests, the biologically dead are beyond harm and benefit. But the biographical lives of those once alive can be affected by posthumous assessments, reactions, and discoveries, and in this sense, the antemortem Machiavelli, the subject of a continuing biographical life, is still vulnerable to attacks and open to benefits.[9]

Accordingly, even if no afterlife awaits us, each of us does persist after death to some extent. We leave a certain legacy to those who follow us and depending on the kind of life we lead, we shall be remembered, if at all, as heroic or despicable or, most probably, as somewhere in between those extremes. Much of our behavior while alive is motivated by a desire to leave a positive legacy to those who survive our death. Few of us will achieve the monumental status of Socrates, Christ, or da Vinci, but we surely would rather be remembered in such a way instead of, say, as a Benedict Arnold, Charles Manson, or Bluebeard. Regardless of whether our heirs appreciate what we did, we want to be remembered in light of what we accomplished and the kind of person we were. We *deserve* this recognition based on our past performances and deeds.

Is our desire to be remembered irrational? Surely if annihilation is our destiny we shall never be able to experience pleasant sensations or even be aware of the fond remembrances that others may have of us; but many of us still want to be remembered fondly even after conceding all this. And this desire may be grounded in the principle of desert. We deserve to be remembered in accordance with our past deeds. Our desire to be fondly remembered may reflect our conviction that a principle of justice should be applied properly when survivors evaluate the lives we led.

Glory is a type of external validation—it depends on the judgments of contemporaries and of posterity—and thus rests on the values and understandings of evaluators.[10] For Machiavelli, glory can be temporary or permanent. Although Machiavelli discusses the notion of glory more thoroughly in *The Discourses*, he does not ignore the topic in *The Prince* (P 7, 8, 14, 24, 26). The greatest glory is bestowed on those who found, reform, or lead religions; next are those who found republics or principalities; then those who lead armies that expand the territorial holdings of their native land; next are exemplary practitioners of literature and art; and, finally, all others who earn glory through achievements in their professions and occupations (D I 10).

Success is not sufficient to confer glory in politics. Although the masses typically judge only by results, they fail to understand fully that favorable *fortuna*, among other thing, may well have caused military triumphs and political benefits. Contrary to mass opinion, the principles upon which chief military and political officials acted and their demonstrated *virtù* are critical when properly ascribing glory. Machiavelli understands that one can lose admirably and thereby merit glory. Machiavelli denies Agathocles glory because of his villainous methods and tyrannical aspirations (P 8). Machiavelli claims that men seek glory and wealth (P 25), but more precisely he is referring only to certain men—those with *grandezza d'animo*. He understood keenly that most of us lead obscure, quiet lives that do not vie for, much less attain, enduring glory. Even among politicians and military careerists, glory is earned by only a few: "*Gloria* . . . may be aptly defined as 'very great fame or honor that is generally recognized, acquired through extraordinary merits or talents, through valorous deeds or great enterprises.' Glory is a reputation for great deeds in the public sphere."[11]

In *The Prince*, Machiavelli is addressing those who would dismiss the false comforts, easy conformities, tepid projects, trivial idleness, and unbearable softness of *animo effeminato*. Instead, he dares those with *grandezza d'animo*—those seekers of glory whom Machiavelli admires and joins—to accept the challenge and compete for the only reward that persists beyond a life span and that levies scorn upon the demons of mortality.

But the quest for deserved, enduring glory must confront daunting obstacles orchestrated by *Fortuna*. Machiavelli sometimes writes as if *Fortuna* is a personified, natural force that consciously and capriciously plays with the circumstances of human beings. At other times, he writes as if *Fortuna* is only the set of circumstances within which human beings must operate and choose alternatives (P 25).

Although he entertains and admits being drawn to the proposition that *Fortuna* completely governs the affairs of the world, he rejects that view. Citing the existence of free will, Machiavelli carves a spot for human agency and prudence. *Fortuna*, he speculates, controls only about 50 percent of human actions. Wise human beings can take proactive and reactive measures to lessen *Fortuna*'s fury. In an example that anticipates Hurricane Katrina's devastation of New Orleans and Hurricane Sandy's wreckage of the Jersey Shore, Machiavelli describes how precautions can be taken against natural disasters. By building strong, effective barriers and banks, human beings cannot prevent torrential rivers from rising, but we can mitigate the amount of damage. Likewise, once a natural disaster has struck we can erect the fortifications required to anticipate and mollify the next occurrence. The Gulf Coast had insufficient barriers and inadequate levees. As a result, Hurricane Katrina devastated the area frighteningly. That Hurricane Katrina struck was unavoidable, but the amount of damage was due to a lack of foresight and preparation.

The message to rulers is even crisper. Do not depend on past favorable *Fortuna*. Your fortunes will change. No person enjoys positive *Fortuna* forever. Leaders must be flexible and adjust their policies as circumstances permit. If a ruler's attributes and actions are not compatible with present needs, then he will fail. Sometimes caution wins the day. Sometimes boldness succeeds. The character of the times is dispositive. If a man continues behaving in his customary way then eventually he will be defeated when unfavorable *Fortuna* appears. Only if a man could alter his character as time and the situation warrant would his luck be consistently favorable. Next follows the shocker: But Machiavelli has not found a man of such great prudence. Men are either unable to go beyond their fixed characters or are unable to convince themselves to change because their past style has been so successful. *Fortuna* changes, but men cannot adjust enough.

Fortuna, like all women for Machiavelli, is both threatening and malleable. She is not only capricious and thus beyond the deterministic schemes of fate, but also subject to being overwhelmed by bold, masculine action. Unlike other women, though, *Fortuna* has an endless bag of relentless tricks, while even the greatest men are limited by their relatively fixed characters and the seductions of past success.

Machiavelli does not explicitly spell out the conclusion of this argument: All men must fail in the long run. The worst of us will supplicate ourselves before *Fortuna* and submit meekly in defeat. The best of us will defeat *Fortuna* most of the time. None of us will defeat *Fortuna* all of the time. Even those of the grandest *virtù*, if they live long enough, will eventually confront *Fortuna* so unfavorable that they will fail due to inherent limitations on human flexibility of character. Men flourish when their character and actions mesh with circumstances *Fortuna* fashioned. Men fail when their character and actions are out of step with the times. As a guideline, Machiavelli advises that boldness and ruthlessness are preferable to caution: "For *Fortuna* is a lady. It is necessary, if you want to master her, to beat her and strike her. And one sees she more often submits to those who act boldly than to those who proceed in a calculating fashion" (P 25).

Machiavelli astutely grasps that success requires a happy marriage between a man's character and his situation. For example, the question, "Would Russo be a great president?" should be replaced by, "Would Russo be a great president at this time under these circumstances?" A person's temperamental range and his ability to adapt to fortune are limited. Instead of seeking a great ruler *as such* we are better advised to assess carefully the prevailing context and select the person best suited to flourish in *that* environment.

Machiavelli's sagacious, famous call for flexibility and adaptability as crucial to military and political success is deflated by the dreary, insightful conclusion that human beings must fail in the end. This does not mean enduring glory, the highest prize for Machiavelli, is impossible. Part of that glory is fighting the strong lifelong battle against an unconquerable foe, refusing the easy consolations of lesser men and relishing the contest as an opportunity to manifest one's mettle. We are born of dust and to dust we shall return. But along the way, if we retain our nerve, energize our spirit, activate our understanding, and greet the world with *brio* and *virtù*, we, too, may earn a measure of glory.

Machiavelli's tragic view of life understands fully the inevitability of human suffering, the flux that is the world, the Sisyphus-like character of daily life. Yet in one's response to tragedy one manifests heroism or bland resignation, *grandezza d'animo* or *animo effeminato*. We cannot rationalize or justify the inherent meaningless of our suffering. We cannot transcend our vulnerability and journey to fixed security. We are contingent, mortal beings and will remain so.

But we are free to create ourselves: we bear no antecedent duties to external authority; we are under the yoke of no preestablished goals, other than those endorsed by God who presumably mirrors the patriotic fervor Machiavelli embodied. We need not recoil squeamishly from the horrors of existence; instead, we can rejoice in a passionate life of perpetual self-overcoming. Machiavelli forces us to confront the paramount questions of human existence, invites us to live—and not merely contemplate—our answers, and challenges us to take responsibility for the persons we are becoming.

Accordingly, part of Machiavelli's tragic view of life is that the greatest among us will nurture evermore challenging first-order desires that will present more daunting resistances that will probably eventually lead to greater defeats and possibly to death. Even those who achieve felicitous, immediate results will in the end fall victim to the limits of their own flexibility and the caprices of *Fortuna*.

Machiavelli is himself a case study of his own account. He was more flexible and adaptable than most human beings. His willingness to adapt to his times is reflected in his willingness to serve republics and principalities, as the circumstances warranted. In the end, *Fortuna* ground him down and he was not trusted completely by advocates of either form of government. He died disillusioned, the product of high expectations and unfulfilled political promise. Although he did not live long enough to know and experience it, Machiavelli eventually earned enduring glory as a writer, theorist, and provocateur—a deserved response to his artistic *virtù*. Fittingly, Machiavelli's life mirrors his teachings on the caprices and power of *Fortuna*.

Accordingly, deserved, enduring glory remains the highest prize. Throughout his work, Machiavelli preserves the distinction between tyrants and leaders embodying *virtù*, and the distinction between mere notoriety and glory. Machiavelli, for example, derides Giovampagolo Baglioni as a vulgar tyrant who murdered his relatives to seize control of Perugia. Worse, when he had the chance to cut down the militarily threatening Pope Julius II and the entire College of Cardinals—which could have in one fell swoop rid the country of internal oppression—he cravenly withdrew (D I 27). Baglioni was at times gratuitously cruel and at other times excessively timid. He failed to master the art of distinguishing when evil was well-used from times when it was ill-used.

Tyrants such as Baglioni confuse selfishness with enlightened self-interest: They seize power to plunder and destroy a state instead of reforming it. They do not merit glory because they are indifferent or hostile to the common good. Tyrants mistake infamy for glory. Their states stagnate because they are bound together only by fear of the coercive power of law and arms. Any benefits that accrue to such a state flow only to the tyrant. No sense of a common good exists. Anyone who demonstrates military or political *virtù* must be destroyed by the tyrant lest his own position weaken. Civic *virtù* is impossible in a tyranny because its prerequisites are ignored or discouraged. Mistaking power as such as the highest goal, the tyrant invites the hatred of his subjects and his denunciation by history (D I 10, 17, 25, 33; D II 2: D III 3, 6, 26).

The Significance of the Value of Patriotism

Loyalty and service to a particular nation is the hallmark of patriotism. But only those possessing the requisite nationality can be patriotic. Foreigners can appreciate and benefit another nation, but they cannot be patriotic toward that nation. The significance of the value of patriotism is the tension it produces between the impersonal morality of the Ideal Observer and the explicit partiality and particularity of the robust patriot.

To ascend to the impersonal vantage point of the Ideal Observer is to evaluate independently of one's own interests, preferences, and social relations. From this perspective, a life lost in one country is, all other things being equal, no more or less regrettable than a life lost in another country. But patriotism, which requires particularity and partiality, is incompatible with such an outlook: a life lost in *my* country, all other things being equal, is more regrettable than a life lost in another country.

Of course, the patriot cannot advance the interests of his or her country without regard for the rules of impersonal morality. I cannot act on the principle, "my country right or wrong" simplistically. I cannot steal, lie, and kill foreigners indiscriminately merely because doing so advances the cause of my nation. We might be tempted to conclude that the dictates of impersonal morality are inviolable constraints upon the actions of ardent patriots. But such a conclusion is mistaken.

Even if Machiavelli overstates the zero-sum context that structures the world, he is surely correct in thinking that given the relative scarcity of natural resources, occasions will arise such that two (or more) nations must compete for the same desired prize. Impersonal morality would have no preference as to which nation should prevail, while the patriot must strive mightily to ensure that his or her nation prevails. The very nature of patriotism precludes indifference in a zero-sum contest.

A critic might rejoin that all this is still acceptable: the patriot may pursue the preferences of his nation and compete vigorously for the desired resource as long as the patriot does not violate impersonal morality in so doing. Thus, patriotism can still be manifested compatibly with the imperatives of impersonal morality. On this reading, abrogating utter indifference to outcomes in zero-sum contests is not automatically a violation of impersonal morality. So no necessary conflict between patriotism and morality has been demonstrated.

If only the matter were so simple. As Machiavelli continually points out, patriotism sometimes requires advancing the interests of one's nation in enterprises that are not always in the interests of human beings taken collectively. At times patriotism requires using evil well—in ways that win zero-sum contests at the expense of foreigners. The difficulty is in distinguishing when and to what extent the imperatives of impersonal morality limit zealous patriotic action. The true but trivial conclusion is sometimes but not always.

The duties of military and political office require leaders to place special value on the interests of their constituents. In fact, a strong case can be made that the entire moral enterprise, understood properly, presupposes the partiality in personal relations. That is, the sorts of dispositions and virtues that comprise the moral enterprise can be acquired only through the experiences and habits learned in personal relations characterized by partiality. Personal relations are nonfungible: if X has a personal relationship to Y, then Y is one of X's ends and that end is precisely Y and not any other person. The particularity of the other person grounds the value and bond of friendship, at least in part. Also, the intimacy of friendship promotes general virtues such as honesty, loyalty, empathy, and self-making. Intimacy requires partiality—by definition, we cannot be intimate with everyone—and treating family and friends preferentially is often sound.[12] By extrapolating and refining this principle we may well conclude that the partialism embodied by patriots on the national level is also well-grounded.

We must recognize that the unique and valuable ends of family and personal relations cannot be achieved without the socially recognized institutions of family and friendship. While the precise nature and strictures of these institutions are reimaginable, some form of family and friendship are necessary lest important values evaporate. By viewing morality merely as a set of abstract rules and principles, impartialists—those who insist that everyone's interests must be considered equally in all cases—open themselves to the charge that they ignore paramount functions of morality such as developing and nurturing personal relationships as well as trusting local communities.

Partialists also illustrate the alleged poverty of viewing the value of personal relations in purely instrumentalist terms. If some impartialists are willing to admit a certain level of partiality only because doing so has an instrumental value for the general moral enterprise, they miss the mark. Personal relations bear value for their own sakes. Imagine being in a personal relationship and discovering that the other party has done certain actions for you only out of a sense of duty or from an ideal of universal beneficence or for reasons of general moral development. You would most likely conclude that the other has misunderstood the nature of personal relations. Personal relations are not merely different in degree from impersonal relations; they are metaphysically different in kind: the metaphors of mutual bonds, connectedness, attachments, although faintly capturing the truth, are too effete. Again, the parallels between patriots and their nations are clear.

Personhood presupposes partiality in the sense that one's identity and personal integrity must consist in part of projects, aspirations, and life's plans that have unique status in one's priority of values simply because they are hers. To require people to calculate impartiality would be to alienate them from their attitudes, convictions, projects, and actions. Also, a world in which I considered everyone's interests equally would be a world in which profound affection for others no longer existed, a world that eliminated the values of specialness and belonging. Intimate friendships involve the parties' recognition of each other as special, noninterchangeable people. They and only they have certain unique qualities, or combinations of them, or ways of embodying and expressing them. We do not live in a sea of undifferentiated "humanness."

But patriotism, if overly inflated, morphs into rabid nationalism. In Machiavelli's work the differences between the two are subtle. Viewing the world as a series of zero-sum contests where increased *virtù* is a prize emerging from territorial expansion entails that the common good extends primarily to one's own people. Territorial boundaries, however, are constantly changing and the circle of one's own people also expands with time, socialization, and assimilation. Machiavelli makes no appeal to master races, chosen people, or genetically superior tribes. Human beings are inherently flawed and potentially vicious. But within us is the capability to rise above our wantonness if and only if a healthy, expansionist state bestows its guidance.

The task, then, is to carve out an appropriate place for partialism in moral theory and practice. Not all partialism in personal relationships is fair. Nor does legitimate partialism in international affairs—the times when promoting the interests of one's country is warranted—underwrite ignoring the well-being of the world community generally. This is especially the case if international affairs are not conducted in a Hobbesian state of nature. In addition, political leaders will face excruciating decisions where they must choose between advancing the well-being of the greater portion of their citizenry by sacrificing the interests of a minority.

Churchill and Coventry

This is an illustration of a patriotic statesman having to choose between advancing the common good and protecting the interests of a relatively small number of his constituents. During World War II, English operatives broke a German message code and concluded that the Nazis were about to bomb Coventry. If the citizens were warned and evacuated, the Germans would have been alerted that their code had been broken. This breakthrough was thought to increase the probability that the Allies would eventually defeat the Axis powers, but if the Germans knew about it they would devise another code. Winston Churchill allegedly decided not to order the evacuation of the town, thereby preserving the illusion that the German codes were still effective. Doing so, failed to adequately protect the citizens of Coventry. Assuming the probabilities and consequences of the action were correctly calculated, many would argue that Churchill's action was warranted under a lesser-of-two-evils or lose-a-battle-to-win-the-war theory. True, the innocent citizens of Coventry were used as mere means for a greater good, but evacuating them would have resulted in much greater overall carnage. Some thinkers, call them moral optimists, would conclude that Churchill's action was justified or completely excusable, that he was innocent of wrongdoing, and that he should feel no guilt about his decision.

Other thinkers, call them moral pessimists, might conclude differently. The sacrifice of innocent citizens, without their knowledge and consent, is morally objectionable. The situation does not appear to be a supreme emergency wherein the force of moral prohibitions eases. Churchill's action is excusable, but not entirely so. Some residue guilt is, therefore, appropriate.

Here are some details: As World War II loomed, Coventry, England, was an industrial city of almost 250,000 people. As one of the leading munitions centers in the United Kingdom, Coventry was the source of 25 percent of all British aircraft manufactured during World War I. During World War II, the Germans launched more than fifteen relatively small bombing raids on the city between August and

October 1940. But the massive raid of November 14, 1940, merits our attention and underscores the problem of dirty hands.

On that evening, 515 German bombers conducted operation Moonlight Sonata with the intention to destroy Coventry's factories and industrial capabilities. Collateral damage to the city and its residents was inevitable and foreseen. The raid was a German success: more than 4,000 homes were destroyed, almost 70 percent of Coventry's buildings were damaged, two-thirds of the city's factories were razed or badly damaged, between 350 and 600 people were killed, more than 800 people were badly injured, and 400 more sustained lesser injuries. Coventry's air defenses managed to shoot down only one German bomber. A greater number of casualties was averted because many citizens traveled out of the city at night and slept in nearby towns in reaction to the earlier German raids. Coventry also contained about eighty public air raid shelters that protected thousands of other citizens.

This would be only another piece of historical trivia but for the contention that Winston Churchill knew that the raid would occur and intentionally failed to alert officials in Coventry in order to preserve valuable intelligence information that he would later need. If true, rather than compromise a paramount source of intelligence, Churchill knowingly sacrificed the interests of the citizens of Coventry to the merciless designs of the German Air Force. The details of Churchill's alleged connivance are as follows: either two days prior to or at least earlier in the day of the raid, the name "Coventry" appeared clearly on a decrypted German message (codenamed "Boniface" and later "Ultra," designations British military intelligence adopted for wartime signals intelligence obtained by breaking high-level encrypted enemy radio and teleprinter communications Germany's Enigma machine generated). This presumably signaled that Coventry was to be the primary target of a massive bombing raid on the evening of November 14, 1940. After this information was brought to the attention of Churchill, he conferred with Sir William Stephenson, senior representative of British intelligence, who advised him that "Boniface" was too valuable a source of intelligence to risk. If Churchill alerted officials in Coventry, he would expose the intelligence source and render it useless in the future. Thus, Churchill decided to conceal the information, Coventry was not evacuated, and citizens therein were in effect sacrificed for what the Prime Minister took to be the greater good.[13] As an aside, some have also accused Churchill of using his foreknowledge of German aid raids for self-aggrandizement. Christopher Hitchens writes: "On the nights when he knew that [German] bombers would overfly London on their way to, say, Coventry, he would make a point of standing on the Air Ministry roof, or of taking a stroll in the Downing Street garden, thus impressing his staff and subordinates with his pluck and daring and sangfroid. On the nights when Enigma gave him private information about a raid on London itself, he would decamp to the country house of a wealthy friend."[14]

Whether the story of Churchill's actions regarding Coventry is true is a matter of dispute. Some argue that Churchill and his advisors did not know the location of the primary raid of operation Moonlight Sonata, and in fact suspected that London, not Coventry, was the actual target. In the past, Churchill had acted on intelligence information that stymied German operations, why would he not do so in regard to Coventry? To conclude that Churchill would not act upon intelligence derived from the Enigma machine because the target was Coventry requires a fuller explanation. Moreover, the German codes the Enigma machine generated were changing frequently and it was unlikely that British intelligence had permanently broken those codes. That Britain would invest extensive time, money, and manpower in breaking the German codes, even if temporarily, and then not act on information garnered as a result seems peculiar. Finally, even if Churchill had been aware a few hours prior to the attack that Coventry was the primary target of the German raid, that city probably could not be evacuated in a timely fashion. Also, Churchill's Royal Air Force was already overextended and unlikely to be capable of defending Coventry even if the Prime Minister had known of the attack and had desired to defend the city. Accordingly, that Churchill knowingly and intentionally sacrificed some British citizens for what he took to be the greater good is highly unlikely.[15]

This is not the forum to establish the truth about Churchill's actions in this matter. For the record: I conclude that the more charitable and reasonable interpretation—given conflicting evidence, much of which arises from eyewitnesses to the events—is that Churchill did not knowingly and intentionally sacrifice the interests of the citizens of Coventry in service of what he took to be the greater good. Of course, Machiavellian statesmen would fabricate conflicting evidence in order to retain plausible denial of their deeds.

But suppose the story is true and the facts leading to Churchill's decisions are as presented within it. What would Machiavelli say?

Iran-Contra

This is an illustration of a statesman operating in the international arena in possible violation of his country's laws and policies. The Iran-Contra affair, which took place sometime between 1985 and 1987, consists of a series of events with more twists and turns than a rollercoaster. A simplified version would read as follows: The U.S. Congress under the Boland Amendment prohibited funding of the Contra rebels in Nicaragua. The Contras were anticommunist rebels waging guerilla war against the then-Marxist government in Nicaragua. The Contras were merciless, violently abusive, and disdainful of basic civil rights, but President Ronald Reagan strongly supported their anticommunist cause. Meanwhile, an Islamic group with Iranian connections had taken seven U.S. citizens hostage in Lebanon. The Reagan administration concocted a scheme whereby the United States would sell military arms to Iran, then engaged in a war with Iraq, with assurances that Iran would facilitate the release of the hostages. This was conceived at a time when Iran was subject to an arms embargo and in violation of the government's stated refusal to negotiate with terrorists. When the plan was first formulated, Israel was to act as middle agent between the United States and Iran. Later, Lieutenant Colonel Oliver North, a military aide to the U.S. Security Council, engineered modifications to the plan that included using some of the proceeds of the arms sale to fund the Contras and eliminating Israel as middle agent.

This scenario could well be depicted as a dirty hands situation. The Reagan administration saw two worthy ends: freeing American hostages and supporting an anticommunist movement. But the means necessary to attain those ends violated both the administration's publicly stated policies and the prohibitions of Congress: arming Iraq, funding the Contras, and in effect negotiating with terrorists. Along the way, a host of deceptions would be required to ensure that President Reagan retained the possibility of plausibly denying what was occurring or, at least, his foreknowledge of the scheme.

In late 1986 a Lebanese magazine reported the weapons-for-hostages arrangement, a report later confirmed by the Iranian government. President Reagan soon thereafter gave a national address in which he denied that the motivation for the arrangement was straightforwardly weapons-for-hostages and, instead, tried to fashion it as the beginning of newer, more salutary, American-Irani relations. The President created the Tower Commission, a special review board that conducted hearings and concluded that President Reagan seemingly lacked full knowledge of the scope of the program, but criticized him for lax supervision of his subordinates.

In a host of subsequent statements, President Reagan, himself, seemed to be unsure of whether he knew the salient details of the program. Reagan was impaled on the horns of a dilemma: If he engineered or knew of the paramount details of the scheme he was implicated thoroughly in illegality; if he was unaware of such details he was grossly negligent or stunningly incompetent in executing the duties of his office.

The International Court of Justice awarded a judgment against the Nicaraguan government that mandated the payment of compensation from the United States. But the United States refused to comply with that judgment and as a permanent member of the U.N. Security Council stymied every Nicaraguan attempt to enforce the judgment.

From August 1985 through the fall of 1986, the terrorists released a few but not all of the hostages. A different Islamic terrorist group in Lebanon took three more Americans hostage in September and October 1986.

In the spring of 1987, President Reagan expressed regret in several national addresses, taking responsibility while still denying full knowledge of the scheme. He also finally conceded that what began as a strategic warming of relations with Iran deteriorated into an arms-for-hostages arrangement during its implementation. By November 1986, Reagan's approval rating dropped from 67 percent to 46 percent, but rebounded to 64 percent by January 1989. Eventually, fourteen government officials were indicted and eleven convictions resulted, some of which were reversed on appeal. President George H. W. Bush pardoned the remaining officials in the final days of his presidency in 1992. What would Machiavelli say?

I will speculate on Machiavelli's assessment of Churchill and Coventry and the Iran-Contra affair after we collect more evidence as to his view on the nature of dirty hands in politics. Much of Machiavelli's work grapples with the conflict between the impersonal standpoint of conventional morality and the obligations of statesmen to their constituents and rulers to their subjects. Those in authority who insist on keeping their hands clean—by avoiding any actions that infringe on the imperative of impersonal morality—will sometimes thereby violate their duties to their constituents. Those in authority who are excessively and narrowly patriotic—those who too eagerly get their hands dirty in order to advance the interests of their nation—will too easily dismiss the imperatives of impersonal morality and will thereby soon lose their souls. Only statesmen who can balance the often conflicting normative demands of impersonal morality and patriotic zeal can risk their souls without losing them. Such leaders must distinguish carefully between using evil wrongly and using evil well; they must come to their authority with a keen understanding of the imperatives of impersonal morality; but they must learn how not to be good on appropriate occasions; they must recognize that clean hands are the province of children, saints, and martyrs, but not of military and political heroes; and they must endure the ambivalence and agony accompanying their political choices and deeds. Machiavelli's secret is the internal life of statesmen. Although he never addresses the internal life of statesmen explicitly, Machiavelli leaves readers all the clues required to piece the puzzle together. We must continue to amass that evidence by probing Machiavelli's view on the proper role of religion and his understanding of morality.

2

Religion and Morality

We must comprehend Machiavelli's views on religion and morality in order to see how the value of patriotism animates his general normative outlook and to unravel the problem of dirty hands that confronts military and political leaders.

Although Machiavelli disparages certain Christian virtues—such as humility, contemplation, self-abasement, and contempt for worldly goods as contrary to the requirements of a robust republic—he accepts the conventional morality of his day that is grounded in Christianity (D I pref.; D II 2). Pernicious priestly interpretations of Christianity have rendered its followers indolent, compliant, and deficient in civic *virtù*. However, to interpret Machiavelli as an extoller of paganism is an error. Machiavelli insists that "our religion [Christianity] teaches us the truth and the true way of life" (D II 2).

The Values and Uses of Religion

In *The Prince*, Machiavelli only alludes to his misgivings about the role the Church had played in Italian politics (P 7, 11, 21). Given that his audience for that book was the Medici family, one of whom was the current Pope and several of whom had been high-ranking prelates, doing so was prudent strategy. In *The Discourses*, though, Machiavelli relishes the opportunity to brandish his case against the Church.

Most important, Machiavelli celebrates religion as a forceful instrument for establishing order and security, promoting military discipline, reinforcing good laws, and coercing people to behave well. In his ranking of glorious men, Machiavelli places leaders and founders of religion in first place (D I 10). Religion is the most powerful agent of social control. A robust religion nourishes the homeland, energizes patriotism, and promotes military defense (D II 2). Accordingly,

Machiavelli reveres the majesty of religion and takes it most seriously: "Ours [Christian religion], because it shows us the truth and the true way, makes us esteem less the honor of the world; whereas the pagans [pre-Christians], greatly esteeming such honor and believing it their greatest good, were fiercer in their actions. . . . Ancient religion attributed blessedness only to men abounding in worldly glory, such as generals of armies and princes of states. Our religion has glorified humble and contemplative men rather than active ones. . . . It prefers that you be adapted to suffering rather than doing something vigorous" (D II 2).

Any powerful agent, however, can be used in service of Machiavelli's most cherished principles or against those values. Unhappily, the Catholic Church is the major villain in *The Discourses*. In fact, Machiavelli's criticisms of Christian religion flow through all his writings. While he recognizes and celebrates the role that religion *should* have in creating a healthy, expansionist republic, he sharply rebukes the role that Christianity has taken in Italy.

Specifically, Machiavelli bemoans the *values* Christianity has embraced. Roman religion advocated greatness of spirit, bravery, boldness, physical action, vigor, passion, and the quest for worldly glory. Christianity venerates humbleness, contemplation, softness, suffering as the road to redemption, and disdain of worldly honor. In a critique that prefigures that of Nietzsche, Machiavelli argues that Christianity has weakened the conditions required to promote military and political *virtù*, and has thereby fostered civic corruption and *ozio*. Christianity has substituted the supposed value of enduring suffering without complaint for Machiavelli's preferred value of overcoming resistance and obstacles. Casting a too-appreciative gaze toward eternal salvation, Christianity has debased the material values that spawn earthly glory. As a result, Machiavelli concludes that the people have degenerated to the status of *animo effeminato* (D I pref.; D II 2; D I 11). The Church keeps weak men feeble by offering easy consolations and excuses. The Romans were more freedom-loving and braver than Renaissance Florentines because of the different values their respective religions promoted. These differences do not merely reflect Machiavelli's abstract aesthetic preferences. They bear practical implications: the Romans lived in freedom, while contemporary Florentines and other Italians live in various forms of servitude (D I 11, 13; D II 2; D III 33).

In addition, Machiavelli attacks the *political strategies* Christianity favored. Constantly aligning itself with this or that foreign dominator, the Church ensured that Italy remained fragmented and easy prey for barbarians. Instead of subjugating regional princes, the Church brought in a foreign oppressor to subdue any Italian prince who was seemingly strong enough to unify the country. In so doing, Christianity kept sharp focus on its own aggrandizement and power to the exclusion of developing wider civic *virtù* (P 12; D I 12; P 6, 3). Consequently, the Church has kept Italy divided and politically weak. In sum, the Church has promoted and has benefited from a divided, corrupt Italy (D I 12).

Furthermore, the Florentine laments *opportunities squandered*. Religion has special authority to command the obedience of human beings, to establish order and security, to ordain salutary laws, to reinforce military and civic discipline, and to energize respect for the common good. Instead, Christianity, by the values it embraced and the self-serving political strategies it employed, nurtured only civic weakness (D I 12, 13, 1, 11).

Finally, Machiavelli excoriates the *hypocrisy of the church hierarchy*. While living as pampered and corrupt authorities, they preached the virtues of poverty, austerity, and humility. The result was a loosening of piety and religious devotion among the people. Lacking glowing religious examples, the people, to the detriment of the common good, have become irreligious and evil. Church leaders have talked piety and reverence but practiced wickedness and blasphemy. As a result, the people bear superficial allegiance to Christian values but remain corrupt. The Church has squandered its moral authority and its potential for being a force of necessity that could make men behave well (D I 12; D III 1).

Could Machiavelli have seriously concluded that an appropriate rendering of religion could facilitate the unification of sixteenth-century Italy? Remember, the unification of Italy, the *Risorgimento*, did not occur until the mid- to late nineteenth century. In the sixteenth century, Italy's regions and city-states were in such disarray and the military power of foreign countries was so dominant that it would seem only a utopian dreamer of the most gullible stripe could have taken the unification of Italy seriously.

Conditions in Italy were, indeed, dim at that time. The five principal regions—Milan, Venice, Florence, the Roman Papacy, and the Kingdom of Naples—treasured their independent power. Transitory alliances and coalitions with foreign powers thwarted any region that threatened the balance of power. Machiavelli bristled when chronicling the Church's dogged role in preventing Italian unification (P 12;

D I 12), but also saw it as a potentially powerful tool for reformation. This potential was never actualized. Any strong, unified Italy would prove a secular threat to the Church's near monopoly of authority. The divisive policies of the Church continued beyond Machiavelli's lifetime: when Machiavelli's works were published posthumously, the Church immediately placed them on its index of forbidden reading. Later, the Church was indifferent, at best, and hostile, at worst, during the nineteenth-century *Risorgimento.*

Still, Machiavelli understood that the major political achievements in Europe were being accomplished by strong princes with unified countries (D I 12). Given his private correspondence, we may reasonably conclude that Machiavelli was gravely pessimistic that Italian unification would occur soon. Yet he harbored a dream—that sometimes distorted his political vision—of an Italy freed from the domination of foreign government and united, to some measure, in common cause. When reflecting soberly on the chaos of his country and the machinations of the Church, realism and pessimism enveloped him. When consulting his heart and when overwhelmed by his overflowing *ambizione,* the dream seduced him. He fantasized a movement, led by the Medici family in Florence or Rome, guided by a politically savvy statesman, Machiavelli himself, that would leave an illustrious, indelible imprint on the pages of history.

Accordingly, for Machiavelli, the Roman Catholic Church required a complete redirection, perhaps a return to founding principles, in order to assume its rightful function in the revitalization of Italy.

Refashioning God and Religion in Service of Patriotism

To illustrate the power of religion united robustly with political reformation, Machiavelli recalls the lives and triumphs of Moses (ca. 1392 BCE–ca. 1272 BCE) and Numa Pompilius (ca. 750 BCE–ca. 673 BCE) (see Appendix B).

Machiavelli esteems Moses for being an armed prophet (P 6); for taking an enslaved people and pointing the way to reformation (P 26); for being a lawgiver with concern for the common good (D I 9); and for understanding that "in order to have his laws accepted and his proposals adopted, [Moses had] to murder vast numbers of men, men who opposed his plans for no other reason but envy" (D III 30). Moses is an exemplar of military and political *virtù,* an embodiment of the necessity of using violent means to attain worthy ends, underwritten with a divine imprimatur. Although not explicitly recognized in Machiavelli's writings, Moses exhibits other worthy Machiavellian traits. Prior to the killings of the 3,000 worshipers of the golden calf, Moses refused God's invitation to start a new nation and, after the killings, Moses offered to have himself expunged from the divine book (Exodus 32: 10–13, 32–33). Moses, then, was a kindred spirit to Machiavelli: he loved his country more than his own soul. Machiavelli expects nothing less from great liberators and founders.

In sum, Moses antecedently understood how to be good, but he learned how to be bad on the proper occasions; he dirtied his hands and risked his soul in service to his countrymen; and he demonstrated military and political *virtù* that prefigured the salutary transformation of his people. Moses is thereby a sterling example of Machiavelli's ideal military and political leader.

Machiavelli also invokes the legendary tale of the founding of Rome to underscore the importance of religion. After Romulus had died, probably slain by conspiratorial senators, Numa Pompilius was selected to be the next king of Rome. Numa, contemplative and philosophical by temperament, was reluctant to accept the post. Rome was an uncivilized mosaic of Sabines, Romans, runaway slaves, fugitives, and smaller tribes. Numerous disparate traditions and customs coalesced uneasily. Numa, although not a warrior by nature, had shrewd political insight. Rome needed a common culture to bind it more tightly. That culture would most easily be attained through strong religious rituals and institutions. Numa concluded that religion could best sustain the laws and customs that Romulus had initiated. Numa Pompilius prefigured the glorious Machiavellian union of strong arms and strong laws, underwritten by a vital religion that promoted military and political *virtù*. Civic *virtù*, territorial expansion, security, order, and prosperity were highly likely to follow.

For Machiavelli, religious worship is required for political greatness. Even the greatest human ruler leads a finite life. The power of religion endures. The crucial question is not whether to nurture religion in the polity. The critical question is what kind of religion to foster. The answer, for Machiavelli, is not an emasculated Christianity, with its eye on a transcendent world that rewards the meek, humble, and downtrodden. The solution is a robust religion that promotes the military and political *virtù* required to establish or invigorate the security, order, and civic *virtù* necessary for an expansionist republic.

Machiavelli uses empirical data—derived from historical examples and contemporary activities—as a necessary element for understanding human behavior. However, he does not derive his political and moral conclusions from that data. Instead, his understanding of human behavior grounded in empirical data sets limits to the ambitions of political and moral principles. Machiavelli grasps acutely the proposition that we cannot expect the impossible from human beings; human beings cannot transcend their natures.

Machiavelli's appreciation of religion arises from its instrumental uses, broadly understood. Machiavelli insists that religion must not be used for a partisan agenda that undermines the common good. Instead, religion must reinforce and highlight political and moral principles that advance the nation. By promoting the internalization of those principles among citizens—as people embrace the appropriate political and moral principles as their own—religion can transform souls and facilitate civic *virtù*. To establish and maintain a robust nation we must respect salutary customs, sound laws, and appropriate principles of behavior (D I 12). Religion should play a crucial role to that end. The fear and love of God is a powerful motivation in that process.

Properly conceived and vigorously employed, religion can promulgate values and promote excellences that invigorate a healthy state. Machiavelli, then, admires the power of religion to help craft civic *virtù*, transform elements of human nature into robust national character, and nurture national greatness. As always, Machiavelli's primary value is patriotism—his love of country and his veneration of ambitious men embodying expansive souls who are willing to risk everything in the quest for the deserved, enduring glory that constitutes the only immortality available to finite beings. Despite the basic venality of human beings, the cruel vicissitudes of *Fortuna*, and the harsh competitiveness of the international political arena, Machiavelli envisioned magnificent ideals the pursuit of which enlarged human purpose and energized human souls. Accordingly, the instrumental value of religion is broad—it encompasses not only political purposes but also the transformation of individual souls. This is why Machiavelli ranks founders of religions ahead of founders of states in his hierarchy of heroes, and at one point praises Numa Pompilius in stronger terms than even Romulus (D I 11).

Machiavelli distances himself from the rituals, ceremonies, and political pretensions of the Church of his day. While he invokes God often and believes in God in his own fashion, even God primarily serves instrumental purposes. Machiavelli never questions the existence of God, but is selective in the way he uses Scripture to sculpt his conception of God. Machiavelli understands God as enjoining human beings to love and defend their native lands, to be vigorous and forceful in the international arena, and to pursue relentlessly military and political greatness. Happily, Machiavelli's God espouses precisely the same values as does Machiavelli!

In that vein, Machiavelli never appeals to the teachings of Jesus that stress humility, forbearance in the face of attack, and withdrawal from the allure of earthly glory. For Machiavelli, eternal salvation was nothing more than the attainment of deserved, enduring glory grounded in confronting and overcoming obstacles in service of the common good. Religion, properly understood, could elevate human souls and redeem a people. Machiavelli envisions a mutually sustaining marriage between the good citizen and the good Christian. God's love of liberty, justice, and political excellences requires this coupling. Only those who loved their country more than their souls and who evidenced that commitment by acting vigorously in the political and military arenas were genuine apostles of God. Machiavelli was convinced that the interests of salutary republics were in complete harmony with the will of God. Any religion that drained men of *virtù* or tamed their patriotic ambitions was unworthy of the title.

Machiavelli, then, discusses the possibility of redirecting Christianity from a universal, cosmopolitan religion to a national, patria-centered religion. One might argue that Martin Luther during the Protestant Reformation was able to nationalize God and religion such that the state enjoyed supremacy over religion and politics oversaw morality.

Machiavelli's conception of God reflects his own highest value of patriotism: "Men must attempt everything, and not be too frightened of anything, and . . . God loves men who are strong, because we can clearly see how He always uses the powerful to afflict the powerless" (CC 34). Instead of concluding that the pervasive presence of moral evil provides evidence that God does not exist or that God cannot have the three major properties attributed to Him (omnibenevolence, omnipotence, omniscience), Machiavelli deduces that God appreciates the excellences of strong men pursuing military and political glory.

Machiavelli's analysis of God is, of course, profoundly self-serving. He ignores the bulk of Jesus' teachings that interpreted the love commandment. The God of Jesus requires unconditional love, material minimalism, forbearance in the face of evil, humility, and serving the needs of the disenfranchised. The God of Machiavelli instructs human beings to love their native lands and to cultivate military, political, and civic *virtù*. Machiavelli's interpretation of God illustrates his general teaching that religion should serve the common good by sculpting a vigorous national character, transforming human souls, and nourishing national greatness.

A sympathetic critic might argue that serving the common good is how human beings can fulfill the biblical injunction to demonstrate unconditional love.[1] Thus, Machiavelli's understanding of God is not so far-fetched after all. But this will not do. The parables of Jesus are clear that the imperatives of the love commandment—loving one's neighbor and embodying unconditional love—require going beyond the boundaries of tribe, nation, religion, and kinship. For Jesus, the answer to the question, "Who is my neighbor?" is not circumscribed by parochial allegiances. Instead, Jesus teaches that we must love strangers and even enemies unconditionally and attend to their needs. Demonstrating unconditional love is not defined by advancing the common good of a particular city-state or nation-state. For Jesus, the demands of impersonal morality trump the designs of the zealous patriot.[2]

As such, Machiavelli's invocation of the common good is much too narrow to fulfill the biblical injunction as interpreted by Jesus. If one reads scripture fairly, serving one's native land is woefully insufficient for fulfilling the love commandment. In sum, Machiavelli's conception of God is prejudiced by his own political aspirations. Francesco Guicciardini was surely closer to the mark when he observed that "who wants to live totally according to God's will can ill afford not to remove himself totally from the affairs of this world, and it is difficult to live in the world without offending God."[3] Jesus did not structure his life around the Machiavellian values of patriotism, military and political *virtù*, and the pursuit of deserved, enduring glory by advancing narrow parochial interests.

Instead of elevating pagan morality and religion above Christian morality and religion, or advocating that the pagan versions must predominate in the political realm while the Christian renderings must oversee the private realm, as Isaiah Berlin and others have insisted,[4] Machiavelli paganizes the notion of God. That is, he conceives of a God who mirrors Machiavelli's own highest values. He does this by seizing upon the biblical narrative of Moses; deriving lessons from that narrative; universalizing those lessons to apply to all statesmen; while ignoring the massive amount of Scripture that extols values other than patriotism, the pursuit of worldly glory, and the founding of grand republics. By "universalizing those lessons" I do not mean that

Machiavelli endorses the view that statesmen should murder recalcitrant citizens straightaway and easily. Instead, Machiavelli universalizes the lessons of Moses in the sense that he took God's ratification of those particular murders as indicative of God's general propensity to embrace Machiavelli's highest values. Machiavelli does not consider the possibility that Moses' situation and God's response were unique: that the narrative was not intended to be universalized and does not manifest God's general propensities. Indeed, when examining and analyzing the parables and teachings of the New Testament, an unbiased person would be hard-pressed to conclude that the God of Machiavelli exists. The words attributed to Jesus simply do not reflect Machiavelli's highest values. Either Jesus radically misunderstood God's nature or Machiavelli reconceived God to underwrite his own political purposes.

Patriotism, Religion, and the Condition of a Person's Soul

Brushing aside the evident self-interested nature of Machiavelli's interpretation of God, a paradox arises when we analyze that conception in the context of Machiavelli's dramatic call to love one's country more than one's soul and to risk one's soul for one's country. In accord with the example God followed in the case of Moses, Machiavelli concludes that God either antecedently endorses or later pardons those founders of states, reformers of nations, and statesmen who use evil well in order to accomplish their missions. The God of Machiavelli is keenly aware of the need for such heroic figures to employ evil means in the face of necessity. Extrapolating from the example of Moses, Machiavelli concludes that God endorsed and abetted the paramount actions of Cyrus, Theseus, and Romulus.

In this vein, Machiavelli described the state of mind of Cesare Borgia as he terrorized northern and central Italy: "[Borgia] wished to be excused with God and men, if he used whatever means were at his disposal to assure himself of his state. . . . He should be sorry to be obliged to injure others, but he felt that he would be excused by God and by men, and even by the Siennese themselves, as being forced to it by necessity" (Legations 11.44, 11.95).

The idea of God's benevolence toward statesmen who use evil well in order to found states and reform nations is more forcefully expressed in Machiavelli's stirring final chapter of *The Prince*: "And though up to now various gleams have appeared in some Italians from which we might judge them ordained by God for [Italy's] redemption. . . . [Italy] is now praying to God to send someone to redeem her. . . . We see marvelous, unexampled signs that God is directing [the house of Medici]. . . . God does not do everything, so as not to take from us free will and part of the glory that pertains to us" (P 26).

Yet Machiavelli is convinced that these same social redeemers risk their souls when they use evil well and that they demonstrate thereby that they love their countries more than their souls. But if God completely approves of such actions from the outset or fully forgives them after the fact, in what manner have Machiavelli's heroes manifested their love of country over their well-being and thereby risked their souls?

What does Machiavelli mean when he writes, "I love my native city more than my own soul" (Ltr. 331: 4/16/27) and when he comments on certain Florentines of the past that "so much more did those citizens then esteem their fatherland than their souls" (FH III 7)?

I must note that although the phrase "more than *my own soul*" is included in virtually every translation of Machiavelli's correspondence, it is actually an interpretive addition to the text. The original letter was erased at that point in the sentence. The term "my own soul" was apparently added because doing so was consistent with what Machiavelli says when he celebrates several patriotic heroes in his *Florentine Histories* and with patriotic sentiments he expressed in other works. In any case, the entire sentence underscores Machiavelli's patriotic zeal.

Hannah Arendt interprets the phrase in this way: "Machiavelli's 'I love my native city more than my soul' is only a variation of: I love the world and its future more than my life or my self."[5] This strikes me as somewhat misleading. Machiavelli is highlighting the importance of civic responsibility and commitment to the common good, to be sure. But his allegiance, his love, is not directed to an abstraction called "the world and its future." Instead, Machiavelli champions the concreteness and specificity of his native land, whether it is conceived of as Florence or an anticipated united Italy. The world can yield only an ethereal identity: the global citizen is a cosmopolitan, generic human being. Florence or Italy nurtures a robust identity that expands the subjectivity of the individual manageably—that permits the person to retain individuality in the context of a circumscribed community.

In his own case, Machiavelli underscores his priority of placing the common good of his country above personal concerns, whether those interests center on adhering to the conventional pieties of religious worship or the pursuit of petty self-interest. In Machiavelli's case, his highest values focus on patriotism and the pursuit of enduring glory related thereto. For him, the common good and his highest values coalesce. In the case of the noble Florentines of the past, Machiavelli stresses the need to place the common good above even one's higher values that may conflict with the common good.[6] For example, when Machiavelli applauds Cosimo Rucellai as a "worthy man and a good citizen" (AW 1 7), he judges that Rucellai would have sacrificed all his possessions and his own life to advance the larger cause of the common good.

The meaning of loving one's fatherland more than one's own soul, then, converges in the three illustrations of Machiavelli, the ancient Florentines, and Rucellai: Machiavelli and those whom he admires self-consciously adopt the common good of the fatherland as their highest value. Moreover, doing so is compatible with and in fact demands that patriots pursue enduring glory grounded in military and political activities. For Machiavelli, the only immortality worth pursuing can be attained only by loving one's country more than one's own soul, more than one's narrow self-interest, and even more than one's cherished values that are incompatible with patriotic action. A person loves his country more than his own soul only when he embraces the common good of his country and patriotism as his highest values and acts resolutely to advance those values.

Machiavelli suspects that we cannot transcend death, our projects do not last forever, the stamp of our identities smudges with time, and for all but a few our footprints are trampled on and then obliterated. But the experiences; the stream of processes; and the struggles, defeats, and triumphs elevate our lives with meaning. The heroic military and political quest in service of the common good may be his response to the terror of human vulnerability, limitation, and inevitable death. Perhaps an unearned narcissism fuels the journey. Perhaps human life is impossible to live robustly without illusions. Perhaps religious commitment, instead of being the vehicle by which dominant classes solidify power (Marx's critique), or by which the herd deflates the pursuit of greatness by potential nobles (Nietzsche's account), or by which human beings project their need for a Great Father (Freud's explanation), is an especially seductive narrative of the heroic quest for personal immortality. Machiavelli, however, is firmly rooted in this world and therefore yokes religion to political purposes and personal transformation.

We must choose and act in a partly self-forgetful way. A personal perspective, which narrows our focus of concern, allows us to luxuriate in the heroic quest by temporarily marginalizing explicit awareness of death. Yes, this can become inauthentic: we cannot live entirely in personal perspectives without yielding our reflective powers that elevate us from a purely animalistic life. But neither can we live entirely in a cosmic perspective, which radically broadens our focus and calls into question the justification of each conscious moment. The struggle to triumph over life's limitations, the hunt for ersatz immortality, and the yearning for connection with value and meaning render us noble in the face of our terror. Confronting the Grim Reaper at the moment of ultimate Truth can itself crown the meaningfulness of our lives, or not.

Machiavelli is keenly aware of the tragic dimensions of life. Embracing life fully means accepting its tragic dimensions including human limitation, individual estrangement, the temporality of even the highest human achievements, and inevitable death. Celebrants of the Machiavellian ideal distinguish themselves by the quality of their performance: their confrontations with obstacles and suffering, their ability to forge a unified style out of their inherent multiplicity, their recurring self-creations and self-overcomings, their ability to luxuriate in the immediacy of life, and their understanding of life as a sequence of aesthetically self-fulfilling moments—all this accomplished in an international military and political arena bearing zero-sum implications.

A full acceptance of life and the surrounding world includes, for Machiavelli, the realization that prior to death our life has been fulfilling and is in need of no further acts to complete it. As the final curtain falls over his life, the Machiavellian hero savors the whole and wishes only that it could be relived. This is his ultimate satisfaction should he be so fortunate as to attain it. Living with adequate recognition of mortality, yet responding zestfully, vivifies meaning in his life and elevates death above meaningless termination. Mortality is the human context, but not necessarily our defeat. We need not glorify death, we need not pretend we do not fear death, but we should temper Father Time's victory by living and dying meaningfully. Our impulses to generate legacies are honorable even if permanence eludes us. This is part of Machiavelli's secret.

What, then, does it mean to risk one's soul for one's country? Perhaps Machiavelli is speaking metaphorically about risking one's life in service of national interests. Certainly, those who advance their nation's military or political interests are vulnerable to assassination, death in battle or from opposing conspiracies, and the like. But this is unlikely to be Machiavelli's import. To expend one's life in a grand cause is noble but does not automatically risk one's soul. Martyrs, for example, presumably earn eternal salvation under precisely those circumstances.

Machiavelli might also mean that in the course of advancing national interests statesmen must stray from the imperatives of conventional morality and thereby risk eternal damnation for their transgressions. On this reading, Machiavelli's meaning dovetails with his understanding of international politics: leaders must act morally when they are able, but must use evil well at times. The use of evil, even under such circumstances, corrupts the soul and renders it susceptible to punishment in the afterlife. This possible interpretation is also highly unlikely to capture Machiavelli's intent for at least three reasons.

First, Machiavelli's extensive writings reveal no evidence that he feared eternal damnation or believed in the existence of hell. For example, in *La Mandragola*, a character opines that "the worst that can come to you from it is to die and go to hell; but how many others are dead! And there are so many good men in hell! Are you ashamed to go there? Face your lot; flee evil, but, not being able to flee it, bear it like a man" (M 4:1).

Second, a story recalls Machiavelli on his deathbed being told that "the wisdom of this world is the enemy of God," and Machiavelli replying, "I am not tagging along with those ragbags [the ill, weak, weary, and poor who are blessed] to go to paradise. I am staying with that other company [Plato, Plutarch, Livy, and Tacitus, among others], to talk about the state and go to hell."[7] Even if apocryphal, the story attests to Machiavelli's utter indifference to the threat of Hell and the possibility of eternal damnation. As further evidence of Machiavelli's lack of concern for his prospects during final judgment, we have correspondence from his friend, Francesco Guicciardini. Writing to Machiavelli, who was charged with the task of selecting a preacher and adjudicating a perplexing issue of jurisdiction over monasteries, Guicciardini noted, "I believe you will serve them according to the expectations they have of you and as is required by your honor, which would be stained if at this age *you started to think about your soul, because, since you have always lived in a contrary belief,* it would be attributed rather to senility than to goodness" (Ltr. 269: 5/17/21; emphasis added).

Third, Machiavelli consistently ridiculed the Church practices of accepting money for indulgences and offering masses presumably on the behalf of the dead (to soften punishment in the afterlife). He placed no stock in ransoming souls out of Purgatory.

Finally, if God genuinely endorses the patriotic values and heroic nationalistic actions that Machiavelli extols, then God would be unlikely to punish earnest statesmen who use evil well in the context of necessity and in service of the common good. Just as God ratified the harsh measures of Moses, so too would God—at least from Machiavelli's vantage point—approve of evil well-used by statesmen elsewhere and in other times. Accordingly, that Machiavelli intends the expression "risk one's soul for one's country" to invoke the prospects of eternal damnation in the bowels of Christian hell is unlikely.

In my judgment, the most likely meaning of the expression "risk one's soul for one country" focuses on how being implicated in evil deeds is its own punishment. Having to make and to act pursuant to choices that implicate our lives with evil, even if doing so is grounded in political necessity and fervent patriotism, registers effects on who we are *now*: we thereby stain our souls. Machiavelli seems convinced that the quality of our choices and deeds deeply affect our characters regardless of how fortune, other people, and even God respond. We become our sins in that our souls reflect the nature of our deeds. Regardless of how other people perceive us and how luck favors us, who and what we are is an objective matter determined by the way we exercise our freedom—what we choose and do. For Machiavelli, in this sense we reap what we sow on earth. Thus to use evil means, even if doing so is required by the duties of one's office and in service of the common good of a healthy republic, is to alter the topography of the self in potentially unflattering ways. To risk our souls, then, is to jeopardize who we are as the effects of being implicated in evil register on our characters.

Statesmen antecedently know and act upon the good. But often in gaining and after assuming their offices, they must learn how not to be good in order to serve national interests and discharge their duties to constituents. They must avoid losing their souls, in which case corruption and tyranny will follow, but they risk their souls as their characters are challenged and potentially transformed by the deeds in which they participate. Some of these military and political acts require using evil well. As I will examine thoroughly later in this work, for Machiavelli, even when used well evil remains evil and registers dangerous effects on the souls of perpetrators.

If the soul at risk is not the metaphysical entity depicted by religion, then what is it? Although difficult to define precisely, the soul refers to the central or integral part or vital core of a person: a person's character and identity. If what one does greatly affects who one is then Machiavellian statesmen risk much in fulfilling the duties of their office. If Machiavelli is correct in thinking that such statesmen must dirty their hands because of the nature of the world and the partiality their positions required, then they must also jeopardize their internal condition. In my judgment, like ancient philosophers such as Plato and Augustine, Machiavelli assumes that a person's internal condition is an objective matter. Regardless of how a person is judged by contemporaries and how he or she appears to the public, the condition of a person's character and inner core are objective in that they register the effects of that person's deeds. To violate categorical moral rules, even where doing so is appropriate to the duties of a statesman's office, is to assume the burdens of the moral wrong that remains and to stain the soul. Although Machiavelli famously speaks about the importance of maintaining appearances in order to remain in office and exercise power, he is not seduced by his own rhetoric: he understands acutely that appearances are distinct from reality. What a person does greatly affects who that person is regardless of external appearances and the judgments of the masses. Vice is its own punishment and virtue is its own reward in that the inner core of a person absorbs the effects of both. For people to dirty their hands too frequently is to risk losing their souls in that they will alter their characters and identities for the worse; they will become different, less worthy human beings.

We can illustrate Machiavelli's conviction in the context of the seven deadly vices. Arrogance distorts and amplifies the self, alienates us from salutary human communities. and renders us empty and self-absorbed. Envy simmers in its own resentment, diminishes the self, and deepens our sense of inadequacy. Wrath wallows in spite, severs us from righteous elements in the community, and hardens our hearts. Sloth begins in joyless apathy and blossoms into hopelessness and muted self-absorption. Avarice fastens us to a pendulum of frustration and relegates us to a quicksand of rapacious desire; we ignore the interests of others when we should not and become captive to our own insatiability. Gluttony, understood as excessive self-indulgence, diverts us from noble pursuits, weakens the resolve of our wills, and promotes unnecessary suffering. Lust replaces the human need for intimacy and bonding with the yearning to satisfy immediate cravings. As such, lust distances us from loving the proper things in the appropriate measure.

Accordingly, Machiavelli is firmly convinced that complicity with evil is its own punishment, our characters are reflected and formed by the way we exercise our freedom, and the condition of our characters is an objective matter. Indeed, the punishments that Machiavelli's Florentine precursor, Dante, conjures in Hell and Purgatory are metaphors for what sinners have already made of themselves while living.[8] Dante's afterlife reflects infallibly what sinners have become through their choices and acts. Machiavelli, unlike Dante, is not concerned with the afterlife, but understands acutely that the law of personal desert operates on earth: to flunk the test of soul-crafting is to fail life. Regardless of how fortune responds to us and how others perceive us, we are in the process of becoming certain people with particular characters that are forged from the way we exercise our freedom. Appearances and the judgments of others can shroud but cannot alter what we are becoming. If Machiavelli is correct, chief military and political officials—because of the zero-sum nature of international politics and the nature of the world—must dirty their hands and jeopardize their souls on behalf of their fellow countrymen. Machiavelli alludes to this in his writings, but he does not develop explicitly or analyze thoroughly the inner life of statesmen. While he makes clear that they must dirty their hands to honor the common good and he intimates that in the course of nobly fulfilling their duties they must risk their souls, he pursues these thoughts no further. As always, however, Machiavelli has left us the clues necessary for unraveling his secret.

Machiavelli's Morality

To understand fully Machiavelli's normative positive we must first examine, evaluate, and criticize three popular renderings of his view: that Machiavelli separates politics from morality; that he unites politics to pagan morality; and that his considered moral position was a version of tribal, act consequentialist.

An influential interpretation of *The Prince* is most closely associated with Benedetto Croce (1866–1952). According to Croce, Machiavelli strove to separate the moral sphere from the political domain. Conventional morality cannot apply to political maneuverings, which are governed by strategic and prudential prerogatives that elude moral evaluation.

Machiavelli discovered the necessity and the autonomy of politics, politics which is beyond good and bad morals, which has its own laws against which it is futile to rebel, which cannot be exorcised and banished from the world with holy water.[9]

On this view, Machiavelli's political prescriptions are not immoral because politics are independent of moral assessment. Politics is public, morality is private, and this autonomy is required for the proper functioning of social life. Conventional morality does not govern political affairs, and actions and policies operating on different assumptions are doomed to disaster, at worst, or irrelevance, at best. As Machiavelli observes, only if all men were good would this not be the case (P 18). But because human nature is radically flawed, public responsibility and private rectitude are distinct spheres of activity.

Croce's view is reflected in a more general interpretation of *The Prince*: that the book is an exercise in realism; that Machiavelli's writing is purely descriptive. True, he draws conclusions of what a prince should do given the conditions of the world and of politics, but such prescriptions are prudential and strategic, not moral. Machiavelli's methods are the means of his time, indeed all times, and the only ones offering hope for political success. Political leaders sometimes lie, connive, threaten, plot, and coerce in order to attain their ends and advance the interests of their polity. What is the source of the scandal? Not even Plato, who insisted that virtue and knowledge must be joined in the paradigm of the philosopher-king, would be surprised by such news. Plato would bemoan the separation of morality from politics, but he would not deny that as an empirical matter that division existed. Whereas Plato hoped to change the world through his utopian vision, Machiavelli aspires to succeed politically in the world as it is. Machiavelli is not *championing* the autonomy of politics from morals nor is he delighted that the world is as it is. Instead, the successful ruler will learn how to gain the competitive edge in a world not of his making. His subjects deserve nothing less.

True, Machiavelli is also convinced that the world cannot be changed because of inherent defects in human nature, the zero-sum nature of international affairs, and the natural scarcity of desired resources, but this, too, is a description of reality. Strong men will press forward to establish, preserve, and extend their power: "The first law of internal policy is to hold on to power, of external policy it is to extend your imperialism."[10] Again, Machiavelli does not confer moral blessings on these circumstances and events. He does not, as did Thrasymachus, conclude that "might makes right" and that conventional morality consisted of guidelines in the interests of the strongest in society. Instead, for Machiavelli effective use of force and fraud translate to political success, which is beyond moral assessment.

This interpretation at once liberates Machiavelli from charges of immorality and honors him for sharply observing the political world and compiling a handbook for political success. Unfortunately, it overly simplifies Machiavelli's writings.

First, although Machiavelli undoubtedly saw himself as a realist, his vision was clouded. His convictions that the state of the world and of human nature are fixed; that ambition and power-mongering are the key to understanding men; that international affairs are by their very nature zero-sum contests; and that human motivation flows only from self-interest all betray his myopia.

Second, that Machiavelli separated politics from morality, although a popular mantra, is false. Machiavelli subjected politics to moral assessment at numerous crucial junctures and in subtle, complex ways. Part of Machiavelli's innovation and genius resides in his intuitive feel for the nuanced ways morality intrudes on politics, and for the inner tensions simmering within conventional morality itself. Although Machiavelli rarely addresses such matters explicitly, they implicitly underwrite many of his major themes.

To begin to understand these connections, we must examine a second rendering of Machiavelli's normative position: the challenging interpretation of Machiavelli's work that concludes that at the heart of *The Prince* is a clash of two incompatible value systems—conventional (Christian) morality and pagan (ancient Roman) morality. In that vein, Giuseppe Prezzolini offers a subtle, challenging interpretation of *The Prince*. Machiavelli does not separate politics from morality, only from a certain version of Christian morality. Machiavelli weds politics to a pagan morality that places state interests above all religion and honors only those religions that render the masses "loyal and governable."[11]

Prezzolini finds the origins of Machiavelli's position in a pessimistic Christianity best exemplified by St. Augustine. The great theologian bifurcated the City of God from the City of Man as two distinct ways of life. Damned by original sin, human beings could not legitimately hope to attain justice and moral goodness in worldly, political communities. The state ministers to those who are morally deficient. Only if all people abided by Christian morality would the state be unnecessary.

But people do not abide generally to Christian morality. Thus, only in the afterlife will perfect justice be realized. Earthly governments, then, will always transgress against moral law. St. Augustine foreshadowed Machiavelli's notion that to succeed politically leaders must often cast aside conventional morality. St. Augustine's position itself is prefigured in the Bible where Jesus advises Pontius Pilate that "My kingdom is not of this world" (John 18:36).

Isaiah Berlin echoes Prezzolini's view, but erases the references to pessimistic Christianity. *The Prince*, says Berlin, details a clash of two value systems: a pagan (Roman) ethic and the conventional (Christian) morality. Instead of conceiving Machiavelli as positing two autonomous guiding-action realms, the moral and the political, Berlin sees the conflict in Machiavelli waged within morality itself. Machiavelli, then, is not advocating the separation of politics from ethics, but only the marriage of politics to a morality different from the conventional, Christian version. "[Machiavelli plants] a permanent question mark in the path of posterity. It stems from his *de facto* recognition that ends equally ultimate, equally sacred, may contradict each other, that entire systems of value may come into collision without possibility of rational arbitration, and that not merely in exceptional circumstances, as a result of abnormality or accident or error . . . but (this was surely new) as part of the normal human situation."[12]

The pagan or Roman morality embodies goals as ultimate and legitimate as those celebrated by Christianity. Christianity treasures faith, hope, charity, love, mercy, adoration of God, forgiveness of transgressions by enemies, selflessness, compassion for others, redemption of the soul, suspicion of worldly goods, and focus on earning a blissful afterlife. This, for Machiavelli, is an ethic for private people seeking transcendent salvation. Roman religion stressed the establishment, preservation, and expansion of a well-ordered social whole. This required men of character: "inner moral strength, magnanimity, vigor, vitality, generosity, loyalty, above all public spirit, civic sense, dedication to the security, power, glory, expansion of the *patria*."[13] Through glittering displays, bloody sacrifices, sound laws, and carefully defined education, the Romans sanctified pagan virtues: "Power, magnificence, pride, austerity, pursuit of glory, vigor, discipline . . . this is what makes states great."[14] This, for Machiavelli, is an ethic for leaders in public roles striving for personal (worldly) glory and the founding, reforming, or preservation of a healthy, expansionist polity. Such social ends, Machiavelli insists, are natural and prudent for men to pursue.

To welcome Christian morality wholeheartedly is to consign oneself to political fecklessness. To embrace Roman morality uncompromisingly is to risk losing one's soul. Machiavelli notes that Christianity, instead of being misconstrued in the spirit of *ozio*, could have been designed in ways that facilitated military and political *virtù* (D II 2; D I 12). Unfortunately, the corrupt Church in Rome molded spiritual doctrine in unpatriotic, *effeminato* ways. While Machiavelli does not condemn conventional morality, he advises public officials to learn how not to be good (in the Christian sense) and, instead, cultivate the craft of the fox and the intimidation of the lion (P 15, 18).

For Machiavelli, the importance of Rome as an example largely flows from the extent and duration of its power; that Rome could have influenced so many peoples for so long a time makes it the supreme case of collective civic *virtù*. Through his study of ancient Rome, Machiavelli found support for his instinctive personal values: passion for competition, zest for honor, yearning for community, and distrust of other states. The Romans recognized no difference between moral excellence and reputation; praise was what every citizen most desired; to place personal honor above the interests of the entire community was considered barbaric; citizens were educated to harness their ambition in service to the common good, although in their relations with other states and *stranieri* (strangers), no such limitations constricted their competitive instincts.[15]

Machiavelli also found ballast in the traditions of Rome for his convictions that the quest for *virtù* was a zero-sum competition that required valiant combatants taught through proper laws, family values, and military and political contests:

> Ruthless competition was regarded as the basis of all civic virtue. . . . Hardness was a Roman ideal. The steel required to hunt out glory or endure disaster was a defining mark of a citizen. It was instilled in him from the moment of his birth. . . . To raise heirs successfully, to instill in them due pride in their bloodline and hankering after glory, these were achievements worthy of a man. . . . "Gain cannot be made without loss to someone else." So every Roman took for granted.[16]

Men, then, have two choices. Those entering public life cannot effectively be responsible for the lives and security of their constituents while obeying the imperatives of Christian morality. Those who do choose to diligently follow those commandments should focus on their personal salvation, but refrain from military and political leadership. Berlin is clear: "This is not a division of politics from ethics. It is the uncovering of the possibility of more than one system of values, with no criterion common to the systems whereby a rational choice can be made between them . . . men choose either a good, virtuous private life, or a good, successful social existence, but not both."[17] Accordingly, for Berlin, Machiavelli's originality consists in his evisceration of a foundational tenet of Western philosophy: the conviction that all genuine values are ultimately compatible.

Berlin does not allege that Machiavelli's conscious intention was to challenge the moral thinking of Western philosophy. On the contrary, Machiavelli's purposes were practical: to have an effect on the political world and to advertise for employment. But a careful reading of this work leads Berlin to conclude that he has identified a hitherto ignored source of Machiavelli's innovative thinking. The incommensurability of two, clashing, internally legitimate moral systems is the fuel that implicitly drives Machiavelli's writings.

The Prezzolini-Berlin interpretation is insightful: Contrary to popular judgment, Machiavelli does not divorce politics from morality. Still, this interpretation is too clean and tidy. The relationship of conventional morality to Machiavellian politics is more complicated than they suppose.

Political leaders must follow conventional (Christian) morality if they can, but must be prepared to do wrong if necessary (P 18). Politics, then, is not simply divorced from conventional morality. Complying with the imperatives of conventional morality remains the default position. More important, conventional morality continues to evaluate political actions. To call evil "well-used" is not only to highlight the necessity of cruel measures but also to underscore that those means remain "evil"—as judged by conventional morality (P 8). When the masses judge only by results they stray from the principles of conventional morality and from the guidelines for wise assessment of political efforts (P 18, 25; AW I 29–32; D III 35; D I 9, 53).

In fact, Machiavelli's political program is required primarily because of a breakdown in conventional morality and a weakness of human nature. If all human beings obeyed conventional morality, Machiavelli explicitly recognizes that his advice to political leaders would be woefully inadequate (P 18). The pagan (ancient Roman) morality of *The Prince* is required because of the failure of conventional morality, probably because of defects in human nature itself, to command strict allegiance. Moreover, Machiavelli disparages tyranny: politics are conducted morally when directed toward the common good, not when pursued only for selfish advantage (P 8; D I 10, 17, 29, 34). When certain means are partially "excused" because of the critical importance of the ends they attain, the excuse is rendered from the perspective of conventional morality (P 18; D I 9). That harsh means are only excused and that they remain "evil" even if well-used implies that the wrongness of the actions persists for Machiavelli even though the actions were warranted. This can be a judgment only from the perspective of conventional morality. Pagan morality, presumably, would have no reason to excuse or to label as "evil" what it would take to be perfectly reasonable and acceptable measures to secure its ends.

The strictures of conventional morality must also underwrite the sound laws and disciplined education required to nourish the moral and civic *virtù* of the masses. The imperatives of ancient Roman morality are needed to promote the military and political *virtù* of government leaders. Moreover, ancient Roman morality, or something akin to it, is required to establish the order, security, and framework that make conventional morality possible.

Machiavelli requires a reformation of religion, which he takes to be the foundation of all moralities. He accepts conventional morality and understands his society cannot simply turn back the clock and act as if Christianity never occurred. They cannot merrily trip back to the era of the Roman republic, accepting its religions and superstitions as their own while erasing the history of Christianity. He recognizes that Christianity is not inherently incompatible with a robust religion that could advance state interests (D II 2; D I 12). He, of course, understands well that the Church in Rome will resist vigorously the required reforms. The Church had its own secular, not merely religious, power and prerogatives to preserve. (For example, the Church fought strenuously for centuries to retain Latin, not Italian, as the official language of the peninsula, a strategy designed to retain a source of its ideological hegemony.)

In sum, the relationship of Machiavellian politics to morality is more complex than the Prezzolini-Berlin interpretation suggests because (1) Machiavelli accepts absolute principles of conventional morality—principles that are absolute not in the sense that they cannot be legitimately overridden, but because violations of these principles retain an element of wrongness even if excused; (2) Machiavelli keenly appreciates the tension between impersonal morality and the particular duties of public office—the extra responsibilities borne by chief military and political officials; the imperative to advance the interests of constituents over those of foreigners; and the need to advance the collective interest embodied by the state; and (3) Machiavelli underscores the necessities of international affairs—the intrusions of *Fortuna*, the zero-sum nature of the contest, the deficiencies of human nature, and the natural scarcity of resources. Machiavelli does not merely argue that Roman (pagan) morality oversees politics, while conventional (Christian) morality governs private life.

The life of a political leader is lived in tensions among the three competing vectors sketched in the previous paragraph. It is not as if such a leader merely casts off the cloak of conventional morality when he enters his office or job quarters, and adorns himself in the liberating dress of a Roman pagan. Such action would increase the likelihood of his degenerating into a tyrant or an official who used cruel measures when they were not required. Machiavelli never explores the interior life of his imaginary prince or those of his historical princes, some of whom are merely mythical anyway. To say that Machiavelli's political leaders, if proper to their posts, would suffer existential angst seems a legitimate inference. But Machiavelli never says that or even touches on the possibility. Perhaps the implications of the meanderings of his argument eluded him. Perhaps he never clearly recognized his own internal conflicts. But he left us a series of clues: the competing moral and political vectors pressing down on a Machiavellian ruler are deep, dark, and dense. Their conflicting demands cannot be simultaneously fulfilled.

A third, popular rendering of Machiavelli's normative position concludes that he was a tribal act consequentialist. A tribal act consequentialist or, more narrowly, tribal act utilitarian, strives to select the course of action that, under the circumstances, best advances the collective interests of *his* group. He is not a classic utilitarian who impartially considers the interests of *every human being* (or every sentient being) affected by actions spurred by moral choice. Instead, he restricts his domain of concern to a small unit—perhaps country, city, organization, or family. Unlike nonconsequentialist moralists, who insist that individuals have rights that insulate them from being used for the public good or in service of advancing the interests of the majority, the tribal act consequentialist has only the communal good at the forefront of his moral calculations. Individual rights, under this view, are respected only insofar as doing so promotes the best overall results. Moreover, they are subject to recurrent scrutiny as new situations and circumstances arise.

Initially, labeling Machiavelli a tribal act consequentialist seems fair.[18] He is willing to transgress conventional morality in deference to the common good; he considers the interests of his city-state or nation as monumentally more important than the interests of foreigners or the international community as a whole; he is willing, at times eager, to sacrifice individuals for what he takes to be the common good; and he carefully calculates the respective outcomes of contemplated actions.

But first judgments are often deceiving. Machiavelli advises statesmen to follow conventional (nonconsequentialist) morality if possible, both domestically and internationally. In a well-grounded polity, doing so domestically will be the norm. Some excusable transgressions, though, will occur. "The sons of Brutus" must be eliminated if they threaten the safety and security of a republic; founding or preserving a healthy, expansionist state, or reforming a corrupt state will require evil well-used; promoting the common good will occasionally demand the removal of recalcitrant elements. But, domestically, not *every* action is subject to consequentialist moral or political calculations. The default mindset is compliance with conventional morality grounded in nonconsequentialist considerations. Violations of those norms are more circumscribed than the number occurring under tribal act consequentialism. Demonstrating that a marginal gain in the collective interest can be attained by, say, oppressing a minority group or exploiting an individual is insufficient to trigger an excusable transgression under Machiavelli's view.

Internationally, conventional morality is followed if and only if strategically and prudentially sound. But given the structure of the world as a zero-sum game, the nature of human beings, and the need for preemptive military and political action, Machiavelli scoffs at the possibility of a brotherhood and sisterhood of nations. Accordingly, his judgments on such matters are grounded in expediency; his military responses are often disproportionate; and he extols the principle of doing-unto-others-before-they-do-unto-you. Even here, though, the structure, boundaries, and composition of the tribe change. As foreigners are defeated and brought under the umbrella of Machiavelli's expansionist republic, they gain the moral status he would previously deny them. Eventually, they become citizens worthy of domestic consideration. Machiavellian membership has its privileges.

In sum, unlike a tribal act consequentialist, Machiavelli does not derive an action's or a principle's moral quality after assessing its consequences. Instead, he accepts the absolutist inclinations of conventional morality: even when used well, evil remains evil. That in the instant case it was the appropriate means to employ does not transform a generally evil means into a moral method. For Machiavelli, then, the consequences of an action do not determine its moral quality. This is another reason why he observes dryly that the masses judge events only by outcomes and are fascinated by mere appearances. Machiavelli understands well that such assessments are crude, partial, and inadequate.

The Popular View of Machiavelli on Morality

The most popular understanding of Machiavelli's normative position is an offshoot of two views we have just examined: that Machiavelli separated the moral and political realms, and in the political realm he embraced tribal act consequentialism. The popular understanding of Machiavelli's understanding of morality is that he proudly advocated that the ends justify the means, at least within the political realm. Even if absolute moral principles held sway within private relations, they must yield to the exigencies of political necessity. Thus, if a goal is politically useful then its pursuit through whatever means are necessary is justified. Furthermore, the artful statesman should conceal from the public his expedient uses of fraud, treachery, and force to the extent he is able.

The renowned twentieth-century political theorist Leo Strauss expresses forcefully the popular view: "Contemporary tyranny has its roots in Machiavelli's thought, in the Machiavellian principle that the good end justifies every means. At least to the extent that the American reality is inseparable from the American aspiration, one cannot understand Americanism without understanding Machiavellianism which is its opposite."[19]

In two sentences, Strauss accuses Machiavelli of having spawned tyrannical movements such as fascism and communism; of espousing triumphantly the principle that the good end justifies every means; and of conjuring an anti-American political philosophy even though Machiavelli died about 250 years prior to the founding of our republic.

Strauss goes on to charge that Machiavelli, sensing that he needed to soften and misdirect readers from the harshness of his principles, cleverly added the final chapter of *The Prince* to stir hearts and to cloud minds: "The information regarding the political prerequisites of the liberation of Italy is withheld in [chapter 26,] which is explicitly devoted to the liberation of Italy because Machiavelli desired to keep the noble and shining end untarnished by the base and dark means that are indispensable for its achievement. He desired this because the teaching that 'the end justifies the means' is repulsive, and he wanted the *Prince* to end even more attractively than it began."[20]

Moreover, Strauss insists that Machiavelli understood and advocated that freeing Italy from the barbarians required nothing less than a political and moral revolution: "The liberation of Italy means a complete revolution. It requires first and above everything else a revolution in thinking about right and wrong. Italians have to learn that the patriotic end hallows every means however much condemned by the most exalted traditions both philosophical and religious."[21]

Rarely has so distinguished a scholar drawn such crude, mistaken conclusions.

Justifications and Excuses

Did Machiavelli ever write that "the good end justifies every means"? In a word: No. The closest he came is in *The Prince*: "*e nelle azioni di tutti gli uomini e massime de' principi dove non è iudizio a chi reclamare, si guarda al fine. Facci dunque uno principe di vincere e mantenere lo stato: é mezzi saranno sempre iudicati onorevoli e da ciascuno laudati; perché il vulgo ne va sempre preso con quello che pare e con lo evento della cosa*" (P 18).

In some English and American translations of that work, particularly those composed in the first half of the twentieth century, the phrase "the end justifies the means" appears. For example, the Modern Library edition of *The Prince*, based on the Luigi Ricci translation in 1903 as revised by E. R. P. Vincent in 1935 reports: "In the actions of men, and especially of princes, from which there is no appeal, *the end justifies the means*. Let a prince therefore aim at conquering and maintaining the state, and the means will always be judged honorable and praised by every one [*sic*], for the vulgar is always taken in by appearances and the issue of the event" (P 18; emphasis added).[22]

Those translators projected a principle or phrase unknown to Machiavelli upon his work, perhaps to make it relevant to contemporary readers. In every translation I have read in the past, say, thirty years that phrase is absent. For example, David Wooten's translation is an example of contemporary English renderings: "In the behavior of all men, and particularly of rulers, against whom there is no recourse at law, *people judge by the outcome*. So if a ruler wins wars and holds on to power, the means he has employed will always be judged honorable, and everyone will praise them. The common man accepts external appearances and judges by outcome" (P 18; emphasis added).[23]

From a philosophical standpoint the difference between what Machiavelli wrote and what some translators and interpreters have attributed to him is profound. Machiavelli is making an *empirical* claim: the masses, as a matter of fact, evaluate actions, especially those of politicians, by their results. Even the Ricci–Vincent translation recognizes that the masses are deceived by appearances and evaluate actions only by their outcomes. Machiavelli is not lodging a *normative* claim: he is not concluding that human beings should evaluate actions only by their outcomes. He is not arguing that the ends justify the means as a feature of sound moral principle. In fact, Machiavelli's observation that "the common man accepts external appearances" is more redolent of condescension than affirmation.

The implicit message is: Wise men, spurning mass opinion, would do well not to evaluate actions only by results. In fact, Machiavelli rejects the proposition that the results of actions are necessary or sufficient for properly evaluating those actions (P 25; AW I 29–32; D III 35; D I 9, 53). But Machiavelli insists systematically throughout his writings that politicians must operate on the way human beings are, not as they ought to be. Thus, rulers must recognize the manner in which their actions will be evaluated by most people.

Critics might agree that Machiavelli never penned the words nor vividly understood the normative implications of the phrase. Still, they might counter, large amounts of his doctrine tacitly endorse Strauss's interpretation. And not just what Machiavelli says in *The Prince* about the salutary uses of fraud, force, coercion, and the like. In the *Discourses*, Machiavelli is unrepentantly enthusiastic when recalling the stunning cruelty of Romulus killing his brother (D I 9), Brutus overseeing the execution of his sons (D III 1, 3), and Moses helping to slay 3,000 countrymen (D III 30, 41). The Florentine relentlessly exalts strong men of robust military and political *virtù* who are willing to dirty their hands in service of founding or preserving a healthy, expansionist state, or reforming a corrupt state. What is this other than implicit agreement that "the good end justifies every means"?

As an aside, the imagined critic's strong case obliterates one of Strauss's points: that Machiavelli tried to honey coat his political messages in *The Prince* by adding an emotional finale. In his unabashedly republican paean, *The Discourses*, Machiavelli reveled in the horrifying deeds of Romulus, Brutus, Moses, and a host of others. He never tried to whitewash their slayings; instead, he used such mind-boggling actions to graphically underscore his unyielding political message: The great leader bent on securing military and political glory must not shy from bloody business that would petrify lesser men. In *The Prince*, Machiavelli offered twenty-five chapters of strategies, much of them relying on force and fraud, to found a principality. To speculate that one patriotic chapter at the end of that book would deceive readers is unreasonable. Even the most simpleminded supporter of Machiavelli cannot successfully turn him into a liberal humanist. Nor would the Florentine aspire to that label.

To demonstrate my conclusion that Machiavelli did not hold, even tacitly, the principle that "the good end justifies every means," I must begin with two sets of distinctions.

The first distinction is between *justifications* and *excuses*. To *justify* an act is to defend the act as just, right, and appropriate. The perpetrator of the act admits performing it, but advances reasons that claim to show the act was proper; he accepts responsibility for the act, but argues that he should be exonerated from blame because the act was not blameworthy under the instant circumstances: "I did act X and was responsible for X, but I should not be blamed for X because X was not wrong because of R (the reason or set of reasons allegedly supporting the performance of X)." Human beings try to justify acts that are typically viewed as unjust, wrong, or inappropriate by appealing to the special set of circumstances giving rise to that act. "I lied to spare grandma's feelings" may be a valid justification. Imagine that grandma is a wonderful lady but mediocre baker. She spends time and effort concocting an apple pie for your enjoyment. When you visit, she proudly slices you a piece. Having tasted her cooking efforts in the past, you would rather swallow a locust washed down with motor oil than consume her pie. Still, you choke down the dessert, praise it effusively as one of the best confectionaries you have ever sampled, and thank your grandmother. Although lying to your grandmother is almost always wrong, in this case you may well be justified because you know how sensitive she is to criticism. Acts that are typically wrong are sometimes justified by appeals to self-defense, necessity, emergency, unavoidable conflict of interests, avoidance of gratuitous harm, and the like. Such conditions may demonstrate that an action that is usually or almost always wrong is, under the circumstances, morally right.

To *excuse* an act is not to defend the act as just, right, and appropriate. Instead, perpetrators petition to be exonerated from blame, either partially or entirely, because they were not completely responsible for performing it. The agents of such an act may claim that they did not actually intend to perform the act, perhaps because they were incompetent at the time they did it or because they were coerced into doing it: "I did act X and X is morally tainted, but I was not (completely) responsible for doing X because of C (some special set of circumstances such as coercion, incompetence, lack of intent, or the like)."[24] An excuse presupposes wrongdoing and precludes justification. If an act is justified then an excuse is neither required nor appropriate. "The dog ate my homework" is a classic excuse. Student claims she did her schoolwork, but she cannot turn it in to her teacher because her curious canine gobbled it up. The student is not asserting a justification—she is not asserting that failing to turn in homework is appropriate—but instead says that she is not responsible for the failure. Assuming she was neither negligent nor reckless in placing the homework too close to her pet, she may have a legitimate excuse. Actions are excused because they were done inadvertently, accidentally, through mistake, or under duress or other necessity, from nonblameworthy ignorance, by someone with diminished mental capabilities, while temporarily deranged, while under the influence of drugs in a nonblameworthy way, while suffering from a mind-altering disease, while insane, and the like. All such underlying conditions mitigate or erase the moral agent's responsibility for wrongdoing.

The second distinction, one Machiavelli makes, is between *evil well-used* and *evil ill-used* (P 8). The distinction turns on traditional moral considerations: intention, motivation, foreseeable and actual results of actions. *Evil well-used* is aimed at securing the most valuable goals: founding or preserving a healthy, expansionist state, or reforming a corrupt state; driving out foreigners as a prelude to the other ends; facilitating the common good by removing obstreperous elements as a last resort; and the like. Such evil occurs in one fell swoop, it does not persist. And the means used are compelled by necessity; they are required for the valuable goals. Finally—and this is probably redundant—the valuable goals serve the common good.

Effective mercy may require evil well-used, harsh measures needed for order, security, and unification. A statesman should not shrink from being considered cruel if his purpose is to keep citizens united, faithful, and safe. The sensitive ruler—who is too squeamish to use evil well—may, through misguided short-term compassion, permit rebellions and insurrections to develop that do more long-range harm than the cruelest ruler (P 18, 19, 21; D III 3, 9, 30; Ltr. 9/16/12).

Evil ill-used is, at bottom, gratuitous cruelty. It is not required to attain the most valuable goals and may be counterproductive to those ends. Evil ill-used is often disproportionate, recurrent, and frustrates the common good. Moreover, it sometimes advances the cause of tyranny.

Machiavelli's Corollary Principle of Morality

Using the two sets of distinctions, I would argue that Machiavelli never calls evil anything other than evil.[25] Accordingly, Machiavelli does not enter the realm of justification, only that of excuse (P 18; D I 9). Military and political leaders are often forced by necessity in service of the most valuable ends to perform actions that are normally morally abhorrent and remain morally tainted even during exigency. Such leaders take responsibility for the choices they make, but not for the circumstances that induced those selections. The exercise of military and political *virtù* often requires unpleasant choices that issue in morally tainted, but excusable, actions. Leaders must choose between degrees of evil, avoid unnecessary cruelty, and follow conventional morality if possible, but be prepared to exercise harsh means when unavoidable to attain paramount goals (P 17; D III 3). Moreover, even when evil is well-used it registers potentially dangerous effects on the perpetrator's character—it jeopardizes the quality of his soul. The excuse rendered under the appropriate circumstances, then, is only partial: it does not completely exonerate the agent from all culpability.

Machiavelli rejects the notion that every means are permissible for any valuable goal. The means must be necessary to attaining the most valuable political goals; they must pass the criteria of evil wellused. The private ambition of founders, preservers, and reformers of states is insufficient. The common good must be implicated in the goals. Furthermore, the nature of the state is crucial. The state must be effective, aim at the common good, and have the requisite purposes. In sum, tyrannies are unworthy. Not every action that serves every state is a candidate for Machiavelli's approval. Crucially, Machiavelli's program is not a general moral theory, but a recommendation only for political leaders: the prince in a principality, the monarchical or executive element in a republic. The Florentine is not counseling private citizens in their everyday dealings, despite the laughable ways that contemporary writers of self-help literature struggle to trade on his name.

Accordingly, the language of justification is misapplied to Machiavelli; not every good goal is a candidate for his approval—only the most valuable political ends; not every means are acceptable even for those most valuable political ends; the private *ambizione* of military and political leaders is always insufficient; the domain of his advice is restricted to statesmen in healthy principalities and republics; he does not think the most refined evaluations of political actions focus solely on outcomes; he never calls evil anything but evil; he argues against the rule of offsetting good against evil; and he often invokes necessity as the coercive engine of political actions. Necessity compels human beings to act as reason demands under the given circumstances (D I 24; D III 12).

If the actions of statesmen were always morally *justified*—in the typical sense of being unambiguously morally right under the circumstances—then they would not need to learn how not to be good. Yet Machiavelli takes that knowledge to be crucial for effective statecraft (P 15; D I 9, 18). The capability and willingness to use evil well are uncommon personal attributes, but required of those aspiring to exercise robust military and political *virtù* (D I 18). Aspiring leaders must overcome moral squeamishness and dirty their hands as they perform morally dubious acts. The attainment of earthly power and enduring glory are the rewards Machiavelli identifies for those few who can accomplish the mission (P 8, 26; D I 10). Of these, the more important is deserved glory, which confers on men a spark of immortality and permits them a measure of revenge on the Pale Rider.

Furthermore, Machiavelli accepts the validity of conventional morality for ordinary citizens and in the private realm. He also takes conventional morality as relevant for leaders and commanders, especially when they are managing internal affairs. Power obtained through inhumanity and evil ill-used cannot reap enduring glory (P 8; D I 10; D III 40). Nor does Machiavelli, contra Berlin, embrace Roman (pagan) morality as the sole appropriate guide for political and military leaders. One of his major themes is the conflict between the imperatives of conventional morality and the duties required by the political and military offices of power. The imperatives of impersonal morality do not simply evaporate.

In sum, Machiavelli, contra Strauss, is not inciting a revolution in values. Nor does he state or implicitly adopt an obtuse slogan such as "the good end justifies every means." Nor does he tack on the final chapter of *The Prince* as the ultimate manipulation of shallow readers. Nor does he embrace tyranny, either consciously or tacitly. If Machiavelli advances a normative doctrine on these matters then the relevant principle is "*a few ends partially excuse some (typically horrifying) means.*"

Under Machiavelli's corollary principle of morality, a statesman must follow conventional morality if possible, but be prepared to transgress morality if necessary (P 18). Only a few ends partially excuse the use of means that are almost always wrong: Founding or preserving a healthy, expansionist state, or reforming a corrupt state; driving out foreigners as a prelude to founding or invigorating a state; facilitating the common good by removing obstreperous elements as a last resort; and the like. These ends, for Machiavelli, are required for a social life that can transform the people in positive ways, allow military and political leaders to satisfy their yearning for glory, and confer on a nation the reward of immortality.

A fragmented, corrupt city-state ensures the further degeneration of citizens, foreign domination, and the collapse of civic and moral *virtù*. Without a strong nation-state, citizens are vulnerable and insecure, suffer from a poor competitive position in relation to other nations, and endure an impoverished quality of life. A strong nation-state thwarts foreign invasion, teaches citizens to rise above selfish individualism, nurtures communal bonds, increases public wealth and the spiritual quality of life, and promotes civic and moral *virtù*. For Machiavelli, the choices are few and stark: A nation will either be fragmented, corrupt, and vulnerable to foreign domination or a nation will be unified, saturated with civic *virtù*, and able to dominate. The difference between the two types of situations begins with the degree of military and political *virtù* embodied by a nation's leaders; it continues with the quality of a nation's armed forces, laws, religion, and education.

For Machiavelli, because of a scarcity of resources and the nature of human beings, the world is a zero-sum contest (P 3; D II pref.). Competition between states is inevitable; governments will always wage war on one another; a successful state is one that has a strong, well-prepared military and expansionist aspirations; the freedom of my homeland may well depend on the defeat of yours. Enduring peace can be purchased only at the cost of enslavement. Henry Wadsworth Longfellow (1807–1882) observed that, "In this world a man must be either anvil or hammer." Having observed his native city used too frequently as an anvil, Machiavelli prefers being a hammer.

In addition, under conditions of supreme emergency—when the safety and survival of your country is at stake—Machiavelli advises that "you should pay no attention to what is just or what is unjust, or to what is kind or cruel, or to what is praiseworthy or shameful. You should put every other consideration aside, and you should adopt wholeheartedly the policy most likely to save your homeland's life and preserve her liberty" (D III 41). Contemporary ethicists define supreme emergencies in terms of imminent, horrifying danger. Respecting moral laws prohibiting harm to innocent people may facilitate, under such circumstances, the enslavement or extermination of a nation by a wrongful aggressor: "A world where entire peoples are enslaved or massacred is literally unbearable. For the survival and freedom of political communities—whose members share a way of life, developed by their ancestors, to be passed on to their children—are the highest values of international society."[26] For Machiavelli, failure under such circumstances invites servitude, the breakdown of sound arms and laws, and the collapse of civic and moral *virtù*.

Finally, Machiavelli recognizes a distinction between a politician managing internal matters and a military commander manipulating foreign affairs: "There is a moral element in Machiavelli's notion of political glory, he thought there were modes of conduct incompatible with political glory, whereas this element is absent from his notion of military glory, for this sort of glory is achieved through deserved success in war, whatever the methods used."[27] General William T. Sherman famously intoned that "War is hell." Machiavelli would disagree: War is worse than hell. At least in hell people presumably reap what they have sown; they receive deserved retribution for their freely chosen deeds. In war, appeals to notions of desert and merit lack an audience.

In the 1970 movie *Patton*, lead actor George C. Scott appears before an American flag and instructs his troops, "No bastard ever won a war by dying for his country. Wars are won by making the other poor, dumb bastard die for his country." We must imagine Machiavelli smiling.

3

The Problem of Dirty Hands

Having discussed Machiavelli's highest value, patriotism, and how that value animates his views on religion and morality, and having identified Machiavelli's corollary principle of morality, we are prepared to explain and critically evaluate his position on the problem of dirty hands.

How Political Hands Get Dirty

In politics and elsewhere, we sense at times that a particular action is the best course to pursue, but that our efforts nevertheless involve doing something wrong. Statesmen must often transgress clear, paramount moral principles and are rightly required to do so by the demands of their positions. The paradox of being *morally required* to *violate moral standards* seems irresolvable and deeply unsatisfying. Michael Walzer eloquently poses the critical questions for the problem of dirty hands: "Sometimes it is right to try to succeed, and then it must also be right to get one's hands dirty. But one's hands get dirty from doing what it is wrong to do. And how can it be wrong to do what is right? Or, how can we get our hands dirty by doing what we ought to do?"[1]

The notion of dirty hands is as old as the Bible. Pontius Pilate, Roman governor of Judea, offers the crowd a choice of prisoners, one of whom would be released. The crowd selects Barabbas as the fortunate son, while understanding that such a choice would result in the crucifixion of Jesus. Pilate's query, "But what evil hath he done?" only hardens the crowd's resolve. Fearing a possible riot should he push his case, Pilate washes his hands before the multitude and self-servingly judges that "I am innocent of the blood of this just person" (Matthew 27: 15–24). Pilate sought to evade dirty hands by deferring the decision of life or death to the crowd. If only the problem of dirty hands was so easily dissolved.

The phrase "dirty hands" is found in Jean-Paul Sartre's play of the same name in which the revolutionary protagonist declares: "How you cling to your purity, young man! How afraid you are to soil your hands. . . . Purity is an idea for a yogi or a monk. You intellectuals and bourgeois anarchists use it as a pretext for doing nothing: To do nothing, to remain motionless, arms at your sides, wearing kid gloves. Well, I have dirty hands. Right up to the elbows. I've plunged them in filth and blood. But what do you hope? Do you think you can govern innocently?"[2]

In the same spirit, Machiavelli often derides sensitive, self-righteous politicians who, in the name of morality and their own exalted rectitude, refuse to do what is necessary to establish or preserve a healthy, expansionist state, or reform a corrupt state; or who are reluctant to expel military barbarians as a prelude to founding or invigorating a state; or who decline to slay the "sons of Brutus" in order to save the republic (P 21; D I 38; D II 13, 14, 15; D III 3, 9, 30; Ltr. 203: 9/16/12). Preoccupied with their own self-images as virtuous people, timid leaders self-indulgently sacrifice their countries on the altar of their moral egos. Military or political leaders, then, who aspire to moral purity may become strategically paralyzed, fail the duties of their office, and jeopardize the well-being of their country and its citizens: "The integrity of the martyr is saved at his own expense, whereas the statesman's refusal to compromise is paid by his people."[3] Dirty hands situations typically involve overriding the claims and interests of an individual, group, or humankind to promote the collective interests of the unit that the moral agent represents.

Dirty hands situations embody moral conflicts but are not identical to moral dilemmas. All moral dilemmas are moral conflicts, but not all moral conflicts are moral dilemmas. A moral dilemma is the type of moral conflict where none of the alternative actions are morally endorsed or, to put it differently, where each of the available actions seems equally wrong and thus neither action is more necessary or compelling than the other. A dirty hands situation is a type of moral conflict where necessity or role-differentiated duties decree that an imperative arising from impersonal morality must be violated in deference to promoting the common good of a limited constituency. Here the role-differentiated duty and conditions of necessity compel a violation of impersonal morality and the main question is whether such actions are overall justified thereby exonerating the agent from all guilt or whether such actions provide only a partial excuse thereby leaving moral disvalues and an agent with dirty hands.

Bernard Williams sketches the systematic nature of the paradox of dirty hands for politicians: "A politician might find himself involved in, or invited to, such things as: lying, or at least concealment and the making of misleading statements; breaking promises; special pleading; temporary coalition with the distasteful; sacrifice of the interests of worthy persons to those of unworthy persons; and (at least if in a sufficiently important position) coercion up to blackmail."[4]

Other, more dramatic dirty hands enigmas include "the justification of political assassinations as an action that can dramatically correct the course of history; whether it can be right to yield a targeted judge to terrorists in exchange for the safety of many innocent hostages; what to do if one should meet a guerrilla leader who stipulates that if one will personally slay just one small peasant he will spare the rest of the otherwise-doomed group; and whether, as a leader of a country in civil war, one ought personally to order that a captured opponent be tortured to extract information that one expects will save lives."[5]

The paradox of dirty hands apparently rests on two convictions: seemingly absolute moral prohibitions sometimes must yield in political and in everyday contexts; and a good person will feel and be guilty from having broken those prohibitions, while a person bearing political and moral *virtù* will understand the necessity of sometimes doing so. Some dirty hands cases flow from social forces demanding wrongdoing, where wrongdoing is elicited as unintended consequences of social processes.

Chief military and political officials, acting on our behalf and in our name, sometimes act in ways that are incontestably condemned by conventional morality except that under unusual circumstances such acts prevent great harms or achieve great goods. Choosing under imperfect conditions and with only probabilistic evidence, the officers judge that no other morally permissible alternative exists and that the likelihood of securing the desired ends is high. The contemplated act is experienced, simultaneously, as required and prohibited. Thus, good people seem forced to compromise their moral principles for the sake of accomplishing crucial goals. They are pressured by necessity into violating absolute principles of impersonal morality in order to advance the interests of their constituents.

Machiavelli's advice concerning moral conflicts involving dirty hands is consistent for both princes and republican rulers. His prescriptions in *The Prince* are reflected in *The Discourses* (P 15, 18; D I 9; D III 34).

For Machiavelli, moral leadership sometimes requires performing actions because of the strength of duties to a limited constituency, but doing so transgresses absolute moral prohibitions. Such prohibitions are absolute not in the sense that they cannot ever be overridden, but in the sense that even when properly overridden they leave serious moral remainders: disvalues that are not erased by the overall evaluation of the action from which they arise. To call this "doing wrong in order to do right" is somewhat misleading and gives rise to the apparent contradiction Walzer identifies.

The crux of the paradox of dirty hands for political officers, then, is the partialism their stations demanded. Impartial, impersonal morality, where everyone's interests are equally important, competes with the partiality of the executive, who is charged with advancing the particular interests of his own citizens or specific group. While the degree of warranted partialism is contestable, the existence of a duty to be partial is clear. This tension also appears, typically less strikingly, in everyday morality wherein moral agents advance the interests of their families, friends, and loved ones instead of promoting the more abstract general good.

The problem is one *within* morality because conventional moral imperatives permit a sphere of partiality in numerous everyday matters. Advancing our own interests and those close to us in ways that do not advantage and perhaps even disadvantage others is often allowed or recommended. In our social relations we are connected to a host of roles that bear moral currency. Our actions not only produce consequences more direct and substantive upon those closer to us, but we also owe those closer to us greater consideration than we owe the general public. Thus, if I can rescue only one of two equally needy people where one is my mother and the other a stranger, saving my parent will not engender moral disapprobation (unless, perhaps, my society is grounded in the strictest Kantianism.). In fact, if I reported that under such circumstances I saved the stranger that would require an explanation because it would strike listeners of good faith as a peculiar choice. Conventional morality does not demand that we act always as Ideal Observers.

The partialism of statesmen is even more apparent. They are responsible for the well-being of a circumscribed group and act in the name of their constituents. The state emerges as an institution that is created by its members to serve their interests. The very existence of the state presupposes a distinction between members and nonmembers. The state itself is necessary to attain numerous important human purposes. Although this does not confer upon statesmen license to disregard totally the interests of humanity, it does sanction considerable latitude in preferring and privileging the interests of their constituents over the interests of other nations or at times even over the interests of the global community. Morally permissible actions undertaken by one state to benefit its members will often affect nonmembers and other states adversely. The practical necessity that governs the activities of statesmen does not arise, then, from an autonomous normative sphere ("politics") that competes with morality. Instead, it is a constitutive feature of morality itself. Perhaps the activities and necessities that frame the decision-making contexts of statesmen highlight this particular characteristic of conventional morality, but they do not define it. As the state's reason for being is to weigh unequally the interests of members with those of nonmembers, it represents the clearest but far from the only illustration of the power of partialism in conventional morality. At its core, conventional morality is internally limiting in that its imperatives and considerations are at times incommensurate and on other occasions qualified by social practice. Machiavelli employs the broad term "necessity" to describe the circumstances of social practice. Accordingly, morality as practiced must coexist with the circumstances of necessity.

Government officials, as agents of the public, are responsible for greater, more enduring consequences than private citizens. Unlike everyday people, they have control of the coercive, violent apparatus of the state. Their roles often require that they advance the interests of their citizens above those of the international good. To shrink from using evil well is to betray the trust of their constituents.

Statesmen, upon assuming their office, incur duties to serve particular functions and to advance the interests of constituents. These duties can limit or conflict with the claims that other moral imperatives lodge on them. These duties also, of course, are not unlimited. That is, they cannot substitute for or replace entirely the imperatives of impersonal morality. To ensure their country's political success, statesmen cannot be given a blank moral check. They are not permitted to ignore completely the general interests of humanity in order to advance the interests of their constituents. The proper balance between honoring the imperatives of impersonal morality and particular duties to limited constituencies is an ongoing matter of dispute.

As Thomas Nagel argues:

> This great division between personal and impersonal, or between agent-centered and outcome-centered, or

subjective and objective reasons, is so basic that it renders implausible any reductive unification of ethics—let alone of practical reasoning in general. The formal differences among these types of reasons correspond to deep differences in their sources. . . . The two motives [arising from a person's special duties to family, friends, or colleagues and from a detached, vantage point that comprehends everyone] come from two different points of view, both important, but fundamentally irreducible to a common basis.[6]

Viewing life from several perspectives, which lodge different and often competing moral claims upon us, human beings confront moral conflicts. Some of these moral conflicts are dilemmas in which two incompatible courses of action are equally supported by reason and morality, while other of these moral conflicts are dirty hands situations in which a course of action may seem overall appropriate even though it involves transgressing a paramount principle of impersonal morality.

As Stuart Hampshire puts it: "the relevant criterion for a great national enterprise is lasting success; and success is measured by a historian's yardstick: continuing power, prosperity, high national spirit, a long-lasting dominance of the particular state or nation in the affairs of men. So Machiavelli argued. Below the level of state politics, any representative role or official position, which confers power, to some degree imposes a responsibility for the well-being of persons not directly known."[7]

Morality is directed toward the appropriate navigation of the roles we undertake in our web of personal relationships. Politicians assume a role most of us never face. They act in the name and on behalf of an entire nation, state, county, or city. They control the coercive power of those social units. Their responsibilities are wider and deeper than those of ordinary citizens. They sometimes take risks or are called on to make decisions with frightening foreseeable and numerous unforeseeable consequences. Thus, the problem of dirty hands is a critical feature of military and political life. Still, all of us engage in personal and professional relationships, some of which conflict at times, and are thereby subject to gravely ambiguous moral choices.

Moral Theory and the Problem of Dirty Hands

Several standard moral theories provide possible responses to the problem of dirty hands—situations where doing what is normally evil will produce an overall balance of good over evil or will prevent an even greater evil from occurring:

Strict absolutism insists that a moral agent must never choose to do evil even where doing so would produce the best consequences available. Moral rules are categorical and always determine what we should do, no matter what the consequences or catastrophes, no matter what the circumstances. Some things must never be done, regardless of what unwelcome consequences ensue from our not doing them. The horrible consequences that sometimes ensue from following strict absolutism result from the actions of the agents of evil who crafted or the natural events that created the context forcing the unpleasant alternatives. By refusing to collaborate with evil, the moral agent who embraces strict absolutism evades causal and moral responsibility for the horrible consequences that sometimes ensue. This view is sometimes grounded in the conviction that acting in accord with categorical moral rules is demanded by a Supreme Being who will reward such behavior in the afterlife; other thinkers ground their conviction in the demands of reason (e.g., Kant).

The main problems with strict absolutism are striking: What should we do when two categorical moral rules conflict? If we find ourselves in a situation in which we cannot honor both categorical moral rules, which of the two imperatives should we obey? At the very least, conflict situations will ensure that adhering to moral rules absolutely is impossible even where the antecedent will to do so is firm. Also, by "washing our hands" are we still not partly responsible for the horrible consequences that ensue? Surely, on at least some occasions, we are responsible for our inactions or our omissions that permit harm or evil to succeed. Finally, what should we do under a supreme emergency where the consequences of following strict absolutism could result, say, in the destruction of an entire people? In sum, strict absolutism is vulnerable to counterexamples that ratchet up the severity of the horrifying consequences accompanying inflexible allegiance to categorical moral rules that cannot be overridden. From Machiavelli's vantage point, statesmen who are strict absolutists will inevitably sacrifice the common good of their nations in deference to their own presumed moral purity.

Flexible deontology concludes that moral rules are not categorical, but instead create prima facie moral duties. While violating these duties is always wrong, doing so under certain circumstances is sometimes morally permissible. Sometimes we must violate one prima facie moral duty because it conflicts with another prima facie moral duty. For example, if we must lie in order to prevent serious harm to others we violate our prima facie moral duty to tell the truth but we do so in service of another, weightier prima facie moral duty. To determine which of two conflicting prima facie moral duties should govern a particular case we must either appeal to an adjudicating principle if one exists, or merely reflect on the situation at hand and determine the better course of action through moral intuition. At other times, we must violate a prima facie moral duty as a necessary evil to avoid an even worse evil. Thus, on this account, moral rules always persist as prima facie moral imperatives—they always provide a powerful moral reason for compliance—but they will sometimes conflict and violating a prima facie moral imperative in such cases is unavoidable and morally permissible, at least where our choice of which imperative to violate is the correct one. For example, if telling a lie is necessary to prevent serious harm to others and we refuse to utter the falsehood à la Kant, our choice is subject to moral disapprobation under this account.

Threshold deontology holds that categorical moral constraints can be overridden when the disvalue of the consequences that would result if they were obeyed is far out of proportion to the particular values the moral constraints promote. When the consequences of obeying categorical norms become so dire that they exceed the specified threshold, the moral constraints of the norms are justifiably overridden. Such a view is designed to soften the excesses of strict absolutism, tighten the manipulability of flexible deontology, and yet avoid consequentialism. For example, suppose the relevant threshold states that torturing people is almost always morally wrong but torturing people to save 500 innocent lives is permissible. If so, torturing someone, even an evil-doer, remains morally impermissible unless doing so will directly save at least 500 innocent lives. Simple threshold deontology would stipulate one threshold, a fixed level of dire consequences that must be crossed for any categorical moral norm to be rightfully violated. Complex threshold deontology would stipulate a host of thresholds that would vary in proportion to the degree of moral wrong being perpetrated. Thus, torturing an evil-doer might require the saving of 500 innocent lives to be deemed permissible, while punching someone in the nose in response to a perceived insult would require crossing a much lower threshold.

That the difference in results between threshold deontology and the other moral theories sketched here depends on the levels of threshold stipulated should be clear. If the thresholds are set stunningly high, this brand of deontology approximates strict absolutism; the exceptions permitting the override of categorical moral norms would be extremely rare. If the thresholds are set quite low, this brand of deontology approximates consequentialism. In practice, the thresholds are set high and favor strict absolutism much more than consequentialism.

Threshold deontology faces several criticisms.[8] First, how should we derive the relevant thresholds? Why, say, is torturing permissible in order to save 500 innocent lives but not 499 innocent lives? Is not any specified threshold, which presumably must be expressed as a bright-line rule, riddled with arbitrariness? Second, if we are just short of crossing the stipulated threshold is it permissible to put one or a few more people at risk in order to cross the threshold and save all innocent lives at stake? What if the means of putting that one or those few people at risk are themselves morally dubious? In that vein, suppose we are rightfully torturing an evil-doer in order to save the lives of 500 innocent people. If a confederate of the evil-doer releases one person must we stop the torture as the number of innocent lives no longer meets the stipulated threshold? Third, in cases not involving saving innocent lives, how are we to calculate the pain and suffering that constitute the projected dire consequences? Should we do so by consulting some form of consequentialism? If so, does that threaten the integrity of the deontological approach?

Despite these and other difficulties, threshold deontology has possibilities for conforming to our moral intuitions about particular cases more closely than does strict absolutism, which is sometimes fanatical ("Let justice be done even if the heavens shall fall") as well as those versions of consequentialism that hold moral imperatives hostage to the circumstances of the moment.

Can Machiavelli be described as a threshold deontologist? One might argue that Machiavelli can formulate thresholds that correspond to those few ends that he deems to partially excuse the use of certain means that are otherwise evil. In other words, these thresholds constitute the distinction between evil well-used and evil *simpliciter*. Such thresholds are set high in order to avoid gratuitous wrongdoing.

When these thresholds are crossed then and only then may we override categorical moral norms.

This is a reasonable description but leaves one paramount issue dangling: the moral remainder of overriding a categorical moral norm. If threshold deontology does not recognize such a remainder—that is, if it insists that crossing the stipulated threshold implies that the resulting action is fully justified—then this view, like consequentialism and flexible deontology, eliminates the problem of dirty hands. This is the case because the statesman who acts in accordance with threshold deontology has performed the right action all things considered and the totality of circumstances purifies his deed. The statesman would at most regret to some degree but not be remorseful for his action.

Threshold deontology might, however, insist that overriding a categorical moral norm does leave a moral residue that implies a duty on the part of agents to compensate, apologize to, or at least think about the person who was subject to the overriding of the categorical moral norm. In my judgment, this would come closer to Machiavelli's position but still seems too weak as I will soon argue.

Strong consequentialism maintains that the point of moral action is always to produce the best overall consequences for those affected by the action. The best overall consequences are defined typically by the greatest balance of good over evil or occasionally by the least evil where the circumstances do not permit the production of good. This view demands that we judge, as best we can, the results of the alternatives we are considering and select the alternative that produces the best consequences. Numerous varieties of strong consequentialism exist, but most share the conviction that the factors to be weighed are commensurable and careful, impartial calculations performed by a moral agent acting in good faith will produce right answers to moral questions.

Under consequentialism the problem of dirty hands dissolves. No moral conflicts of that sort or deeply ambiguous moral choices should arise when every moral choice is made with an eye toward maximizing the good in the instant situation, and only if every relevant reason for and against an action in that situation is taken as a moral reason, and only if all moral reasons are measurable by a common standard. Sometimes our calculations will be difficult to sort through and the long-range effects of our actions are typically speculative, but at least in principle a correct, justified moral answer should exist. Even in rare cases of a quantitative and qualitative tie—two alternative actions produce the same overall good effects—we would be justified in choosing either course. Although fallible human beings acting in good faith will surely make some mistakes in perceiving and computing the possible results of their actions, that does not vitiate the fact that a morally right answer exists.

Weak consequentialism differs from strong consequentialism in that it does not require that moral agents should aim always at producing *the best* overall consequences, everything considered. Instead, its point of departure is the denial of strict absolutism: it rejects the position that categorical moral imperatives exist that by their very nature cannot be violated because they determine in all circumstances correct moral action. Consequences are always relevant to the question of what is the morally right thing to do. There are thus no acts that we can rightly conclude should never be done without considering the particular circumstances and consequences of the decision at hand. On this account, if circumstances prevent the production of good—if whatever we do or fail to do produces or sustains evil—we do the morally right thing under the circumstances by choosing the lesser of two evils. Although under typical circumstances our action would be gravely wrong, under the instant circumstances they are morally right when everything is considered. Where the only choices are between evils of different magnitudes, it is always morally right to choose the lesser evil.

Both strong and weak consequentialism are problematic. Act consequentialists apply the principle of consequentialism to each moral instance. But act consequentialism is untrue to moral experience. That all reasons for and against an action are commensurable is highly unlikely; that all the relevant reasons for and against an action are moral reasons is equally suspicious; that the good must be tallied and maximized on each occasion (strong consequentialism) does not square with how we make moral choices; and that deeply ambiguous moral choices can be whisked away by abstract theory falsifies the anguish of numerous political and moral decisions. In addition, act consequentialism wrongly excludes the dispositions of moral agents and how they factor into perceptions of actions. The only relevant dispositions under this view are the inclinations to maximize good consequences in particular cases (strong consequentialism) or to evaluate actions or principles only by their consequences (weak consequentialism).

Rule consequentialism, which takes moral standards as mere guidelines that may be overridden in particular cases, fares only a tad better. Rule consequentialists derive their moral guidelines from what generally promotes good results. But when those of us who are not consequentialists violate our moral guidelines we justify those transgressions in ways that honor the status of our moral standards independently of their utility in previous cases. We do not take our moral rules to be grounded in and dependent upon only their capability of maximizing good or minimizing evil in particular cases or generally. We do not ground the authority of moral principles only in their usefulness. Accordingly, justified variances from our moral rules are less frequent than rule consequentialism would sanction.

But perhaps I have been unfair to consequentialism in an important respect. The consequentialist and flexible deontologist could admit a place for regret or feeling badly in dirty hands situations even though they would insist that the agent has done no wrong and her actions were fully justified. We often feel badly or regret or even feel guilty in the absence of moral wrongdoing. The consequentialist or flexible deontologist will describe choosing to act on the lesser of two evils or violating the lesser of two prima facie duties as justified, but concede that the agent, although cleansed of wrongdoing, will still experience regrettable side effects arising from the instant circumstances. This phenomenon is common and explainable.

For example, suppose a motorist accidentally runs over a squirrel. The motorist understands that she is not morally responsible for killing the innocent animal, yet she will probably feel badly about the event and regret being causally responsible for the death. Now suppose she accidentally ran over and killed a pedestrian. The negative feelings would intensify exponentially even though everyone recognizes that the motorist was not morally culpable for the death. That feeling badly or regretting or even feeling guilty can occur even where moral culpability is lacking is clear.

Now let us heighten the point by considering the following bizarre but illustrative example: You are an utterly scrupulous motorist, but in the course of only one year you accidentally kill ten people. In each case, the victim leaves a suicide note declaring that he or she is at wit's end and has decided to run into an automobile in order to end his or her life. In an unfathomable run of bad luck, you are the motorist that happens to appear when each victim decides to execute the plan. Video cameras and eye witnesses record and testify that in every instance you were completely blameless. In fact the tale of your stunning misfortune is publicized and you gain the sympathy of an entire nation. Still, having been the involuntary instrument of ten deaths will undoubtedly exact a great mental toll on you. You will not merely feel badly or suffer pangs of regret, but could well be devastated even though you recognize cognitively that you are morally blameless for the ten deaths.

A moralist could argue that you may *feel* guilty about the ten deaths, but you are not morally guilty for any of them. Such a moralist could analogize your situation to that of statesmen in dirty hands contexts: if their actions were overall justified then they bear no moral guilt even though they may feel guilty for their involvement in numerous deaths.

For Machiavelli, this analogy is inapt. In the example of your killing ten people bent on suicide you have not risked your soul: you have not knowingly violated absolute moral principles; instead, you have accidentally become an instrument of death. Although you feel horribly, perhaps guilty in some sense for the deaths, that you bear no moral blame implies that the condition of your soul remains intact. You cannot suffer the effects of wrongdoing because you have done nothing wrong. Repeated accidents of this sort may lead you to lose your mind, but cannot engender the loss of your soul. In the case of statesmen they feel guilty, assuming they have not already lost their souls because they are guilty of transgressing absolute moral principles even when their actions are overall appropriate. To feel guilty in such instances evidences sound moral character, one that is instinctively adverse to wrongdoing. Feelings of guilt in dirty hands contexts are warranted by the moral rules and principles that command us to keep our hands clean. These rules and principles are not merely external imperatives from the vantage point of an Ideal Observer, but have been recognized and accepted by the nations within which statesmen operate. Accordingly, pointing out that people often feel guilty even though they are not morally guilty does not soften the paradox of dirty hands for a Machiavellian.

Feelings of guilt will also intensify in dirty hands scenarios. Here we are no longer talking about accidents. The agent intentionally and knowingly chooses to act on the lesser of two evils or to violate the less weighty of two prima facie moral duties. Thus, the agent is no longer implicated in the events by misfortune, and she explicitly recognizes that something regrettable has occurred even though her choice and action are prudent. The negative feelings that ensue are understandable and natural. Still, the consequentialist and flexible deontologist will insist that the agent is not guilty even though in some cases she may feel guilty.

Machiavellian deontology insists that the morally disconcerting feature of a dirty hands situation both figures into the overall value of the contemplated act and again independently of the overall value of that act. This view takes moral principles to be categorical: to transgress such a principle leaves a moral remainder (moral disvalue) even when the act in which it takes place is overall appropriate. Machiavelli derives categorical moral principles from his observations of and reasoning about human capabilities, desires, and dispositions that he regards as timeless. The overall evaluation of the act that concludes it is appropriate in the instant circumstance does not erase the partial evaluation that the means are evil. Accordingly, the means remain evil well-used: they remain a moral disvalue within the whole. The contemplated act is the correct choice but it is undertaken at a high moral price. Knowing that they are implicated in evil, as all proper Machiavellian statesmen must, the agents *feel* guilty because they *are* guilty. As reluctant but ultimately willing participants in using evil well, agents embody the moral remainders of their deeds: these moral disvalues exert direct effects on the agents' souls. Such agents risk their souls because they do not simply perform deeds that are overall justified. Instead, they use evil well and struggle with the moral remainders of their patriotic choices and actions. They must acknowledge both the severity of the evil means they employed and the necessity of their deed. As argued previously, for Machiavelli acting properly in a dirty hands situation provides only a partial excuse not a justification.

Strong consequentialists would insist that no moral disvalues remain if a dirty hands action was overall morally proper. They recognize no categorical wrongs because only a calculation of overall consequences determines right and wrong. As a balance of good over bad consequences constitutes completely their moral universe, strong consequentialists deny that an immoral remainder persists in dirty hands situations. But weak consequentialists could accept that certain moral imperatives are categorical ("torture is always wrong") in the sense that they are always evil even though acts that include such means are sometimes morally permissible. Thus weak consequentialists can argue that the moral prohibition against, say, torture can be rightly overridden to avoid dire consequences; that overriding such a categorical moral prohibition is an unpleasant process; that the agent who authorizes or administers torture will typically feel guilty; but that the agent is not morally guilty because he or she did what was, all things considered, the morally right thing to do. Weak consequentialists, then, will count the moral disvalue of torture only once—in the overall calculation that determines the morally right thing to do. They recognize no moral remainder, but concede that if a categorical moral prohibition has been rightfully overridden the authorizing or administrating agent will feel guilt.

The critical difference between weak consequentialists and Machiavellian deontologists is that the latter insist that agents with dirty hands feel guilty because they are guilty. This is the case because the moral wrong of overriding a categorical moral prohibition remains even after the calculation that doing so is appropriate in the instant circumstances. Most important is that the moral disvalue registers effects on the person an agent with dirty hands is becoming.

The problem of dirty hands calls into question the consequentialists' assumption that all genuine values are commensurable. In such contexts, the vantage point of the Ideal Observer applying the imperatives of impersonal morality may produce a different moral conclusion from that emerging from the perspective of the ardent patriot applying principles appropriate to the national interest. Walzer's way of framing the issue is somewhat misleading. In dirty hands scenarios, the same act is not both right and wrong, at least not in the same sense. Instead, the act involves performing a moral duty that implicates the agent in evil in that he must transgress against a moral principle that is absolute not in the sense that it cannot be overridden but in the sense that even when properly overridden a moral disvalue remains, one that is not cleansed by an overall assessment of the deed.

Statesmen cannot simply act as Ideal Observers who apply the dictates of impersonal morality. Instead, they are charged, among other things, with safeguarding and advancing the ideals, allegiances, and guiding principles of their respective nations against other nations that do not necessarily share those values. At times, even when other nations reasonably oppose the values of a country's statesman he may appropriately advance his nation's values. Thus, sometimes but not always, a statesman may act in a way that is both right (from the standard of moral duty to a limited constituency) and wrong (from the standpoint of the impartial imperatives of impersonal morality). However, such cases do not produce a moral contradiction because the act is not both right and wrong in the same sense or from the same standpoint. In dirty hands scenarios, statesmen know that they have done the best thing in the circumstances in terms of their partialist patriotic duties, but they have transgressed an important principle of impartial morality.

By virtue of their role, statesmen confront the problem of dirty hands on behalf of their constituents, not only in emergency situations but on routine and minor matters. Background institutions must recognize and sustain the tension between the respective standpoints of impersonal morality and nationalistic partialism. That requires, in part, understanding that when statesmen transgress categorical moral principles (in the Machiavellian sense) while advancing the common good they are implicated in using evil well and the moral disvalues that partially constituted their deeds persist. Thus, public vigilance, investigative journalism, and the possibility of a public accounting upon exposure are critical. We should not confer a blank moral check on our statesmen both for our good and theirs.

Marxism denies that economic scarcity, the pursuit of individual self-interest, and class division are inevitable features of social life. Marxists herald the day when communist relations of production will unleash creative labor, extinguish class antagonisms, and attain the glorious union of individualism and community. At that historical point and presumably thereafter the fundamental sources of societal conflicts of interests will have withered away: our private interests and the interests of humanity will be at one. Machiavelli, of course, would scoff at Marx, the anti-utopian who was so utopian in his perfectionist yearnings that he was willing to sacrifice human well-being in the present to his long-term fantasies. Machiavelli understands acutely that the tension between the imperatives of impersonal morality and the demands of nationalistic partialism will endure.

But understanding situations engendering dirty hands as conflicts between impersonal moral imperatives and partialist duties to limited constituencies is problematic. What could underwrite the duties to limited constituencies other than general moral imperatives? If so, then how can the duties to limited constituencies at times morally trump the general moral imperatives from which they arose? In my judgment, the answer is that the scope of impersonal, impartial moral imperatives is not boundless. Human beings are not Ideal Observers impartially allocating their goods, resources, efforts, and time. We embody personal perspectives that permit us to craft our lives and sculpt our souls. Acting only as Ideal Observers would render us slaves to the community and extinguish our individuality. Not even impersonal morality makes such a demand on us. For example, suppose you and a stranger are both drowning in a lake. Because of an odd set of circumstances, you can save either yourself or the stranger but not both. From the vantage point of the Ideal Observer, all other things being equal, it matters not who is saved as long as one of you is saved. Yet impersonal morality does not require that you, figuratively speaking, flip a coin or choose randomly whom you will save. You are permitted to save your own life rather than that of the stranger. Should you choose to save the stranger and die in the process, you would be cheered as a hero or a saint for your supererogatory act; or perhaps some would deride you posthumously as a fool. Should you save yourself, the court of morality would not indict you for wrongdoing. Thus, a partialist preference for self-preservation is permitted by the imperatives of general morality to trump the conclusion arising from the standpoint of an Ideal Observer. This partialist preference extends to wider constituencies such as family, relatives, friends, and nation.

Patriots rightfully further the interests of their respective communities. These interests often conflict. Also, not every nation subscribes to the same allegiances, ideals, and principles. These interests are often different and reasonably so. Assuming that the respective patriotisms are not antecedently oppressive or wrongfully aggressive, zealous participation in advancing the prosperity and interests of one's nation is morally permissible. Thus, within morality reside the seeds of the problem of dirty hands: the tension between the perspective of the Ideal Observer and the vantage point of the enthusiastic patriot, and the uneasy coalescence between impersonal imperatives and partialist preferences. National communities presuppose that at times they must deny the moral claims of nonmembers. In so doing, they sometimes appropriately privilege their partialist preferences above the imperatives of impartial morality. What is controversial is not the well-recognized permissibility of partialist preferences within impersonal morality, but the proper scope of those preferences (that is, to what extent can they supersede impersonal considerations) and the occasions, if any, on which pursuing those preferences can appropriately transgress specific imperatives of impersonal morality (one aspect of which is the problem of dirty hands).

The core debate on the problem of dirty hands is between moral pessimists and moral optimists. Moral pessimists are nonconsequentialists. Moral optimists are typically but not necessarily consequentialists. Moral pessimists find an intractable guilt in morally ambiguous cases even where our actions are *excused*. Moral optimists argue that if our actions in such cases are *justified* we are innocent, and if our actions are *excused* we are not responsible for any wrong and thus are not guilty.

Walzer argues for the moral pessimists. When recognized moral rules are overridden, their normative force remains: "We know we have done something wrong even if what we have done was also the best thing to do on the whole in those circumstances. . . . This does not mean that it isn't possible to do the right thing while governing. It means that a particular act of government may be exactly the right thing to do in utilitarian terms and yet leave the man who does it guilty of a moral wrong."[9] If a statesman violates conventional morality in service of, say, Machiavellian-endorsed goals—if he uses evil well—he is both simultaneously morally right and morally wrong: he may be establishing or reforming a corrupt state, but he is also employing evil. If a statesman refuses to soil his hands and abides by conventional morality, he is also both simultaneously morally right and wrong: he honors conventional morality, but at the expense of the polity: "It is by his dirty hands that we know [the moral politician]. If he were a moral man and nothing else, his hands would not be dirty; if he were a politician and nothing else, he would pretend that they were clean."[10]

Walzer is not concluding merely that a politician will sometimes *feel* guilty, but that he will *be* morally guilty in such circumstances. He argues that the best solution is for the politician to pay a socially expressed penance or penalty proportionate to his deeds. The politician's felt angst, guilt, and internal suffering are insufficient because they depend too much on the sensibilities of the particular politician and they lack social expression. The politician's acts were committed in our name and on our behalf. The measure of his atonement is his willingness to publicly accept a proportionate penalty or penance. Walzer notes, sadly, that there are no authorities who could administer the appropriate penalty and no social institutions up to the task.[11] Moreover, statesmen have a duty to conceal their dirty hands from us to the extent possible. Citizens may know, abstractly, that their leaders must soil their hands but are usually shrouded from the exact occasions.

Walzer's formulation—an act can be the best moral alternative yet be morally wrong—underscores the paradox of dirty hands, but stuns logicians. Walzer seems to be violating the basic laws of logic when making the point in this fashion. That logical frailty is assaulted by moral optimists.

Moral optimists[12] argue that if an act is truly the best moral alternative—whether based on consequentialist or nonconsequentialist grounds—then the act is justified. If the act is justified then the politician who commits the act is responsible for it, but is innocent because no wrongdoing has occurred. If the act in question is morally excused then the action was not, strictly speaking, morally right but the politician is not responsible for wrongdoing because his compliance was involuntary in some sense. Involuntary acts exonerate moral culpability. Accordingly, the conventional logic of the relationships between voluntariness, responsibility, moral culpability, justification, and excuse militate that no act is simultaneously both right and wrong in the sense moral pessimists describe.

If, after performing certain political acts requiring horrifying means, a statesman *feels* guilt that is a psychological problem. He has no reason to feel such if his action was, indeed, morally justified or excused. Perhaps he needs a short lecture on basic moral concepts. Or as one moral optimist puts it: "[Walzer's moral pessimism] is confused philosophy and bad psychology. If our good politician knows that he is doing wrong, then he should not do it: no one can act rightly by acting wrongly. Given that he acts rightly and conscientiously, then, if he *believes* himself to be guilty, what he needs is therapy, not penance."[13] In sum, feeling guilty in such circumstances is not a sign of a morally sensitive politician, but a person who is either morally confused or irrational.

Machiavelli and Dirty Hands

Machiavelli sensed the problem of dirty hands acutely. He points out that founding or reforming a corrupt state requires extraordinary, violent, and cruel means. Morally virtuous men are unlikely to be drawn to such tactics. Morally evil men gleefully adopt the necessary means, but are unlikely to promote the good thereafter. The desired combination—a morally good man willing to temporarily embrace evil and use it well—is extremely rare (D I 18). This accounts for the gushing praise Machiavelli lavishes on the few who fit the bill: Moses, Romulus, Theseus, Lycurgus, and their like.

A common solution commentators pose concludes that Machiavelli advances two autonomous, often competing, realms of value: the political and the moral.[14] At times, proper political action requires violating the demands of morality. Chief military and political officials act in our name for wider purposes, but their roles demand that they perform deeds that violate our morality.

This solution is appealing and has a long, distinguished genesis. Unfortunately, it is unpersuasive. Machiavelli does not posit two independent moral spheres of value. As I argued earlier, for Machiavelli politics is constrained by conventional morality. Variances from conventional morality are partially excused by several critical purposes domestically; while internationally Machiavelli places morality in the context of the conditions of the world and of human beings. Although this position bleeds from conceptual and empirical wounds, it does not advance two independent moral spheres—the political and the moral. Machiavelli concludes that political necessity sometimes partially excuses the transgression of conventional moral principles.

No form of consequentialism can solve the problem of dirty hands for Machiavelli. He is not a moral consequentialist bent on maximizing the good on each occasion or committed to judging the morality of actions or principles by their results in particular social contexts. In Machiavelli's view, only imprudent and unwise people judge solely by the results of actions (P 18, 25; AW I 29–32; D I 9, 53; FH VIII 22; D III 35). Even the most prudent *consigliere* cannot predict results with certainty. Actions that appear useful antecedently to capable advisors often generate unwelcome outcomes. Statesmen must always choose between alternate courses of action prior to knowing their outcomes. Also, judging only by results is open-ended: the long-range consequences of actions extend beyond the moment of such judgment, whenever that may occur. Accordingly, to judge decisions and deeds only by their results is unwise. In fact, evaluating only by results is the feckless method of the *ignoranti*. Instead, the reasons for engaging in a course of action must be evaluated prior to instituting policies or rendering decisions. Assessing the reasons that led to a course of action and the context that framed their persuasiveness is critical to sound judgment. In addition, the means statesmen use will influence the nature of the ends attained.

Although he does not sketch explicitly an ethical theory and never invokes natural laws, Machiavelli's writings assume a conventional morality that identifies good and bad acts apart from their instant context. He tacitly accepts the existence of moral standards that are not hostage to recurring calculations of utility in immediate or general circumstances. Machiavelli's moral standards are conventional. Although he deeply admires Roman (pagan) morality, he neither accepts it as a wholesale replacement for conventional morality nor does he unveil a new morality. Habitual responses and internalized dispositions, nurtured by good laws and vigorous religion, are pivotal to civic *virtù*. But military and political leaders must learn to use evil well; they must navigate their roles and social relationships outside the comforting embrace of easy moral justifications. Only if Machiavelli was a full-blown consequentialist would military and political leaders be advised only to become better calculators and discerners of the good. Machiavelli's counsel would be purely epistemological and, perhaps, psychological. But Machiavelli is not a rabid moral consequentialist and he insists that military and political leaders must learn how not to be good, how to live in the quagmire of ambiguity where their actions are not fully morally justified, but only partially excused because of the pressures of necessity and the conditions of the world.

Machiavelli was neither a moral theorist nor an academic philosopher. He is, though, invariably cited in discussions about the problem of dirty hands, and he is sometimes credited with being the first writer to articulate the paradox.[15] He suggested that statesmen, those exercising robust military and political *virtù*, must be willing to risk their souls in fulfilling their duties in service to their country. Machiavelli, though, never explores explicitly the interior life of those historical figures he admired. He never acknowledges explicitly the emotional experience of moral transgression that pervades contemporary accounts of the paradox of dirty hands.

Although he does not examine their internal lives, Machiavelli fastidiously, even excitedly, reports the shocking deeds of Romulus, Moses, Brutus, Borgia, and several others. He never questions whether alternate actions were available to them. Might Romulus have reasoned with his brother? Was there a way short of murder that could have resolved the situation? Did Moses truly have to help execute the 3,000 fools intent on worshipping a golden calf of their own invention? Was his method really a last resort? Might Brutus have finessed the judicial problems of his sons yet preserved the republic? Machiavelli never explores or even raises such queries. On one level, then, he endorses such bloodcurdling exploits as understandable and as partially *excusable*. But Machiavelli does not view the actions as *justifiable* in the contemporary, philosophical sense of that term. His heroes have learned how not to be good.

The most charitable philosophical reading of Machiavelli's position is that although the mortifying acts of Romulus, Brutus, and others are excused, the agents of those deeds nevertheless bear a measure of moral culpability. Unlike fervent moral optimists, Machiavelli does not take these types of excuses to completely cleanse moral agents from *all* responsibility. These excuses greatly mitigate responsibility, but do not erase all vestiges. That is why chief military and political officials risk their souls.

Machiavelli, then, is a moral pessimist, but he does not locate the paradox of dirty hands in a logical puzzle: How can it be morally wrong to do what is morally right? Instead, the problem of dirty hands arises from the inability of some excuses to totally exonerate moral agents from all responsibility, culpability, and guilt. For Machiavelli, some moral excuses do not cleanse completely, some military and political actions are not entirely coerced, and the moral agent bears some responsibility for the deeds to the extent his action was voluntary. When shocking acts that typically offend the conventional moral conscience are performed under circumstances where they are excused from a Machiavellian vantage point—when evil is well-used—the deeds are still problematic even though required to promote the greatest values. Although consequences play a major part in Machiavelli's strategic calculations, he is not a straightforward consequentialist in matters of morality. Despite his systematic recognition of necessity, he does not take that circumstance as a complete justification of human action. Nor does Machiavelli take necessity as a *complete* excuse that totally cleanses human agents of all moral responsibility: "Dante and Petrarch also seek the redemption of Italia, but Niccolò is the only one to point out that the agent of that redemption must enter evil and risk his soul."[16]

Whereas classical ethical theory sought to eliminate or soften evil, Machiavelli aspires to find a preacher to teach the people "the way to go to the Devil . . . and learn the way to Hell" (Ltr. 270: 5/17/21). Machiavelli wants people to learn how to cope with evil in order not to fall prey to its allure and be defeated by it.

What does it mean to risk one's soul in fulfilling one's duties to country? As noted earlier, Machiavelli is far from explicit. It might mean eternal damnation in the fires of a theological hell, but it probably does not. Perhaps the additive culpability of numerous instances of evil well-used is enough for a man to lose his soul. But did God not cheer Moses for wiping out the 3,000? Will God not lavishly honor the prince who liberates Italy? For Machiavelli, the cost is worth the enterprise. In his play *Mandragola* the lover Callimaco rages, "the worst that can come to you is to die and go to hell; but how many others are dead! And there are so many good men in hell! Are you ashamed to go there? Face your lot; flee evil, but, not being able to flee it, bear it like a man; do not prostrate yourself, don't degrade yourself like a woman" (M 4:1). For Machiavelli, "Hell is an exclusive club. For real men only."[17] Machiavelli insists that he loves his "native city more than my own soul" (Ltr. 331: 4/16/27). He lauds those citizens who "esteem their fatherland [much more] than their souls" (FH III 7; AW I, 7).

Machiavelli, though, is hopeful that God will not permit men of admirable military and political *virtù* to fry in hell because of a few moral technicalities. Aside from the biblical examples of Moses, Peter, and David, Machiavelli suspects God's forgiveness is more expansive than commonly thought.[18] After all, God, too, is neither a moral theorist nor an academic philosopher.

As I have argued previously, risking one's soul can also bear an earthly connotation. The appropriate use of evil transforms the agent. What we do reflects and reinforces the values we embrace, or not. The number, magnitude, and far-reaching effects of violent acts tear into the fabric of personal character. Might not chief military and political officials become morally desensitized? Might they not rationalize the use of evil where it is not well-used? Might not each use of evil strike a corrupting influence? Is not the common good hostage to the statesman's capability of maintaining his soul in the face of many confrontations, internationally and domestically, with the forces of evil? Those of *grandezza d'animo*—who passionately sculpt their characters and pursue deserved, enduring glory—must use evil well recurrently and thereby jeopardize the condition of their souls.

The healthy polity does not want to be led by militarists and politicians who have lost their souls: "Only those who are reluctant or disinclined to do the morally disagreeable when it is really necessary have much chance of not doing it when it is not necessary."[19] Yet to run that risk is precisely what such leaders must do. Although Machiavelli does not delve explicitly into the interior life of his heroes, the ability to rise with full hearts, despite countless temptations and situations that militate otherwise, is pivotal for leaders to preserve a healthy, expansionist state. Is it possible for such leaders to preserve their sensibility to moral costs yet continue to use evil well? Does occupying public office permit a leader to depersonalize his morally disagreeable acts?

Although many of a politician's decisions in dirty hands situations are rightly concealed from public scrutiny, even those that are revealed will be judged by the multitude only by their success in attaining critical goals, according to Machiavelli (P 18). The public, then, is an untrustworthy evaluator of a politician's actions in such cases. Success may have blossomed through good luck or accident. Failure and disappointment may have resulted from bad luck or an unavoidable sequence of events. Judging actions only by their results is an unreliable guide. Appropriate social expression, evaluation, and limitation of a politician's anguish in dirty hands contexts are unavailable. Are chief military and political officials, then, the only rightful judges of their own cases? Must they retain a supra-moralism that empowers them to evaluate what they do independently from their doing it? Or does Morality, in imagined personified form, hover over a politician's decision making? Or God?

For Machiavelli, that statesmen must sometimes dirty their hands and soil their souls in service to their countries is clear. While Machiavelli is firm that performing morally proper actions are often useful, he does not conclude that such actions are morally good because they are useful. The results of actions do not bestow moral imprimatur. Instead, principles are categorically moral. Machiavelli consistently distinguishes what is expedient from what is morally right (D I 26).

Machiavelli concludes that "though the deed accuses [the founder of a state], the result should excuse him; and when it is good, like that of Romulus, it will always excuse him, because he who is violent to destroy, not he who is violent to restore, ought to be censured" (D I 9). Thus, even where evil is well-used the act accuses in that the immoral remainder of violating a categorical moral principle survives. Because such an act is required to promote or even to establish the common good of a nation, however, the perpetrator should be excused. The excuse makes public censure of the perpetrator inappropriate, but does not remove entirely the immoral remainder. The perpetrator has still used evil, even if well (P 8, 18). Accordingly, the excuse is only partial in that it eliminates the appropriateness of public censure, but it does not transform the evil means employed: they remain evil even if well-used.

But must the deed be a "success" to have that effect? Suppose Romulus had failed in his efforts. Would failure to attain the desired goal alone transform evil well-used into evil ill-used? In my judgment, the answer must be "no." Potential founders of nations cannot ensure the success of their actions by dint of their volitions, desires, and efforts. As Machiavelli often disparages those who judge only by results, to take success as a necessary condition for the partial excuse conferred on those who use evil well is unreasonable. Of course, the agent's good intentions are not sufficient to gain a partial excuse either. We would think that the deed must have a reasonable chance of success in the context in which it occurs. The court of morality cannot exonerate reckless adventurers even if they invoke establishing or promoting the common good as their motivation for acting.

Moral costs arise from the immoral remainder of using evil well. Agents may suffer in terms of their popularity and reputation. Moreover, damage to categorical moral principles and to the characters of the agents will take place. Statesmen must be steadfastly vigilant that they risk but do not lose their souls. To that end, Machiavelli cautions statesmen to retain their moral rectitude and limit their use of evil to the extent required to ward off wolves and to evade traps. In that vein, they should use evil means only when securing the most valuable goals in service of the common good and when compelled by necessity (when no other means could secure those goals). Also, statesmen should execute the evil means swiftly in order to eliminate lingering effects. To the extent possible, they should also avoid recurrences (P 8).

Case Study in Dirty Hands: President Truman

Consider President Truman's 1945 decision to attack Hiroshima with an atomic bomb. Spurred by concern that Nazi Germany was on the verge of building an atomic bomb, scientists urged President Roosevelt to beat Hitler to the discovery. The scientists succeeded in their pleas, atomic bombs were produced, and eventually dropped on Hiroshima and Nagasaki. President Truman gave three reasons for his decision to use these weapons of mass destruction: Japan had attacked the United States without warning at Pearl Harbor; Japan had violated international law by treating prisoners of war (POWs) inhumanely; and the bombing of Japan would shorten the horrors of the war by forcing an immediate surrender.[20]

Moralists would raise immediate concerns. Atomic bombs cause wide-ranging harm to innocent citizens—those who are civilians, those opposed to the war, those who are inherently innocent because they are infants or mentally incompetent, and those belonging to future generations who will endure the residual effects of the bombing. Even if the government and the leaders of Japan forfeited certain rights because of their transgressions of international law it does not seem that all of the people of Japan forfeited their basic human rights. Moreover, the use of atomic bombs—at that time the most destructive weapon devised by human beings—might well be a disproportionately grave response to the wrongs committed by Japan against the United

States. Using such fearsome weaponry was unprecedented and seemed to assume that once wrongful aggression takes place the defending nation may rightfully use any means to attain victory; that the defenders are exonerated from all moral blame regardless of their methods; that having a just cause in war guarantees that a nation's means of engaging in that war are automatically purified.

Advocates of Truman's policy argued that the leaders of Japan, sensing the war was lost, were bracing for a last-ditch defense. Amassing about 2 million soldiers, Japan hoped to make the upcoming battle so costly that the Allies, suffering high casualties, would negotiate a peace. The Allies calculated that an invasion of Japan could result in 1 million Allied deaths with Japanese losses much higher. The use of atomic bombs, on the other hand, would be so psychologically terrifying—if the United States could drop bombs on two Japanese cities with such ease and horrifying effects, they could in principle destroy the entire Japanese mainland—that the war would end more quickly with fewer deaths on both sides.[21]

The U.S. estimates of casualties were based on the premises that Japan would fight tenaciously to the end and that the United States would accept only unconditional surrender. Walzer argues that these premises are suspect: "The Japanese case is sufficiently different from the German so that unconditional surrender should never have been asked. Japan's rulers were engaged in a more ordinary sort of military expansion, and all that was morally required was that they be defeated, not that they be conquered and totally overthrown. . . . If killing millions (or many thousands) of [innocent] men and women was militarily necessary for their conquest and overthrow, then it was morally necessary—in order not to kill those people—to settle for something less."[22]

Accordingly, some critics will argue that Truman's decision was straightforwardly immoral as it traded off the *certainty* of killing or seriously harming an enormous number of actual human beings for the *possibility* (probability?) of saving an undetermined number of other human beings. Walzer draws the same conclusion on different grounds: "dirty hands aren't permissible (or necessary) when anything less than the ongoingness of the community is at stake, or when the danger that we face is anything less than communal death."[23] Such extraordinary circumstances were not in place at the time of Truman's decision. Walzer adjusts his understanding of the scope of appropriate dirty hands action in several of his writings. Although his earliest view did not specify the proper scope of dirty hands activity, he suggested that such deeds were virtually unavoidable for statesmen.[24] Walzer's more recent view is that only a supreme emergency or imminent catastrophe can render dirty hands actions permissible.[25]

Thus, the bombings of Hiroshima and Nagasaki might be viewed as straightaway immoral because they involved targeting thousands of innocent civilians in the hope that doing so might promote an earlier end to the war and thereby save a greater number of lives overall. One might argue that President Truman did not face an either/or situation: that he was not compelled by necessity to choose either to bomb the Japanese cities or to accept an extended war that would result in a greater number of casualties.

I will suppose, however, that Truman's articulated calculations were reasonable and that he had no other path to shorten the length of the war. Whether he wrongfully amplified the strength of his moral duties to his nation and wrongfully deflated the power of his moral obligations to humanity is contestable. That he did not face a supreme emergency—he could not have reasonably concluded that if he did not bomb the Japanese cities the United States would lose the war and its national identity would be jeopardized—deepens the problem. In my judgment, Machiavelli would endorse Truman's decision. Although for Machiavelli only a few paramount ends partially excuse means that are inherently evil, those ends are much broader in scope than supreme emergencies. Like Walzer's earliest suggestion, Machiavelli is firmly convinced that dirty hands deeds are unavoidable for statesmen.

Whether the use of atomic bombs on Hiroshima and Nagasaki was morally justified by contemporary standards is not crucial to the illustration. We do know that President Truman, although he expressed confidence publicly in the rightness of his decisions, harbored misgivings privately. He was concerned that destroying hundreds of thousands of Japanese people, almost all civilians, was frightening. He told confidants that atomic bombs were not *military* weapons at all, but used to kill women, children, and unarmed citizens. Truman gave orders to stop atomic bombing.[26]

Let us *assume* that the bombings of Hiroshima and Nagasaki were morally justified or excusable. If President Truman felt guilty for his decisions even though he suspected that they were appropriate under the circumstances, would that guilt be misplaced, properly remedied by psychological therapy, or a sign of irrationality? In a world where our calculations of results are uncertain but where extreme devastation is stark and incontestable, our moral universe is more ambiguous than philosophical niceties permit. To say, "Well, if the bombings were unjustified then they should not have occurred. If the bombings were justified or excusable then no guilt is appropriate because no wrong has been done," is too facile. We often wonder whether our actions were justifiable or excusable given the complexity of the contexts in which we make choices. Those doubts are not always easy to dismiss. Perhaps we feel guilty because we are unsure whether we did the right thing and a short lecture in the relationship between moral concepts is not enough to assuage our guilt. Nor would psychotherapy remedy our lot.

Still, moral optimists would insist that *feeling* guilty does not mean you *should* feel guilty or that you *are* guilty. Moral pessimists, such as Machiavelli, would rejoin that excuses are often only partially exculpatory. For pessimists, Truman should feel guilty because he does bear some guilt for ordering the bombings even if we assume that his decisions were, all things considered, warranted by the duties of his office. In fairness, Machiavelli could never imagine weapons as indiscriminately destructive of life as atomic bombs. The existence of such weaponry might have precipitated a revision of his principles. Perhaps he would have further limited the occasions when evil could be used well in deference to the massive destruction generated by modern technology.

We may now return to the cases of Churchill and Coventry and the Iran-Contra affair outlined in chapter 1. What would Machiavelli say? Machiavelli, assuming he did not view the situation as a supreme emergency, would cast his vote with the moral pessimists.

If so, Machiavelli would applaud Churchill's willingness to dirty his hands and risk his soul in order to preserve his nation. Machiavelli would partially excuse Churchill's refusal to alert officials in Coventry of the imminent raid yet hold the Prime Minister responsible for the subsequent deaths of citizens and destruction of the city. If Churchill knowingly and intentionally sacrificed innocent lives, he should *feel* morally guilty because he *is* guilty despite having chosen the proper course of action. He has used evil well, but his hands remain dirty and his soul is stained. Assuming that the intelligence that would have been jeopardized had Churchill ordered the evacuation of Coventry was critical to the larger aspiration of military victory, Machiavelli would conclude that this was a time for the statesman to put into practice what he had learned: how not to be good.

But Machiavelli should also cheer the subsequent historical debate, the vigilance of citizens calling Churchill's deed into question, and Churchill's own manufacture of conflicting evidence that preserved his plausible denial of the events. Each of these phenomena is directed at paramount aspects of the unavoidable tensions in dirty hands contexts. Vigorous historical debate and the vigilance of citizens are important for reigning in the possible excesses of statesmen on the verge of losing their souls. Retaining plausible denial permits statesmen to avoid public confessions that undermine their authority and potentially jeopardize their ability to advance the common good. The delicate balances between using evil well and gratuitous wrongdoing, and between risking and losing one's soul, persist.

Regarding the Iran-Contra affair, the Florentine would surely have considered the following questions relevant: Was engaging in this venture genuinely important for the national interest? What was the probability that the scheme would eventually be uncovered? If so, would the statesman retain the ability to plausibly deny his involvement without compromising his future authority? Was this enterprise truly one of those few ends for which using evil well was appropriate?

In my judgment, Machiavelli would have deemed Iran-Contra an intricate web of deceit and connivance that lacked a purpose important enough to excuse its transgressions of categorical moral principles. The political machinations were so intricate as to maximize the prospects of their discovery; plausible denial could occur after such a discovery only by portraying the president as hopelessly unaware of the operations of his immediate subordinates; and the national interests at stake were insufficient to trigger an invocation of dirty hands politics. Nevertheless, Machiavelli would have been impressed by President Reagan's recovery of his approval rating.

Moral optimists who are nonconsequentialists may have a better way to resolve the paradox of dirty hands in such cases than the method advanced by their consequentialist comrades. The paradox results, they could argue, from taking moral principles as absolute, at least in the sense that they cannot legitimately be overridden by aggregating public consequences. Yet, in political contexts duties of office require that such moral principles be overridden. Political morality, which depends so heavily on consequentialist reasoning, seems to conflict with private morality, which rests on absolute principles and individual rights whose normative force remains steadfast in the face of aggregate utility. Accordingly, the good politician who discharges his duties of office apparently compromises his goodness as a private person because he violates moral norms. He soils his hands.

This type of moral optimist, however, reminds us that the moral structure of political decisions is no different from that of private morality. Moral principles, expressing individual rights, remain prior to aggregate utilities, but bear different weight in relation to one another. Politicians, instead of servilely following consequentialist winds, make moral decisions where moral principles and individual rights conflict. Citizens and foreign governments must, at times, be deceived and coerced by political acts, but only where more fundamental moral principles and individual rights are in play. Political and military leaders face so-called dirty hands situations more than private citizens because they must protect the rights that have been entrusted to them. Their offices require them to make decisions about conflicts of moral principles and individual rights that are not at stake in private decision-making. Still, political and military leaders should decide from the same framework that animates conventional morality. The test is always which moral principles and individual rights are stronger, not a differentiated morality that privileges consequentialism in politics but absolute principles in private decision-making.

Accordingly, politicians who must override certain principles and rights to honor others more compelling are not guilty and should feel no guilt. They may sense regret for having infringed the rights of some innocent people, but if they accurately judged the case and advanced the stronger moral claims their hands are clean. The paradox of dirty hands, then, emerges from confusion: wrongly concluding that two separate kinds of normative reasoning are required of public officials and private citizens, and that in fulfilling his public duties the good politician must automatically renege on his private moral duties.[27]

This version of moral optimism is the cleanest way to sanitize the problem of dirty hands only if every apparent case of consequentialist political reasoning can be accurately redescribed in terms of (nonconsequentialist) moral principles and individual rights. Under this rendering, violations of moral norms in the name of utility are illegitimate; moral principles and individual rights often conflict; as long as military and political leaders satisfy the more compelling principles and rights their hands are clean even where harms have been inflicted on those with lesser moral claims.

Moral pessimists, however, will doubt whether all consequentialist political reasoning can be accurately redescribed as a struggle between nonconsequentialist moral principles and individual rights. Moreover, Machiavellian moral reasoning often trades off more important rights of foreigners, from the standpoint of impersonal morality, to advance less important rights of his compatriots. To say that such trade-offs are categorically wrong is to erase the problem of dirty hands by semantic fiat. The strong partialism military and political office requires is a prime agent fueling the problem of dirty hands. This is so even under contemporary moral outlooks that would not go as far as Machiavellian partialism. Also, in domestic contexts politicians at times sacrifice paramount interests of a few people for lesser interests of the multitude. To argue in such instances that only a struggle of conflicting principles and rights, and not consequentialist considerations, is in play is unpersuasive.

Moral optimists remind us that conventional moral wisdom insists that if strict necessity is in play—if a moral agent is forced to choose—then her responsibility for moral unpleasantness evaporates because she did not act freely. Those moral pessimists, such as Machiavelli and Walzer, who conclude that some excuses only partially exonerate and that vestiges of moral guilt appropriately dirty the hands of the agent must account for why this is so.

Partial Excuses

One possibility arises from the conditions of choice. When writing philosophy our examples come deftly packaged: epistemological ambiguities are neatly smoothed over, probabilities are easily proclaimed, and calculations of results are tidily stipulated. Sound pedagogical reasons exist for doing so. We want to illustrate a principle or point without having to quibble over distractions. In the real world of military and political decision-making, however, critical choices are often made under conditions of radical uncertainty. Leaders, denied the comforting certitudes of philosophical examples, may well agonize over whether their choices will cause moral unpleasantness without securing the desired benefits. Have they acted in vain?

This possibility undoubtedly accounts for the *feeling* of guilt some leaders bear, but is less successful in demonstrating that excuses only partially exonerate. Leaders facing radical uncertainty—over facts, probabilities, and outcomes—must still act. If they act in good faith, doing the best they are able under the circumstances, they do not seem culpable when events later conspire against them. They might feel guilty from the outset right up until they discover their decision did not trigger the desired effects. But in the court of moral logic it does not follow that they are responsible for any moral wrongs merely because of the conditions under which they choose.

A second possibility is that guilt and the feelings of dirty hands are emotional responses to choosing in a situation where incommensurable values are in play. For example, suppose a political leader was forced to choose between saving the life of one of her children at the expense of the life of her other child; otherwise both will be murdered. The leader might understand intuitively that she could not properly evaluate, from any common criteria, the two possibilities offered. The situation resists rational resolution. To be compelled to press down on one side instead of the other is to be ushered into a hall of irrationality and arbitrariness. Again, this possibility accounts for feelings of guilt, but not the reality of guilt. The leader may have reasons to be guilty and might even be guilty, but the incommensurability of the values in play cannot indict this person in the court of moral logic. If choice was unavoidably irrational it does not follow that the leader is guilty of any wrongdoing.

A third possibility is that guilt arises from the manner in which the official performs the act. Determining what to do—deliberating over ends, means, and alternatives—is only one part of the action. The other part is executing the act in an appropriate spirit. Abraham Lincoln's generous rhetorical gesture, "with malice toward none, with charity for all," addresses what he took to be the proper spirit in which to approach decision-making and to carry out the acts required for restoration of the republic. An agent can perform the right action for morally flawed reasons: I can save a drowning child because I seek to be honored, not because I care about the value of human life or because I recognize that so acting is the morally right thing to do. An agent can also perform morally disagreeable actions in a laudable manner: The restoration of the republic after the Civil War required some harsh measures that Lincoln hoped would be performed in an appropriate fashion.

This possibility, though, can account for feelings of guilt in dirty hands situations only where politicians perform actions from inappropriate reasons or carry out their decisions with a malignant spirit. In such cases, the politicians would have to recognize the wrongness of the manner in which they performed the deeds in order to suffer the anguish. But even there, the deserved anguish is an add-on and not the core of guilt. Politicians need not perform morally disagreeable acts in an improper manner. When they do, they add another dimension of possible guilt—the wrongness of their manner of carrying out the act—to whatever guilt is appropriate to the act itself. Also, when politicians perform morally disagreeable acts in a proper manner, the issue of whether guilt from the act itself is appropriate remains. In sum, this possibility expands the question of guilt but does not touch the primary issue raised.

A fourth possibility is that guilt arises because agents sense their own negative transformation. Performing acts recognized as morally disagreeable can corrupt character. Our settled righteous dispositions, our instinctive responses, and our ethical sensibilities are threatened by a series of situations in which we must transgress paramount moral principles in deference to a supposed greater good. We may feel guilty as we sense that it becomes increasingly easier to carry out such deeds. We may perceive that we are risking our souls—jeopardizing, or at least compromising, our core values that partially constitute who we are. Guilt may dog our sense of incremental corruption.

Again, this possibility raises only the origins of our feelings of guilt, not whether we are in fact morally guilty of anything. In this case, even the feeling of guilt may be too strong a description. Regret, a sense of loss, and ambivalence about the obligations of our occupation may be more accurate than feeling guilty about our personal transformation. Moreover, the core question remains: Independently of our misgivings or even our feelings of guilt, are we guilty?

A fifth possibility creases the mark. Suppose a moral agent is not restricted to only two morally disagreeable choices. For example, no one is burdened with an antecedent duty to become a military or political leader—or to remain a leader once he has assumed the post. In a dirty hands situation, chief military and political officials have another choice beyond the two unpleasant options: they may resign. Strictly speaking, military or political leaders bear some responsibility for not choosing this third option. Even if they cannot resign without gravely jeopardizing citizens at the moment of choice, the fact that they assumed leadership with full knowledge that the job description included facing circumstances that would dirty their hands is enough to render them somewhat responsible for moral transgressions that occur.

Peter Digeser adds ballast to the moral pessimist's position: "By being given a set of alternatives that are morally dubious, politicians can, to a degree, be excused for dirtying their hands. The excuse of necessity does diminish blame . . . but it does not remove blame altogether. Officeholders who are placed in a position in which they must dirty their hands have the option of resignation. . . . The fact that they seek office and desire to hold onto it does imply something about the moral responsibilities that attach to offices."[28]

The idea here is that necessity is not strict in such cases. The military or political officer has a third option. He has an excuse that partially exonerates him from full responsibility, but by not choosing the third option and by assuming the duties of office knowing that he inevitably would confront dirty hands situations the moral agent bears some degree of responsibility.

A sixth possibility is also apparent. "The dog ate my homework" is a feckless response if I placed the paper in Fido's feeding dish, ladled gravy over it, and covered it with the dog's favorite dinner. Or if I was negligent in placing my homework in a spot inviting to my dog, I cannot convincingly brush off all responsibility for the loss. That is, if I am responsible, fully or partially, for the circumstances under which my homework disappeared, I cannot properly invoke my canine's appetite as a legitimate excuse for my failure to produce the work in class. Accordingly, when military and political leaders are partially responsible for the circumstances under which they brave unappealing choices by their antecedent acts, they bear proportionate responsibility and are only partially excused in the court of moral logic.

A seventh possibility is more controversial. Might the *enormity* of the violation of a nearly absolute moral principle warrant only a partial excuse for the moral agent? Murdering a brother (Romulus), helping to slay 3,000 fellow countrymen (Moses), overseeing the execution of sons (Brutus), exploiting a confederate by using him to pacify a region and then slicing him in two when convenient (Borgia) . . . are these not transgressions of moral principles that are absolute or nearly so? Even if the acts were warranted by extraordinary circumstances, should their mortifying natures not render the agents partially responsible? Should their excuses not be only partially exonerating?

The moral optimist would be unswayed. Calling a moral principle nearly absolute just means that it may be overridden on only a few occasions. If the instant case is one of those occasions then no squeamishness about the numerous times when the principle may not be violated is appropriate. If the instant case is not one of those rare occasions, or if the principle is altogether absolute, then the agent should not violate the principle at all. In either case, no guilt or even feelings of guilt should arise.

The moral pessimist, perhaps smuggling in epistemological uncertainty and uncertainty of attaining desired outcome, would insist that some acts are so horrifying, even if warranted, that feelings of guilt would arise in all but the most insensitive moral agents. More telling are those feelings that reflect the partial responsibility borne by the agent who is only partially exonerated.

Moral pessimists press their point. An action may be justified or excused, yet still be somehow wrong. When making an overall evaluative judgment of whether to perform an act given the circumstances—whether based on consequentialist or nonconsequentialist grounds—we may properly conclude that the act is justified or excused. But the morally horrifying features of that act, even if unavoidable, still count against the action and its agent. That is, the overall judgment of what to do—the proper evaluation that we should perform the act—does not expunge all the wrongness of the values that constitute that act. The wrongness of certain parts of the act persists as a disvalue. The feeling of guilt that results is righteous and appropriate, not simply an unwarranted neurosis that merits psychological therapy or a lecture on the logic of moral concepts.[29]

Moral principles are absolute not in the sense that they cannot be overridden under particular circumstances, but in the sense that even when they are justifiably or excusably overridden the wrongness of transgressing them remains. The experience of having dirty hands resonates with that conviction. The most important cases of dirty hands include significant "betrayals of a person, value, or principle."[30] Although Machiavelli lacked the conceptual apparatus of twenty-first century moral philosophy, he intuitively accepted that dirty hands were the inevitable consequence of the clash between absolute moral principles, the requirements of public office, the conflict between impersonal morality and partialist duties, and the necessities of navigating in the zero-sum contest that adjudicates international affairs. The actions, even if excusable in Machiavelli's view, of political leaders nevertheless strain from the persisting wrongness of some of their constitutive values. That is why strong leaders blessed with military and political *virtù* must risk their souls to found, reform, and lead their nations.

Thinking otherwise conflates justified acts that contain no disvalues as part of the overall judgment that they should be performed with justified or excused acts that do. For example, working for famine relief, helping my neighbor paint her house, and feeding my dog are all morally permissible, justified acts that, other things being equal, include no disvalues or wrongful components. Dirty hands situations—which by definition do include disvalues and wrongful components—often result in proper judgments that acts are justified or excused. To assess all justified acts in the same way—they involve no *overall* wrongness, exonerate the agent from all responsibility, and thus involve no guilt—is to distort our moral experience and grossly minimize the anguish of moral choice. Not all justifications are created equal.

Some dirty hands situations implicate the agent in executing the immoral designs of another person. For example, the case I offered in which a political leader was immorally coerced into sparing the life of one of her children at the expense of the other lest they both be murdered. Consequentialists would evaluate the action as justified—in that by choosing to save one of the children the leader minimized the amount of evil possible under the circumstances. Yet, the person senses the stain on her hands or, more accurately, the compromise of her soul. Should the leader feel morally righteous? After all, the person did the best she could under the circumstances? What would it say about the politician if she were able, perhaps after a quick talk on the logic of moral concepts, to brush off the tragedy of having been forced to bring about the death of one of her children? Having the appropriate moral response is crucial to a fully human life. The feeling of guilt is evidence of understanding that even justified or excused acts do not always purify the wrongness or disvalues they embody.

Moral pessimists, such as Machiavelli, insist that the constituting values of an overall evaluation of what to do and how to act do not disappear as values once the evaluation is finalized. What is required under the circumstances may still be bad even though excused. Excused betrayals of a person, value, or principle retain their wrongful features; an accurate, overall assessment that they are the best we can do under the circumstances does not cleanse all wrongness and disvalue.

I am arguing, then, that a morally pessimistic version of the problem of dirty hands is implicit in Machiavelli's work and that I find that rendition compelling. Critics will object. First, they will accuse me of yoking Machiavelli to a supra-historical framework of analysis and obsessing over the logic of moral reasoning at which Machiavelli would scoff. Second, many will contest the coherency of moral pessimism in this context.

In response, I will go further. With Walzer, I take Machiavelli, with the possible exception of Aristotle, to be the first theorist to understand intuitively and acutely the problem of dirty hands in military and political matters. Yes, I am making his view explicit in the context of twenty-first century moral concepts. I am not claiming he operated with these concepts. But he participated in the tension between accepting absolute moral principles, recognizing the duties (particularly the obligation to advance the interests of constituents over those of foreigners) of public office, and the necessities urged by particular circumstances. Surely for Machiavelli principles are not morally good only because they are useful. Machiavelli is not a consequentialist in that sense. He did not work out the resulting implications nor did he resolve the conundrums. But, then, I am not sure we can smooth out the irregularities either.

An eighth possible explanation of why some excuses only partially exonerate revolves around the problem of questionable partiality. Suppose the hypothetical leader's choice was between the lives of both her children or the lives of fifty equally innocent strangers: If the leader chooses to save the lives of her children, the fifty others will be slaughtered; if the leader chooses to save the fifty, her children will be slain. If the politician chooses to save the lives of her children, does she bear any responsibility for the deaths of fifty innocent strangers? Is such partialism justified or fully excused or only partially excused? Let's change the case again. The leader's choice is between having her two children tortured excruciatingly for two weeks or saving the lives of fifty equally innocent strangers: If she chooses to save the lives of the fifty others, the children will be tortured; if she prevents the torture, fifty strangers will be murdered. In this case, the values to be compared are no longer lives to lives, but lives to periods of torture. Suppose the leader chooses to prevent her children from being tortured. Is the leader partially responsible for the deaths of the fifty others?

A final possibility of why some excuses are only partially exculpatory combines epistemological, psychological, and theoretical considerations. As I have argued previously, the Machiavellian tension in dirty hands situations is not between the conflicting demands of two normative realms—the political and the moral—or between the imperatives of two moralities—the pagan and the religious—but instead arises *within* conventional morality. The impartiality required of the Ideal Moral Observer often rests uncomfortably with the partialism permitted when moral agents are discharging obligations to special, limited constituencies. This theoretical tension within conventional morality is not merely conceptual but experiential. Human beings confronting dirty hands situations feel the force of competing moral vectors. Unable to satisfy the imperatives of both vectors, they search for an objective way to arrive at the right answer all things considered. But the actuality of arriving at such an overall evaluation presupposes that the elements that comprise our moral calculus are commensurable. Unfortunately, this is not always the case. Conventional morality is not so neatly packaged that all values are compatible with one another or susceptible to being weighed on a single scale. Although I have presented dirty hands situations as distinguished partially by the feature that the agent knows what to do—in contrast, say, to moral dilemmas—that knowledge is not the result of an objective calculation of commensurable but conflicting moral values. In international relations, Machiavelli's statesmen know what to do because they typically (too often?) privilege the interests and common good of their limited constituencies over the well-being of other nations or even over the well-being of the global community. Domestically, statesmen sometimes privilege the common good of the nation over the civil liberties of some individuals: the sons of Brutus must be slain; harsh measures are often required to found or maintain a healthy republic; means that are typically evil must be employed to advance national interests.

Statesmen employing evil well do so resolutely. They must swallow all doubt and perform their duties as they must. But the horizon of their choices and actions lingers: They cannot derive what they should do conclusively from the materials comprising conventional morality; they will feel great pressure to privilege their national interests over the well-being of other countries; they may find doing so easier and more natural after several past occurrences; they understand keenly that the means used to attain their goals remain evil even if required by what they take to be necessity; and, finally, the conditions they take to constitute necessity often expand as past successes promote future overreaching.

Taking excuses under such circumstances to be only partially exculpatory serves several purposes: doing so serves as a caution to overreaching; it recognizes and underscores epistemological uncertainty; it tacitly acknowledges the incommensurability of values pervading conventional morality; and it highlights that even when used well, evil remains evil. Statesmen willing to risk but determined not to lose their souls cannot merely alternate between the impartial imperatives of and the partialist exceptions conventional morality permits. Conventional morality cannot draw that line so neatly because of the incommensurable values it embodies, the epistemological obstacles haunting determinations of necessity, and the psychological sirens luring decision-makers to privilege their own causes.

Accordingly, statesmen willing to risk but determined not to lose their souls must not embrace too easily the excuses and justifications so readily available to them when they dirty their hands in service to their nations. While this rationale of why some excuses are only partially exculpatory is most persuasive in the context of statesmen who confront dirty hands situations recurrently, it also applies to private citizens who confront them less frequently. Although not all of the underlying purposes of the rationale apply to those who face dirty hands situations rarely, the persuasive power of some of those purposes remains.

Military and political officers are required by their job descriptions to promote the interests of their partisans over the interests of the international good. The extent of warranted partialism is contestable—no contemporary moralist would endorse the degree of partialism Machiavelli advocated in international affairs. But might some responsibility and some guilt for harmful outcomes to foreigners arise from implementing partialistic reasoning under conditions of uncertainty? Might some occasions of preferring the interests of our own to the interests of outsiders exonerate moral agents incompletely?

In all such appeals, moral optimists will insist that a right answer exists. If the act is permitted then it is justified and the moral agent incurs no guilt. If she feels guilty that is a psychological, not philosophical, concern. Only if the act is unjustified does guilt ensue. In such cases moral agents should feel guilty because they are guilty. Moral pessimists rejoin that moral experience is not so neatly arranged. Degrees of uncertainty pervade our assessment of circumstances, weighing of alternatives, deliberation over means, and evaluation of different ends. The duties of public office complicate matters further because the ideal moral vantage point of impartialism is compromised systematically: military and political leaders must promote the interests of their country.

Machiavelli must remain a puzzle for contemporary moralists. His understanding of necessity, contrary to current usage, does not allow a statesman to lodge a legitimate claim of justification. Necessity permits only a claim of excuse that does not fully exonerate the actor from responsibility in Machiavelli's court of morality. For Machiavelli, limitations on a leader's range of alternatives do not fully exonerate him or her from responsibility. Machiavelli takes moral principles to be categorical. Leaders are sometimes partly responsible for the antecedent conditions that nurture necessity, the horrifying nature of certain of their acts, and their prior understanding of the inevitability of resorting to evil when they freely assumed office combine to make them partially responsible for moral horrors that ensue. Leaders who have already lost their souls—those who feel no pangs of conscience when violating moral norms—are too likely to promote tyranny. The perhaps impossible task for chief military and political officials is to preserve their souls while consistently and systematically using evil well. Machiavelli's model invokes a solitary actor, estranged from simplistic evaluations by results only, aspiring to but suspicious of honors conferred by the masses, commanded by the duties of office to advance the interests of his country above those of the international community. Surrounded by packs of jackals and wolves immersed in a zero-sum contest in which the winners harvest glory, power, and *virtù* while the losers suffer humiliation, impotence, and servitude, leaders must soil their hands and risk their souls.

The multitude will, naïvely, judge only by the results. If the evil used turns out to facilitate desired ends—such as the founding, preserving, or reforming of a healthy, expansionist republic—the masses will judge the means praiseworthy. If the evil used does not succeed, the people will evaluate the means harshly. But actual outcomes blossom from numerous causes, some of which *Fortuna* plants. To evaluate leaders only by results is to bestow too much credit or too much blame for circumstances and events outside their control. Machiavelli stresses the current situation and the reasonably foreseeable consequences of alternative possibilities. Our predicted outcomes and assessment of present circumstances arise from our own acts and evaluations. The actual results occur, at least in part, from things beyond our command.

Is Machiavelli's Doctrine Abhorrent?

Harvey Mansfield warns, "It is sometimes claimed in extenuation of Machiavelli that he never said, 'the end justifies the means.' No, but he said worse: that the end makes the means honorable, and that moral men believe this."[31] I would deny that what Machiavelli said is "worse." More fundamentally, Machiavelli says that the means will be *judged* honorable because the masses are lured by external appearances and evaluate actions only by their outcome (P 18). Machiavelli, then, is not claiming that the judgment of the masses, which he considers vulgar in this context, "makes" the means honorable in any higher sense. Moreover, the problem of dirty hands illustrates how one can argue that an action is tainted with evil but required by the duties of office and *is*, thus, honorable to perform. Moral optimists will dispute that analysis, but the position of moral pessimists such as Machiavelli is at least plausible and in my view persuasive.

I have argued that for Machiavelli only a few ends partially excuse the use of means that are otherwise wrong: Founding or preserving a healthy, expansionist state, or reforming a corrupt state; driving out foreigners as a prelude to founding or invigorating a state; facilitating the common good by removing obstreperous elements as a last resort; and the like. These ends for Machiavelli are required for a social life that can transform the people in positive ways, allow military and political leaders to satisfy their yearning for glory, and confer on a nation the reward of historical immortality.

Still, a critic would respond, those "few ends" cover more ground than first suspected. None of the goals listed is attained by merely a single act. They all require numerous, perhaps recurring, uses of evil. In what way does the doctrine, "A few ends partially excuse some means" amount to a moral improvement over the view that, "The good end justifies every means"?

The critic is correct that my interpretation of Machiavelli's positions still endorses numerous harsh, cruel measures in the name of treasured goals. No whitewash of Machiavelli is possible or desired on that score. But the excuse doctrine narrows the scope of what defines a "good end." Not just any desired goal legitimizes every means used to attain it. Moreover, the excuse doctrine caps the amount of moral disagreeableness at the level of evil well used. Any measures exceeding that cap call into question the ends sought. That is, going beyond the level of evil well used suggests a leader is most probably a tyrant focused on the accumulation and exercise of power as such, instead of a Machiavellian ruler striving for personal glory in the context of transforming citizens for the common good.

Furthermore, the excuse doctrine implicates a leader's conscience in a way that the justification view does not. If my actions are fully justified, as moral optimists never tire of pointing out, I have no reason to feel guilty because I am not guilty: my action was the morally right thing to do under the circumstances. If my actions are excused in a fashion that only partially exonerates me from responsibility, I should harbor some guilt and serious misgivings. If so, perhaps in the future I will be more reluctant—than I would be under the justification view—to use cruelty in circumstances where it is not warranted. Perhaps under the justification view it is easier in the future to rationalize the use of harsh means and to dismiss countervailing reasons.

I must temper my argument by pointing out, again, that Machiavelli does not delve explicitly into the psychology of his historical favorites nor does he examine the interior life of his hypothetical military and political leaders. Accordingly, I am not claiming that Machiavelli stated, or even held explicitly, the contrasts that I am urging. I am proposing, instead, that such contrasts are implicit in Machiavelli's work as we interpret it in a contemporary framework. Machiavelli left the clues. We must now continue to piece those clues together, complete his puzzle, and unlock his secret. The next step is examining how he evaluates certain military and political leaders.

Evaluating Military and Political Leaders

To understand more concretely the trials and tribulations of statesmen we should examine the examples Machiavelli discusses in his works. Let's begin with those whom Machiavelli concludes were military or political failures. (See appendices B and C for a chronicle of the historical events fueling Machiavelli's assessments.)

Gaius Julius Caesar (100 BCE–44 BCE)

Machiavelli is remarkably contemptuous of Caesar. With other members on his list of failed statesmen, he typically mentions the brutal effectiveness of their efforts or their military *virtù* even though his overall evaluation is decidedly negative. With Caesar, Machiavelli is unsparingly critical. The only positive remark about Caesar, despite his undeniable prowess as a warrior and military strategist, in *The Prince* and *The Discourses* is that he used the money of others wisely—Caesar plundered and pillaged his military victims, and used that money generously instead of squandering his own wealth or that of the Romans (P 16). [In fairness, Machiavelli does examine Caesar's military *virtù* in *The Art of War* (AW I 34; II 55–56; III 96; IV 111, 120, 123–24; V 146–47; VI 175–76, 178–79; VII 201, 211).]

Machiavelli contrasts the tyrannical Caesar with the civic-minded Scipio; he chastises those who have been mesmerized by Caesar's power and apparent success; he sneers at Caesar as an evil-doer; as the destroyer of Rome; as the man who placed the yoke of slavery on the necks of Romans, while blinding the people to that reality; he labels Caesar a tyrant who exploited the corruption of the people for his own benefit; he depicts Caesar as a man who greedily abused the office of dictator by extending the term of that office without authorization from the people (D I 10, 17, 29, 34; AW I 17). In contrast to warriors and politicians who channel their personal ambition to found or reform states in the long-term interests of the common good, Machiavelli concludes that Caesar was a rabid opportunist who drove the final nail of tyranny into a corrupt republic. Although I am convinced that his indictment is distorted and misleading, Machiavelli derides Caesar mercilessly as a paradigmatic tyrant.[32]

Oliverotto Euffreducci (Oliverotto da Fermo), CA. 1475–1502

Oliverotto served as one of Cesare Borgia's primary henchman until his plot against his superior was discovered, leading to Oliverotto's death. Why, then, does Borgia earn some appreciative commentary from Machiavelli while Oliverotto suffers Machiavelli's disdain? Although noting Oliverotto's military *virtù*, Machiavelli suggests that Oliverotto, instead of acting to inaugurate a new state or reform a corrupt state, enslaved a state that was otherwise viable. Oliverotto acted selfishly and only in pursuit of his own *ambizione*, not in long-term service to the common good; he murdered a relative and fellow citizens in the course of destroying Fermo; and his purposes did not lead to enhanced order, security, and the preconditions for civic *virtù*. Oliverotto clearly lacked political *virtù*, civic *virtù*, and moral *virtù*. Oliverotto destroyed Fermo and continued evil well beyond the time and extent necessary. Rightly or wrongly, Machiavelli judges otherwise with regard to Cesare Borgia. For the Florentine, Borgia was in the process of reforming the corrupt state of Romagna by ensuring order, security, stability, and new laws—ingredients of the recipe required for developing civic *virtù*.

Agathocles of Syracuse, 361 BCE–289 BCE

Agathocles was an admirable general: brave, strong, overcoming resistance and adversity. But his long-term cruelty ill-used, brutality, and wickedness relegate him to infamy. In short, much like Oliverotto and Caesar, he lacked political, moral, and civic *virtù*. Agathocles, in the short run, used cruelty well as a militarist, but in the long run he enslaved a free state. The selfish *ambizione* and inhumane purposes of the tyrant cannot merit glory, for Machiavelli. Murdering one's fellow citizens and betraying one's friends are acceptable only in service of humane purposes such as founding a state or reforming a corrupt state. Similar brutality perpetrated against a military enemy is often a required part of military *virtù*.

Girolamo Savonarola, 1452–1498

Machiavelli appreciated the wiles that allowed Savonarola to ascend to influence and his passion for cultural reform. Also, Savonarola used religion for political purposes. He convinced numerous Florentines that he communicated directly with God, even though he performed no miracles or extraordinary deeds. His own example, the unwavering certitude of his message, and the conditions of his time were enough to garner short-term success (D I 11). Machiavelli, though, would point out that Savonarola's religious values were unworthy of a thriving, expansionist republic. That the friar understood the crucial connection between religion and politics counts in his favor, but the particular religious and political values Savonarola exalted strike a sour note for Machiavelli. Mildness, meekness, spiritual contemplation, and resolve in the face of suffering are unreliable substitutes for Roman physicality, pursuit of glory, passion, and militarism. Vigor trumps delicacy.

Savonarola was inflexible, fanatical, and focused on the transcendent world—an infallible roadmap to failure. In addition, Savonarola was partisan and failed to comply with a law he himself had urged on Florence. Finally, Savonarola was an unarmed prophet. He was destroyed as soon as his moral authority fell into question because of his fanaticism. Savonarola lacked the means—the strong arms and secular laws—required to harden the resolve of his remaining supporters or to persuade critics to obey his decrees (P 6).

Piero Soderini, 1450–1513

For Machiavelli, Soderini's patience, generosity, and indecisiveness sealed his downfall. Instead of killing the sons of Brutus—those antirepublicans who were doing the Holy League's bidding within Florence—Soderini was conciliatory, offering compromise and gifts. Soderini feared that eliminating the sons of Brutus would require exercising special powers that, even if successful in the short run, would destroy the office of *gonfaloniere à vita*. Soderini failed to understand that the success of the Holy League was radically more likely to destroy that office and the republic of Florence as well. As a result of Soderini's reluctance to dirty his hands, he fell from power, was exiled, and the republic was destroyed. Political hostility is not domesticated by time or mollified by peace offerings (D III 3).

Soderini's ultimate weakness was the frailty that eventually destroys all politicians: inflexibility. During his first nine years in office, his moral *virtù* and civic *virtù* reaped great benefits for Florence. When the times changed—when ruthlessness, decisiveness, and harshness were needed to stem the rising, hostile political tide—Soderini could not adapt. Moral and civic *virtù* cannot guarantee triumph over jealousies, political intrigues, hatred, and a bad turn of *Fortuna* (D III 9, 30).

Giovampagolo Baglioni, 1470–1520

Machiavelli excoriates Baglioni because in order to attain power he was excessively cruel: he killed his cousins and nephews, forced his sister into an incestuous relationship, and wielded power viciously. In short, he ignored the distinction between evil well- and ill-used, and was gratuitously mean-spirited.

More strikingly, Machiavelli derides Baglioni for his cowardice. When the Pope, his bodyguard, and the College of Cardinals entered Perugia, Baglioni meekly surrendered even though he was accompanied by many soldiers. Machiavelli is stunned that Baglioni did not simply strike down his enemies and confiscate their riches. Machiavelli notes that we cannot attribute Baglioni's reluctance to act forcefully to his goodness because he was a "vicious man."

Machiavelli adds that Baglioni "had a perfect opportunity to do a deed for which everybody would have admired his courage and for which he would have left an everlasting remembrance of himself, as being the first who had shown prelates what a low estimate was to be put on men who live and reign as they do" (D I 27). In sum, Baglioni stands as a Machiavellian paradigm of viciousness married to cowardice.

Cesare Borgia ("Duke Valentino"), 1475–1507

Cesare Borgia is a transition figure between Machiavellian villains and Machiavellian heroes. Borgia and Machiavelli were contemporaries who met several times and sized each other up. Machiavelli was among a Florentine legation that spent two months with Borgia. Bishop Francesco Soderini, ambassador of the legation, described Borgia in glowing terms: "This lord is very magnificent and splendid, and so spirited in feats of arms that there is nothing so great but that it must seem small to him. In the pursuit of glory and in the acquisitions of dominions he never rests, and he knows neither danger nor fatigue. He moves so swiftly . . . he knows how to make himself beloved to his soldiers and he has in his service the best men of Italy . . . his wit and eloquence never fail him."[33]

Machiavelli acknowledges that Borgia acquired power through *Fortuna*—namely, his father's influence and allies. Cesare laid the foundations for future power, though, by his military and political *virtù*. His ultimate demise flowed from a change in *Fortuna*—his own untimely ill health and the death of his father (P 7). Machiavelli admired Cesare Borgia's glowing *ambizione*, military insight, ability to practice fraud and administer force, and willingness to do what was necessary to found or reform a state: "I cannot think of any better example I could offer a new ruler than that of his actions" (P 7). Borgia, though, does not occupy the same realm as exemplars such as Romulus, Moses, and Brutus. They were stunningly more successful, establishing communities that endured; they did not commit the sort of major blunders that plagued Borgia; and their success was less dependent on *Fortuna* than was that of Borgia.

The lives of failed statesmen that Machiavelli sketches all embody fatal flaws. Some apparently lacked antecedent understanding of the good (for example, Agathocles, Baglioni); some did not understand the distinction between using evil well and using evil poorly, or even if they understood the distinction could not use evil well because of cowardice (for example, Baglioni) or squeamishness (for example, Soderini); some were overly ambitious, selfish, and unconcerned with the common good (for example, Oliverotto, Caesar), another form of lacking antecedent understanding of impersonal morality; some lacked appropriate religious values even though they grasped the connection between religion and political power (for example, Savonarola); and some were overly reliant on *Fortuna* and may have lost their souls in the course of governing (for example, Borgia).

Romulus, CA. 770 BCE–CA. 716 BCE

Let us now to turn to statesmen whom Machiavelli deems more successful. I have already discussed Moses, so I begin with Romulus. Machiavelli honors Romulus for being an armed founder of a city (P 6); for establishing strong laws that were the preconditions for security, order, and civic *virtù* (D I 1); and for killing Remus and, later, Titus Tatius, a Sabine who had been elected to share office with Romulus (D I 9). Machiavelli insists that the founding of a republic or principality requires one person in charge. While those who resort to violence and cruelty to destroy a thriving city merit guilt, those who do so to found or reform a city are partially excused (D I 9).

According to Machiavelli, history should judge Romulus favorably. He acted in accord with the common good, not from self-aggrandizement. After all, he soon established an effective senate with extensive influence. Romulus retained only the power to command the military once war was declared and the authority to summon the senate. In this manner, the original institutions of Rome were more in line with constitutional and participatory politics, not tyrannical absolutism (D I 9). In sum, Machiavelli concludes that Romulus should be largely forgiven, not blamed, for slaying Remus and Titus Tatius. Establishing the constitution of a republic requires one man of excellence acting for the common good.

Lucius Junius Brutus, CA. 545 BCE–CA. 509 BCE

Machiavelli hails Brutus as "the father of Roman liberty." Recognizing that condemning two sons and supervising their execution is extraordinarily harsh, Machiavelli excuses, even commends, Brutus's action as required for the preservation of freedom. Brutus publicly and decisively destroyed those who sought to overturn the newly formed republic. Machiavelli reminds everyone that hostility to the state is not mollified by time or gifts (D III 1, 3). Brutus's horrifying actions are classic cases of evil well-used. The survival of a new state requires extraordinary men willing to perform, at times, acts that shock the conscience. Machiavelli insists that "killing the sons of Brutus"—a metaphor for destroying those plotting against self-government—is the most effective and reliable means of preserving a state that has recently acquired freedom (D I 16; D III 1, 3). Brutus enforced the law and levied the ultimate punishment on his own blood. Machiavelli nods approvingly and reminds us that he "loves his country more than his soul." Patriotism glistens as his highest value.

Numa Pompilius, CA. 750 BCE–CA. 673 BCE

Machiavelli gushed over Numa's acute vision that religion was essential for civilized life. The power of the gods exceeds that of any man or group of men in compelling citizens to behave. The appeal to divine authority, then and now, is the ultimate political trump. Numa Pompilius, understanding that his own power was insufficient to command complete allegiance, claimed to have a special relationship with a nymph who passed him advice from the gods on matters of governance. The unsophisticated nature of his subjects facilitated Numa's design (D I 11).

Hiero II, 308 BCE–216 BCE

Machiavelli also praises Hiero II of Syracuse, whom he cites as an exceptionally virtuous man and a rare example of someone who became a ruler of a major city from private station. The oppressed people of Syracuse elected Hiero to be their military commander because he was judged prior to his ascension as embodying extraordinary *virtù*. Here Machiavelli seems to be noting Hiero's excellences in all relevant respects: moral, civic, military, and political. Upon being made commander-in-chief, he massacred the standing mercenary army of his city and replaced those troops with his own soldiers (P 6, 13; D ded.). Syracuse prospered under his rule.

Hannibal, CA. 247 BCE–183 BCE

For Machiavelli, Hannibal possessed abundant military *virtù*. By being "harsh and cruel" he promoted the admiration and fear of his troops. For Machiavelli, Hannibal's cruelty was a precondition of his military *virtù*. In fact, Hannibal's cruelty was the "principal cause" of the loyalty embodied by his forces (P 17). Hannibal was able to keep morale high and avoid internal strife within his army because of his deserved reputation for terror (D III 21).

Machiavelli's successful chief political and military officials understood the distinction between evil well-used and evil used poorly. More important, they were willing to participate in horrifying deeds in order to advance the common good. Even Numa manipulated the power of religion for political advantage. Machiavelli underscores how they risked their souls in service of founding or maintaining their countries, but provides no evidence that his stalwarts lost their souls. Like Machiavelli, patriotism was their highest value and they loved their countries more than their narrow ambitions. As facilitators of the common good, they earned the biographical immortality that enduring glory confers.

These evaluations of chief military and political officials provide the final piece of our puzzle. We are now prepared to unlock Machiavelli's secret and describe the soul of his patriotic statesman.

4

The Soul of the Statesman

We can now understand and explain the mindset of a Machiavellian statesman from the clues that the Florentine author provided. If Machiavelli is correct, statesmen must dirty their hands while discharging their duties. They are at the helms of states that embody a monopoly on the legitimate use of violence and coercive means; they operate in a competitive context with numerous unscrupulous agents; they have special responsibilities to their limited constituencies that sometimes require them to infringe on the interests of humanity in general; they must sometimes appear to be what they are not in order to retain their authority; and their decisions involve higher stakes than those of private citizens. Thus, unlike private citizens, statesmen confront dirty hands situations systematically.

At the international level, statesmen confront moral paradoxes generated by conflicts between the imperatives of impersonal morality understood from the perspective of an Ideal Observer and the partialist obligations they bear to their national constituents. This is a conflict within morality and not, as often supposed, a conflict between two types of morality (Christian versus pagan) or between two normative domains (moral versus political). Moreover, as Machiavelli never tires of pointing out, statesmen will sometimes need to use violence or dissimulation in foreign affairs given the nature of the world. Even if he is incorrect in thinking that the world is wholly and inevitably a ruthless forum for zero-sum competition, Machiavelli accurately cautions statesmen that they must embody the power of the lion in order to frighten the numerous political wolves extant among them and the cunning of the fox in order to recognize and evade the traps and machinations of their peers.

At the domestic level, statesmen will often face moral paradoxes generated by conflicts between their duty to promote the common good and their obligation to honor the interests of individual citizens.

In democratic and republican forms of government, they will be required to facilitate deals and broker compromises directed at accommodating diverse interest groups. The decisions of statesmen involve more people and more critical issues than the decisions of private citizens. Often those decisions are enforced through coercive state power. In general, different groups of constituents will lodge conflicting, severe demands on statesmen. Typically operating under conditions of epistemological uncertainty and normative disagreement, statesmen must often arrive at monumental decisions while struggling with incompatible or incommensurable values.

In sum, statesmen who risk but do not lose their souls acknowledge several guidelines: they must often privilege their partialist duties to advance the interests of their constituents over their obligations to support the general interests of humanity; they must sometimes choose to promote the common good of their constituents at the cost of infringing upon the interests of individuals who are also constituents; and they should not advantage members of their own family or their friends at the expense of other constituents. But such guidelines do not soften the burden of discharging the duties of statesmen; instead, they underscore the inevitability of dirtying one's hands and straining one's soul while holding high political office. In this manner, statesmen take the burden of evil upon themselves to secure the common good for constituents.

Piecing the Clues Together

Thus far I have argued that the ideal Machiavellian statesman has a default position: to act in accord with the imperatives of impersonal morality, he must know and act on the good. Knowing and acting on the good is not grounded in consequentialism. Machiavelli accepts that principles and actions are right or wrong independently of the consequences they produce. But statesmen must also learn how not to be good: they must not depart from the good when possible, but know how to enter into evil when necessary (P 15, 17, 18; D I 9, 18; D III 3). Because of the nature of the world, the scarcity of desired resources, and his special obligations to advance the interests of his constituents, the statesman cannot invariably obey the imperatives of impersonal morality. Conflicts will arise between the impartiality demanded by impersonal morality and the partialism required by the duties of a particular nation's office. In such circumstances, the statesman must recognize and act on the distinction between evil well-used and evil ill-used (P 8; D I 45; D II 19; D III 21).

Evil is used well when it is aimed at securing the most valuable social goals: founding or preserving a healthy, expansionist state, or reforming a corrupt state; driving out foreigners as a prelude to the other ends; facilitating the common good by removing obstreperous elements as a last resort; and the like. Such evil occurs in one fell swoop, it does not persist. And the means used are compelled by necessity; they are required for attaining the valuable goals. Finally, these goals serve the common good of the statesman's nation. Effective mercy may require evil well-used, harsh measures needed for order, security, and unification. A statesman should not shrink from being considered cruel if his purpose is to keep citizens united, faithful, and safe. But to get good people to use evil well is a difficult task. The morally sensitive ruler—who is too squeamish to use evil well—may, through misguided short-term compassion, permit rebellions and insurrections to develop, which do more long-range harm than the cruelest ruler (P 18, 19, 21; D III 3, 9; D III 30; Ltr. 203, 9/16/12).

Evil ill-used is, at bottom, gratuitous cruelty. It is not required to attain the most valuable goals and may be counterproductive to those ends. Evil ill-used is often disproportionate, recurrent, and frustrates the common good. Moreover, it often advances the cause of tyranny.

Implicating themselves in evil, even if well-used, leaves statesmen with dirty hands, which connotes a morally-stained soul. This is the case because for Machiavelli moral principles are absolute not in the sense that they cannot ever be overridden, but in the sense that even when they are justifiably or excusably overridden the wrongness of transgressing them remains. Accordingly, for Machiavelli, a few good ends only partially excuse the evil means necessary to attain them.

Statesmen must be ardent patriots who love their nations more than their souls (Ltr. 331: 4/16/27; Ltr. 224: 12/10/13; Ltr. 270: 5/17/21; FH III 7; AW I 7). The wrongful remainders that accompany evil well-used imply that statesmen risk their souls in the service of their countries. To risk one's soul is to jeopardize one's character, to potentially transform oneself unworthily. Statesmen must not lose their souls because if they do they will obscure the distinction between evil well-used and evil ill-used and thereby enter into evil too willingly; they will invariably become tyrants instead of stewards of the common good. Nor can they truculently adhere to the imperatives of impersonal morality and retain their clean hands because in so doing they will renege on the duties of their office and fail as patriots.

We can explain many of the actions and much of the mindset of an ideal Machiavellian ruler from the standpoint of power. At its most general, power is the capability to produce or contribute to the production of outcomes ("power to"). A Machiavellian ruler, of course, must possess an abundance of such power which arises from his *virtù*.

Machiavellian rulers must also wield power-over. A superior party possesses power over a subordinate party when the superior has the capability (the disposition) to affect the outcomes and/or interests of the subordinate by controlling or limiting the alternative choices or actions available to the subordinate. The three major uses of power-over are oppression, paternalism, and empowerment. A superior party oppresses a subordinate party when the superior affects adversely the outcomes and/or interests of the subordinate by controlling or limiting the alternative choices or actions available to the subordinate. Often, and especially in dirty hands contexts, a Machiavellian ruler must oppress a foreign enemy or a segment of his own constituents in service of the greater good of his nation. The second major use of power-over is paternalism: A superior party acts paternalistically toward a subordinate party when the superior tries to affect positively the outcomes and/or interests of the subordinate by controlling or limiting the alternative choices or actions available to the subordinate. A Machiavellian ruler often acts paternalistically toward his constituents, especially in the early stages of his rule when the people lack the civic *virtù* required for full political participation. The third major use of power-over is empowerment: A superior party acts to empower a subordinate party when the superior tries to affect positively the outcomes and/or interests of the subordinate with the aim of favorably transforming the subordinate by controlling or limiting the alternative choices or actions available to the subordinate. Empowerment is often paternalism with the direct aim of transforming the subordinate to the point where the subordinate is no longer in need of direction.

A Machiavellian ruler aims at the transformation and empowerment of his constituents, either as the prelude to the transition from a principality to a republic or the transition from the early to mature stages of a republic. As always, nurturing the civic *virtù* of constituents is critical to the advancement of national interests. When interpreters focus too heavily on the use of power-over as oppression or even define Machiavellian power in those terms, they generate much confusion as to the Florentine's normative message.

Dirty hands contexts in politics are driven by agents who exercise their power to use evil well, but who do not conclude that their deeds arose from wrong choices or from situations in which the reasons supporting alternate actions were equal. Instead, agents who retain their souls will recognize their deeds involved violations of paramount principles of impersonal morality recognized by themselves and their constituents. Also, the victims of such deeds will conclude that they have been wronged by those violations. To risk but not lose their souls, statesmen must retain their reluctance to dirty their hands even where doing so is necessary for the national good. They must acknowledge the moral remainder, the cost, of their necessary actions. Otherwise, such leaders will too easily dirty their hands when doing so is not necessary, thereby losing their souls and jeopardizing the common good of their nations. Machiavellian statesmen must learn how not to be good, but still retain all the goodness permitted by their institutional roles. Again, they must risk but not lose their souls. The nature of the world and the structure of the moral conflicts they must confront prevent them from attaining Plato's ideal of the perfectly balanced soul, but permit them to retain their humanity. Or so we must hope.

Statesmen who risk but retain their souls will garner the highest award available to human beings: deserved, enduring glory that confers a measure of immortality upon the greatest among us (P 7, 8, 14, 24, 26; D I 10). Such a person will have softened the triumph of the Pale Rider to the extent possible for finite beings.

The Inner Life of a Machiavellian Statesman

Walzer suggests that statesmen who dirty their hands in the name of and in service to their constituents should be held accountable for their deeds. Theoretically, at least, "We would simply honor the man who did bad in order to do good, and at the same time we would punish him. We would honor him for the good he has done, and we would punish him for the bad he has done."[1] Doing so, however, may be impractical because "there are no authorities to whom we might entrust the task."[2] Still, statesmen with dirty hands should express publicly their guilt to reassert and reinforce the principles of impersonal morality. Doing so "requires us at least to imagine a punishment or a penance that fits the crime and so to examine closely the nature of the crime."[3] In addition, in Machiavellian terms, public confessions and responses increase the possibility that statesmen will not lose their souls. Walzer, then, rejects the view that statesmen who retain their souls by suffering the effects of their use of evil well in isolation have atoned sufficiently. He recommends that such leaders must pay a public price and so should their constituents on whose behalf and in whose name the deeds were undertaken.

Although he does not explicitly address this issue, Machiavelli would be unconvinced by Walzer's appeal. The proposition that doing evil is its own punishment does not imply that agents must outwardly demonstrate their felt guilt, that they must evince a strong emotional response in the aftermath of using evil well. They should, I would argue, suffer the effects of having chosen, in the face of necessity, to transgress categorical moral prohibitions. But people suffer in different ways. For Machiavelli, public confessions bear no honor. Among other reasons, political effectiveness depends in part on action that is concealed from the public. Widespread disclosure of certain actions often hobbles future possibilities.

Machiavellian statesmen should not wallow in anguish or be overwhelmed with doubt. Such leaders must not permit themselves to vacillate; they must not resort to half measures; they must, instead, firmly recognize what necessity requires and resolutely serve the common good of their nation. But they cannot ignore that employing evil well still stains their inner cores and jeopardizes their characters. To ignore those facts is to lose, not simply risk, their souls. Because they are responsible for the lives and well-being of their constituents, statesmen must tread the narrow path between retaining pangs of conscience and plunging into existential angst. They can neither immunize themselves from guilt nor allow themselves to be its victim. Those who are eager to dirty their hands have already lost or will soon lose their souls, which brings no honor to them or to their nations. Those who insist on moral purity are unfit to lead their nations given the conditions of the world. In Machiavelli's view, statesmen will face dirty hands situations early and often. The delicate balance between the heroism of Romulus and the villainy of Agathocles hovers over each decision.

A proper Machiavellian statesman will suffer in recognition of what he has done and what he may become in the course of acquiring dirty hands, whereas a statesman who has lost his soul will be unconcerned about confessing his supposed wrongs because he either does not recognize that his hands are dirty or he does not care. Worse, such a leader might even utter bogus confessions for his private advantage. Also, public expressions of guilt will sometimes jeopardize national security and will more frequently portray the chief political leader as a whimpering penitent, which will weaken the strength of his leadership at home and abroad. Everyone with average insight understands that statesmen must dirty their hands, but imagine the public relations complications accompanying media caricatures of such leaders should they regularly wring their hands in public.

A nation's procurement of social goods such as glory, honor, security, and material resources largely defines its political success. Yet the means sometimes required to secure such goods will trample on the imperatives of impartial morality. Thus, statesmen who have not lost their souls will endure the internal struggle between their desire to maintain moral rectitude and their duty to maximize the likelihood of political success. The leader who retains clean hands will betray his duty to serve the common good of his country, while the leader who loses his soul will degenerate into a tyrant. Accordingly, statesmen who risk but do not lose their souls, who learn how not to be good at only the appropriate times, will be acutely aware of their irresolvable internal discord. For Machiavelli, the nature of the world and the structure of political leadership ensure that Plato's moral exemplar—the person with a perfectly balanced soul whose resplendent rationality prevents him from ever being an agent of evil—would be a colossal failure as statesman. If Platonic philosophers were kings the common good of the state would suffer.

Leo Strauss insists that "consciousness of excellence on the part of excellent men must take the place of consciousness of guilt or sin."[4] If this means only that chief political leaders must sometimes knowingly violate the moral imperatives they antecedently accept in order to rule effectively then the passage accurately describes Machiavelli's view. But if Strauss intends something stronger—and I think he does—then the passage is misleading. If, for example, Strauss means that statesmen must focus narrowly on attaining enduring glory and must thereby concentrate only on political success he overstates the case. On Strauss's rendering, focusing narrowly on attaining enduring glory implies that moral calculations become irrelevant or that statesmen simply dismiss the psychological force of moral imperatives. But to act in such a fashion is not merely to risk one's soul but to increase recklessly the prospects of losing it. The Machiavellian statesman must live and act with ongoing internal tension because only that felt experience evidences the leader's retention of his soul. To dismiss either vector of the context of dirty hands—the duty to maximize political success or the commitment to uphold the imperatives of impersonal morality—is to bring about either political failure or the loss of one's soul. Machiavelli champions neither of these outcomes.

In that vein, using evil well does not imply merely that what is typically seen as vice has been transformed into virtue because of circumstances of necessity or because political success has been attained. In dirty hands contexts, a moral remainder, a significant disvalue, persists: necessity provides only a partial excuse for the chief political leader's actions appropriate though they may be.

Yet, at least one of Walzer's points remains: chief political leaders cannot be completely unaccountable for their actions. Investigative reporters, the watch dogs of a free society, must monitor abuses of governmental power and call attention to the transgressions of political leaders. The people should react appropriately to governmental actions they perceive unwise or immoral. Furthermore, every society needs strict moral absolutists within the government to soften the inclination toward actions resulting in dirty hands. By refusing to compromise their moral integrity even for valuable national goals, such political agents strengthen a society's commitment to the imperatives of impersonal morality or, at least, remind chief political leaders of the costs of transgressing those imperatives.[5] By underscoring the moral alternative, strict absolutists serve valuable functions even if inflexible adherence to their prescriptions is unwise: "synergy among political actors with different moral dispositions can preserve the possibility of moral action in the political arena. They are also needed to elicit those feelings of guilt to which Walzer subscribes."[6]

Finally, constitutional provisions and policy directives will prohibit certain actions and thereby serve as a constraint on governmental abuses. For example, prohibiting acts of torture by official decree may be sound even though extraordinary occasions will arise where torturing an enemy agent is an acceptable action—a classic case of a deed resulting in dirty hands. Without such a prohibition, leaders might resort to torture too easily without any remorse about their acts. With the prohibition, leaders must give serious pause to torture and even where it is used appropriately understand that dirty hands ensue.

Walzer describes the Machiavellian statesman as follows: "He must do bad things well. There is no reward for doing bad things badly, though they are done with the best of intentions. And so political action necessarily involves taking a risk. But it should be clear that what is risked is not personal goodness—*that is thrown away*—but power and glory. If the politician succeeds, he is a hero; eternal praise is the supreme reward for not being good."[7]

Part of Walzer's description creases the mark and part of it is dangerously misleading. Yes, the Machiavellian statesman must do "bad things" well. He cannot afford to bungle a dirty hands situation such that he is implicated in evil and also fails to attain the good end he appropriately sought. But the statesman does not "throw away" personal goodness for at least two reasons. First, he cannot lose his soul if he is to remain a successful ruler in the Machiavellian spirit. While he must compromise his personal allegiance to the imperatives of impersonal morality he cannot simply "throw away" his personal goodness. Second, for Machiavelli, deserved, enduring glory should be conferred only on those statesmen who succeed in attaining the good ends whose appropriate pursuit implicated them in evil and who also retain their souls. To suggest a separation, as Walzer seems to do, between political success and personal goodness obscures this point. For Machiavelli, political success is a necessary but not sufficient condition of deserving enduring glory. Machiavelli, unlike the masses, does not evaluate people or actions only by results. Statesmen do not earn "eternal praise" as the "supreme reward for not being good." Instead, they deserve enduring glory because they have knowingly compromised their allegiance to the imperatives of impersonal morality thereby risking their souls for patriotic concerns; they have used evil well in dirty hands contexts; yet they have not "thrown away" personal goodness and have instead retained their souls; and they have attained the valuable ends that rendered their personal compromise appropriate.

Accordingly, the penance and punishment accompanying recognition that one's hands are dirty must remain internal to statesmen. The worst of them will suffer the least because they have lost their souls: they will either fail to recognize their wrongful aspects of their conduct or not care about them. But the problem of dirty hands is not entirely resolved within the confines of the individual conscience. If Plato, Dante, and Machiavelli are correct, if evil-doing is its own punishment, then those whose moral consciences are weakest—those who have lost their souls and thereby apparently suffer least from the wrongful moral remainders of their political acts—in fact pay the greatest price. Moreover, they will have forfeited the greatest prize of all: deserved, enduring glory grounded in patriotic adventures.

Numerous excuses are available for political officers seeking to detach themselves from their choices and actions: I was only obeying institutional superiors; I was just discharging my obligations of office; I was compelled by circumstances; I was only safeguarding the welfare of the polity; and the like. For Machiavelli these provide, at best, only partial insulation from moral culpability: they help establish that the political officers made the correct decision. To resort too facilely to such excuses, however, makes it too easy for political officers to dirty their hands when doing so is not necessary. To prevent the loss of their souls and to ensure the well-being of their nations, political officers must assume responsibility for their deeds, recognize the lingering moral costs of their actions, and retain their reluctance to dirty their hands.

Accordingly, Machiavellian statesmen must understand acutely that they are responsible for the people they become under the burden of moral conflict. To use evil well must exact a toll. The nature of the world, scarcity of resources, and conflicts between the imperatives of impersonal morality and the patriotic duties owed to constituents ensure that statesmen cannot always wield their authority with clean hands. The person strictly bound to moral purity should seek alternate employment. The statesman who solemnly and sanctimoniously intones that, "I will never lie to you," has probably already uttered his first falsehood to the audience. If not that, then he has revealed his own naïveté or his own deluded conviction that one can retain clean hands (always follow the dictates of impersonal morality) while serving the public good. Unfortunately, moral judgments do not always come so neatly bundled and all genuine values are not always ultimately compatible: what is good for my country is not always best for the world; what is good for my country may not always be best for every citizen or group of citizens within it.

Machiavellian statesmen must be decisive, squarely confront the moral conflicts emerging from their position of authority, learn to use evil well, and struggle internally with the effects of their deeds. Tribal act consequentialists will lose their souls and too frequently transgress against the imperatives of impersonal morality; strict absolutists will protect moral purity but fail their patriotic duties; and clueless political leaders such as Baglioni will be ignorant of the proper occasions to be good and the appropriate times to use evil well. Only those rulers who can risk but retain their souls in the face of their internal struggles with moral conflict are candidates for the deserved, enduring glory that confers a touch of immortality.

The practical problem is whether actual human beings can accomplish all Machiavellian objectives. Machiavelli alludes to procedural safeguards that might prevent statesmen from losing their souls or might be used to take a leader who has lost his soul to task: public debate in assemblies, the right of citizens to bring evidence casting suspicion on their leaders' rectitude, and rigorous standards of accountability for politicians (D I 56–59). Such institutional safeguards, public scrutiny, republican vigilance, and term limits can ease the problem.

Why Should a Statesman Worry about Losing His Soul?

Walzer is unconvinced. He insists that "we suspect that the suffering servant [statesmen who struggle mightily with the moral conflicts attending their authority] of either masochism or hypocrisy or both, and while we are often wrong, we are not always wrong."[8]

To join this discussion, we must delve more deeply into why statesmen should worry about the condition of their souls. Unlike Plato and Dante, both of whom agonize over the objective condition of the souls of human beings, Machiavelli does not invoke punishment in an afterlife for those whose souls are impure. Plato could argue that the perfectly unjust person—someone who committed numerous unjust acts but who retained a reputation for being virtuous—was not well off because his soul was objectively unhealthy. The perfectly unjust person bears a soul that lacks harmony, balance, and happiness. Upon death the soul of the perfectly unjust person is punished in that it would be denied eternal residence in the World of the Forms and, instead, would endure transmigration into another body to continue the quest for purification.

Dante vividly depicts how people become their sins, how their souls solidify into fixed entities that mirror the fruits of their deeds among their kind in hell. Dante emphasizes the law of *contrapasso*: the punishment inflicted on sinners must reflect the nature of their transgressions; the relationship between the particular suffering in the afterlife and the specific sin must be clear. In that sense, penitents bring about their own destiny. They receive what they willed through their choices and actions.[9]

Plato, Dante, and Machiavelli share the conviction that wrongdoing brings its own punishment: even if evil-doing is not recognized as such by other people and even if it results in no apparent external adverse consequences to the performing agent, it nevertheless alters the inner topography of the perpetrator unwholesomely. But Plato and Dante insist that an unworthy soul will eventually be exposed for what it is and suffer thereby in the afterlife. Machiavelli makes no such appeal. He does not seriously invoke punishment in the afterlife as the certain and just retribution for earthly wrongdoing; instead, when he refers to the afterlife he does so lightheartedly and suggests that hell would be a more interesting place to reside than heaven.

Why, then, should a Machiavellian statesman worry about losing his soul except for prudential considerations such as a negative response from constituents? Imagine the perfectly unjust statesman. He performs numerous wrongful acts from a Machiavellian perspective: he is often tyrannical; he is sometimes vicious and cruel; and he ignores the common good while fanning his selfish (not merely self-interested) ambition. Yet through a combination of skill and luck, the masses perceive him as a leader worthy of Machiavellian enduring glory.

One might argue that history will render the final verdict. Even if contemporaries are deceived by appearances and confer undeserved glory on the perfectly unjust statesman, time is the ultimate editor and arbiter. With the additional information and detached perspective from the passage of time, the unjust leader will eventually be exposed. History will uncover the truth, unmask his motives and relegate the perfectly unjust statesman to his deserved ranking in the lowest depths of the infamous. Because the perfectly unjust political officer sought enduring glory, which is now denied him, he ultimately reaps what he had sown even if no afterlife awaits him. Justice triumphs in the end as the unjust politician's biographical life registers the truth, now and forever.

Only if this hypothetical scenario were realized and the perfectly unjust statesman embodied the requisite antecedent motivations—of earning enduring historical glory—could the argument succeed. But we enjoy no guarantees that historical perspective will correct the distorted views of contemporaries. In fact, the possibility remains that history might enhance the glowing reputation of the perfectly unjust statesman. Lacking infallibility, the consensus of history might even conclude that contemporary judgment underrated the greatness of the perfectly unjust statesman.

We are left with a perfectly unjust statesman who is convinced no afterlife awaits human beings. Why should he worry about the condition of his soul other than in terms of prudential considerations—how others will conceive of and respond to him now?

A Machiavellian might proceed along these lines: A person who did not care about the condition of his soul prior to attaining political office does not understand the good. He cannot learn how not to be good because he lacks the requisite knowledge that is the point of departure. He cannot risk his soul because he has probably already lost it. By acting tyrannically while in office, he will have violated both the imperatives of impersonal morality and the partialist duties of his office. By transgressing on the common good, he fails as a fervent patriot. He is unworthy of enduring glory and has earned only lasting infamy. If he succeeds in securing enduring glory because of extraordinary good luck or the obtuseness of contemporary judgment, he wallows in the world of appearances. A Machiavellian statesman aspires *to be* worthy of enduring glory, not merely *to seem* worthy of it. If the perfectly unjust political officer is indifferent to the distinction, that only adds to his infamy. Because evil ill-used is its own punishment, the perfectly unjust political officer will have collaborated in crafting an unworthy self. His depraved internal condition will manifest itself often in his choices and deeds beyond the duties of his office. He will unwittingly expose the person he has become or, perhaps, always was.

Independently of their appeals to punishment in the afterlife, Plato and Dante would agree with Machiavelli: the effects of evil-doing on the character of perpetrators are direct, immediate, certain retributions for their wrongful acts. Regardless of the reactions and evaluations of other people and how perpetrators fare materially in the world, their internal condition unmistakably is altered by their deeds—and that is their most fundamental punishment. Such a response, however, may be unconvincing to those who insist that suffering negative sensations is necessary for punishment or that our interests are frustrated only by setbacks we experience.[10] Although it is likely that the perfectly unjust statesman will expose the person he has become or always was, we have no guarantees. At bottom, Machiavelli's best response may be that all human beings should worry about losing their souls because our lives focus mainly on the art of crafting a worthy self. To scoff at that project is to deny a major portion of our humanity.

The Puzzle Completed

Despite the popular conception of Machiavelli as a realist par excellence, he does not advise statesmen to simply dismiss or suspend moral considerations in deference to pursuing appropriate political goals. Machiavelli does not privilege the political over the moral. Instead, he recognizes that statesmen must risk but not lose their souls. The paradox of dirty hands, then, resides within the conflicting demands of morality itself. Statesmen who have learned how not to be good must begin by empathizing with those who will become the victims of evil well-used: they must imagine what these victims will feel and what the statesmen would feel if they were the victims in the instant circumstances. But if evil is to be used well, statesmen must overcome their compassion and empathy for the victims. At the international level, they hold the better angels of their nature in abeyance in the name of other moral considerations: fulfilling their partialist obligations to advance the common good of their nation. Even though they use evil well, they acknowledge that doing so involves violating a categorical moral principle—a transgression that remains a wrong and leaves an immoral remainder even though the overall action confers a partial excuse on the perpetrator. Accordingly, the perpetrator has dirty hands and a soiled soul even though he or she performed the proper deed. Statesmen, then, should feel guilty because they are guilty.

But the feeling of guilt is multilayered and unique to dirty hands situations. The feeling is not merely one of regret, a desire that a particular state of affairs had not obtained or a specific result had not occurred. To regret that something happened does not imply that the person was guilty of wrongdoing or that the person wishes that he or she had acted otherwise or even that the person was part of the causal chain leading to the unfortunate outcome. I can regret that John F. Kennedy was assassinated in 1963 even though I played no role in the causal chain that led to his death. I can regret that I injured someone in a motor vehicle accident while understanding that I committed no wrong and without wishing that I had acted otherwise. If the event was genuinely an accident then I am innocent of wrongdoing and could not reasonably have avoided the outcome even though my agency was part of the causal chain leading to the injury of another. The appropriate response for a perpetrator with dirty hands is a special sort of remorse.

Typically, remorse arises when we acknowledge that we have violated a moral principle and we are thereby guilty. We recognize that we acted wrongfully and we should vow not to act in such manner in the future. Typically, such remorse is expiated through some combination of restitution, punishment, suffering, and repentance.

But the remorse in a dirty hands context is different. Here perpetrators knowingly and willingly violate a categorical moral principle in service of other moral values. They must, therefore, accept responsibility for their actions. They must recognize that their hands are dirty and their souls are stained. Perpetrators feel the disquieting weight of the immoral remainder that persists even though the overall action confers a partial excuse on their behavior. While they may regret the circumstances under which necessity pressured their complicity in using evil well, they do not vow not to act in such manner in the future. Instead, if they genuinely used evil well they need not wish that the situation had not occurred. (Although, again, they may regret the power of necessity and wish that there was an alternate way to attain the optimal outcome. They should also hope that similar situations do not occur in the future.) In my judgment, here public expiation is problematic. Punishment is inappropriate unless it is also somehow accompanied by honor—a difficult pairing to conjure. Rehabilitation is inappropriate because the perpetrator's wrongdoing is partially excused and he or she selected the proper course of action overall. Repentance is inappropriate for reasons already cited: if precisely the same situation occurs in the future, perpetrators of the first deed should act in the same way then. Reparations to victims may be appropriate where possible. But even these may be better bestowed privately than publicly. Suffering is appropriate, but if dramatized publicly can undermine a statesman's future authority.

In addition, those who have used evil well should also experience a measure of pride and not simply wallow in remorse. They assumed the burdens of leadership, brought about the better result given the available alternatives in the instant situation, discharged their partialist duties to their constituents well, and did so by risking their souls. Accordingly, the paradox of dirty hands is mirrored in the state of mind appropriate to those who use evil well: a delicate balance of a unique brand of remorse leavened by deserved self-pride. Such a paradoxical emotion can help perpetrators understand the boundaries of morality and underscore the fine line between using evil well and inflicting gratuitous wrongs. The moral identities of Machiavellian statesmen are fragile and cannot be measured solely by the success of the outcomes of their political decisions. The moral consciousness of statesmen is both a check on and an impediment to the discharge of their political responsibilities. They must endure in a context of moral ambiguity: from their (hopefully) superior powers of judgment, insight, and vision arise partial excuses for deeds prohibited to private citizens and profound responsibilities for ensuring the collective well-being of their nations.

To sum up the state of mind of Machiavellian statesmen:

- They must embrace conventional morality as their default position and thereby accept the categorical character of numerous imperatives.
- But they must learn how not to be good and how to use evil well occasionally.
- They must recognize the moral tensions involved in a dirty hands situation when such circumstances present themselves.
- On the international level, when no alternative deed is practical, sometimes they must act resolutely to advance the parochial interests of the common good of their nations over their general duties to the whole of humanity or they must otherwise violate a categorical moral principle.
- On the domestic level, when no alternative deed is practical, sometimes they must act resolutely to advance the common good of their nations over their duties to honor the interests of individual citizens or they must otherwise violate a categorical moral principle.
- In so doing, they must heed the distinction between using evil well and inflicting gratuitous evil.
- Still, even if they use evil well, they must acknowledge the immoral remainder of doing so: violating categorical moral principles engenders moral costs.
- After perpetrating such deeds, they should experience the requisite emotions: a paradoxical remorse seasoned with a deserved self-pride.
- They should make reparations, if possible, to the victims of their deeds, who will often have legitimate grievances adjusted to the circumstances of necessity.
- But they should avoid public confessions or dramatic displays of their moral guilt.
- They must reflect systematically on the deleterious effects using evil well can have on respect for categorical moral values and on their own characters. To that end, they must be vigilant in examining the condition of their souls.
- They must avoid habitual moral transgressions to the extent possible. They must recognize that the more an agent uses evil well the easier it is to resort to evil means in the future and the more likely that the agent will inflict gratuitous evil when doing so is convenient and utilitarian.

Machiavelli's rendering of dirty hands is, unsurprisingly, aristocratic and heroic. Statesmen must not only occasionally dirty their hands, but they also must be thoroughly versed in the ways of evil. Statesmen must risk but not lose their souls by learning how to live with, how to repel, and how to use evil well at times without becoming evil. But the actions of ordinary citizens remain constrained by the imperatives of conventional morality: they "cannot under cover of good do evil" (D I 46). Indeed, the moral corruption and lack of civic *virtù* of the masses are important contributing causes to the problem of dirty hands. Consequently, confronting the problem of dirty hands is one only for solo political agents, those with supreme power and grave responsibilities who operate without overly intense media scrutiny. As princes of monarchies and heads of republican governments during the Renaissance, Machiavelli's statesmen are not subject to an extensive system of checks and balances on their authority. Because of the nature of the world and the general condition of human beings, Machiavelli insists that the actions required to promote the common good cannot be produced systematically by invariably following the imperatives of conventional morality. Also, politics involves inherently gaining at the expense of others: "the purpose of a republic is to enfeeble and weaken, in order to increase its own body, all other bodies" (D II 2). Statesmen have special authority to do what is necessary to establish, maintain, and expand the common good, and they exclusively must bear the burdens of doing so. Walzer's call for public confessions and punishments for statesmen who have dirtied their hands would gain no traction in Machiavelli's historical context. There, statesmen must confront the results of their actions alone or with only a few advisers. Although Machiavelli's writings do not include a report of the internal anguish of statesmen, reconstructing the clues he leaves about the statesman's soul suggests a peculiar sort of remorse flavored with deserved self-pride.

As far back as Aristotle, philosophers have advised that habits structure character (NE II 1–2; NE III 12; NE VII 5–14). The good person embodies stability and constancy of character that facilitates understanding of what is right. Rectitude requires not merely doing the appropriate things but also developing and nurturing the proper internal condition of the soul. For Aristotle, the relationship between character, choice, and action is critical: "acts are called just and self-controlled when they are the kind of acts which a just and self-controlled man would perform; but the just and self-controlled man is not he who performs these acts, but he who also performs them in the way just and self-controlled men do" (NE II 4). The proper way of performing such deeds, then, demonstrates the harmonious internal condition of the just and self-controlled person. Merely performing just deeds does not of itself establish a person's harmonious internal condition.

Thus, if statesmen violate categorical moral principles in a particular set of circumstances, that increases the likelihood that they will transgress those moral values in the future. Repetition promotes desensitization. Moral character is subject to gradual corruption until the agent no longer internalizes the categorical moral principles he or she has knowingly transgressed repeatedly. Moreover, even limited use of a technique such as torture jeopardizes our empathy for the suffering of others, a fundamental emotion promoting a host of categorical moral principles. Machiavelli understands the connection between habit and character.

Accordingly, he describes evil well-used as "those atrocities that are committed at a stroke, in order to secure one's power, and are then not repeated, rather every effort is made to ensure one subject's benefit in the long run" (P 8). The difficulty, however, is that given his view of the world, the general nature of human beings, and the role both play in creating "necessity," statesmen will encounter dirty hands situations on multiple occasions. If they remain in power for an extensive length of time, we may reasonably conclude that they will lose and not merely risk their souls.

A complication is that Machiavelli is well aware that those of high moral rectitude will be most reluctant to become statesmen through the violent means that are typically required, whereas those who are antecedently wicked will embody no such compunctions (D I 18). Thus, government authority is most likely to rest with those who have already lost their souls rather than with those in a position to risk them. As becoming a statesman is not the recommended occupation for those seeking moral rehabilitation, the result will too often be massive, gratuitous evil.

Complicating matters further is the role of the constituents of statesmen. Our leaders soil their hands and stain their souls on our behalf and in our name. Except for the most naïve citizens, most constituents will insist that their political leaders keep faith with categorical moral principles generally but will recognize that they will be required by necessity to violate them occasionally. Constituents tolerate espionage and violations of wiretapping restrictions on certain types of criminal suspects, but prefer not to have these matters brought to their attention. Because statesmen act for our benefit and in our name, we share the guilt: our hands are also dirty and our souls are also blemished. Yet if our leaders go too far we must rein in their excesses and abandon our allegiances to them. Citizens, then, embody an ambiguous role: we turn our eyes away from routine transgressions that involve using evil well, but we must serve as guardians against gratuitous wrongdoing. We play a critical role in ensuring that politics does not become too dirty and that our leaders retain the moral quality of their souls to the extent practicable. Furthermore, when our leaders lose their souls we must call them to account. Accordingly, citizens should have access to sufficient information about the workings of their government: we must know enough but not everything. This suggests yet another delicate balance.

Guicciardini's Critique

Evaluating a thinker who wrote centuries ago invites charges of anachronism: foisting a twenty-first-century perspective on a sixteenth-century writer; expecting the writer to anticipate 500 years of military, political, economic, and historical developments; and stridently chiding the writer for his shortcomings as a clairvoyant. A degree of anachronism is inevitable, even clarifying. But too much is unfair and obfuscating.

To avoid the excesses of anachronism we are best advised to consider objections to Machiavelli's normative vision that arose in his own time. Machiavelli's most acute and systematic critic during that period was his close friend Francesco Guicciardini (1483–1540). Guicciardini, a lawyer, played significant roles in Italian politics as Florentine ambassador to Spain and Papal Governor of Romagna. He also wrote, among other things, *Florentine History*; *Ricordi*, a series of maxims and aphorisms on politics and life; the *History of Italy*; and *Considerations on the "Discourses" of Machiavelli*. While Machiavelli held office in the Florentine republic, Guicciardini eyed him suspiciously as Soderini's acolyte. Once the Holy League ousted Soderini in 1512, the two men shared an enmity toward Medici rule in Florence, although that sentiment did not stop either man from seeking employment with the Medici. In 1521, Machiavelli, while traveling as an emissary to the Franciscan friars in Capri, passed through an area Guicciardini governed. The two men enjoyed lively, profound political discussions and soon began a series of correspondences that ended only when Machiavelli died. Machiavelli had famously written to another friend,

Francesco Vettori, "I love Messer Francesco Guicciardini, I love my native city more than my own soul" (Ltr. 331: 4/16/27).

If Machiavelli represented dispassionate calculation punctuated, and often distorted, by fiery idealism, Guicciardini was the philosophical iceman: unabashedly ambitious, obsessed with personal honor, disdainful of religious sentiment, seemingly devoid of personal warmth, relentlessly contriving, and committed to the primacy of reason over passion and will. Guicciardini was shorn of both illusion and hope. He shared several principles with Machiavelli: the prevalence of deception and guile in politics; a strong conviction that a state was only as enduring as its military might; and the need to free Italy from the oppression of foreign dominators and internal clergy. But Guicciardini, unlike Machiavelli, was not a dreamer. The aristocratic glacier did not entertain thoughts of a savior who could redeem the honor of and unite the factions comprising the Italian peninsula. To perceive a need was not to conjure a solution. Luigi Barzini captures well the core of Guicciardini's outlook: "[Guicciardini] knew that without some renown and respect a man could amass riches but rarely preserve or increase them. He also knew that the lofty ideals he cherished would not interfere with his personal success only if he considered them his own private prejudices. He could speak of piety, honor, liberty, justice, morality, and the hope to see Italy freed from foreign oppressors to a few trusted friends. . . . But his decisions in the world were never to be dictated by a desire to change it."[11]

Guicciardini's objections to Machiavelli are both methodological and substantive. Guicciardini has three major misgivings about Machiavelli's method at arriving at political conclusions. First, he argues that Machiavelli's idolization of ancient Rome skews his political conclusions. He charges that Machiavelli's worship of Rome leads him to ignore differences in historical circumstances and lures him into misleadingly idealizing the policies and actions of the Roman republic as a nearly perfect standard (C I 29, 49; 24; R C 110, 117). Second, Guicciardini accuses Machiavelli of asserting his conclusions too categorically and universally. Too often, Machiavelli writes as if a matter can be settled by a bright-line rule where more nuance is present. For Guicciardini, Machiavelli too often derives broad conclusions from inadequate evidence (C I 3, 26). Finally, Guicciardini rejects Machiavelli's quest to discover political rules of behavior from the dustbin of selective history (C I 39, 40: R C 114). In sum, Guicciardini describes Machiavelli, ironically, as too impractical and idealistic.

On matters of substance, Guicciardini is even more critical. He lodges numerous objections to details in Machiavelli's position. The following six judgments illustrate the trajectory of Guicciardini's criticisms.

First, he rejects Machiavelli's view of human nature. For Guicciardini human beings, contrary to Machiavelli's view, are naturally inclined to seek the good (C I 3; R C 134, 135; R B 4; R Q 4): "All men have a natural inclination to goodness, and, all other things being equal, like good better than evil, and if any have a different tendency, it is so far contrary to what is normal for others, and against the first object given by nature, that he must rather be called a monster than man" (C I 3). Despite this natural inclination to the good, Guicciardini notes that human nature is fragile and easily tempted to stray from righteousness. A system of rewards and punishments must reinforce our natural inclination lest we stumble into moral degeneration (R C 134; R Q 4).

Second, Guicciardini is an unabashed aristocrat who harbored no faith in the judgments of the masses. Whereas Machiavelli took the multitude to be better evaluators of at least a few matters than a prince, Guicciardini relentlessly disputed that finding (C I 2, 5, 7, 58; R C 140, 201; R B 113): "A people full of ignorance and confusion, and possessing many bad qualities, can only be expected to overthrow and destroy everything. . . . One cannot deny that a people in itself are a treasury of ignorance and confusion. Hence, purely popular governments have at all times been short lived. . . . It is too dangerous to make the people judges of the accusations for they are not able to understand or examine well and are easily moved by rumor and false calumny" (C I 5, 58, 7). Ever the aristocrat, Guicciardini insists that rule by the nobles is preferable to placing power in the hands of plebeians: "It would be better to choose the nobles, for as they have greater prudence and good qualities, one may have more hope that they will evolve some reasonable constitution" (C I 5).

Third, Guicciardini, while acknowledging the necessity of harsh measures at times, takes Machiavelli to task for too readily accepting violent means where more humane alternatives are available (C I 26): "The prince must take courage to use these extraordinary means when necessary, and should yet take care not to miss any chance which offers of establishing his cause with humanity, kindness, and rewards, not taking as an absolute rule what [Machiavelli] says, who was always extremely partial to extraordinary and violent methods" (C I 26).

Fourth, Guicciardini undermines a crucial Machiavellian conviction: that the amount of good and bad in the world is constant; that the state of the world is always the same in every age, with only the location of privilege, power, and relative greatness changing. This conviction is important in laying the foundation for Machiavelli's portrait of the world as a zero-sum contest in which one nation's gain must be purchased by the losses of other nations. Guicciardini argues that the amount of overall *virtù*, the quality of art, the level of military discipline, the refinement of literature, the vitality of religion, and the temper of social customs do not remain constant through history. One historical era, overall, is not just as corrupt and as glorious as every other (C II pref).

Fifth, Guicciardini calls into question Machiavelli's understanding of the greatness of Romulus and, by extension, Machiavelli's general depictions of his historical heroes. According to Guicciardini, Romulus was "thought to have been assassinated by the senate for arrogating to himself too great authority" instead of conforming to Machiavelli's account wherein Romulus ceded most of his power to the senate, retaining only the authority to convene that body and to command armies during war time (C I 9). If Guicciardini is correct in concluding that not even the revered Romulus was an ideal statesman, then the practical possibility of such an exemplar emerging in any historical era sadly diminishes.

In that vein, Guicciardini argues that Machiavelli also overestimated the greatness of Numa Pompilius. Against Machiavelli's account that credited Numa with establishing religion and sound laws in an unwelcoming social context, Guicciardini insists that "the Romans were of themselves inclined to wish to organize religion and good laws for the arts of peace, so that Numa found a people already disposed to accept a good system" (C I 11). Guicciardini's evidence for that conclusion was that at the death of Romulus the Romans, although "extremely savage and accustomed to arms" went outside their city and elected Numa as king because of his reputation as a person of justice, peace, and religion. Guicciardini remarks that had Numa been Rome's first ruler the city would have fallen prey to its more militant neighbors: "Numa would not have enabled Romulus to create its army, in the way that Romulus made it possible for Numa to create its religion. Therefore, Romulus was more vital to [Rome's] beginnings than Numa" (C I 11). Thus, for Guicciardini, Machiavelli overestimated both Romulus and Numa, and ranked their respective contributions to the well-being of early Rome incorrectly.

Sixth, unlike Machiavelli, Guicciardini was pessimistic about the practical possibilities of unifying Italy and unconvinced that establishing such a country was desirable. Guicciardini agreed with Machiavelli that the intrigues and influence of the Church had prevented the unification of the country, but he concluded that a unified Italy would bring grandeur to its ruling city but prove disastrous to numerous other cities within the country: "for under the shadow of [the ruling] city [other cities] could not attain any greatness . . . [a divided Italy] has had so many more flourishing cities than she could have had under a single republic, that I think unification would have been more unfortunate than fortunate for her" (C I 12). Guicciardini concedes that his argument applies only to unified republics and not to a kingdom, "which is more common to all its subjects" (C I 12).

Thus, Laurence Arthur Burd observes:

> Guicciardini, a thoroughly practical man . . . regarded any scheme for the unification of Italy as the idle vision of a dream; indeed he was almost inclined to think it undesirable in itself, and to regard the stimulating influence of a number of independent states as a compensation for the weakness of a divided nation. In any case he was convinced that Italy could not cut herself adrift from the past . . . he rejected the idea of a great and general fatherland for all Italians, the notion of which had been gradually permeating the intellectual atmosphere.[12]

Finally, Machiavelli, in a meandering argument, concludes that in a republic that has not been corrupted attacking some citizens whom ought to be rewarded and being suspicious of some who merit confidence are "mistakes" that bear a benefit: citizens remain good and less ambitious because they fear punishment (D I 29). Guicciardini rejoins that "every kind of ingratitude and injustice is always pernicious and the republic must be ordered in such a way that the good are always honored and the innocent not alarmed" (C I 29).

Guicciardini's complaints anticipated the core of modern objections to Machiavelli's writing. Machiavelli claimed to derive his political conclusions from observations about human nature and historical examples, mostly drawn from the Roman republic. Despite his aspiration and subsequent reputation, Machiavelli was far from objective. He selected his examples carefully, choosing only those that supported his foregone convictions. He was not above falsifying historical accounts if doing so supported his conclusions better than the actual events.

Why would a supposed detached political scientist use such unreliable and disreputable methods? Despite his renown as the founder of cool, calculating, dispassionate statecraft, Machiavelli embodied profound idealism and romanticism. Disgusted by the rancid disgrace of being dominated by barbarians, while at the same time observing the skills and courage of individual Italians in duels and competitions involving only a few, Machiavelli placed his trust in the ascent of one great man to wreak vengeance and to drive the *stranieri* from his homeland.

Following the tradition of Plato and Aristotle, he was convinced that once this "Superman" emerged, the masses would be spiritually transformed, a republic could emerge, *virtù* would flourish, and the state would prosper. His treatises are not the labors of an objective scientist, but rather the poems, yearnings, and implorations of a lover. His emotions, passion, and anguish permeate his writings. They frequently cloud his thinking, they sometimes animate his insights, but they always starkly reveal the source of the blood in his veins. For most of us, our shortcomings arise from our excellences amplified and distorted. Such is the case with Machiavelli. In short, the methodological strengths and weaknesses of Niccolò Machiavelli flow from his highest value: relentless patriotism.

The differences between Guicciardini and Machiavelli on human nature are ones of degree and starting point. Although Machiavelli's picture of human nature is harsher—stressing the inherent inclination toward selfishness and short-term benefit—he also details possibilities for transformation. Sound leadership, strong arms, well-crafted laws, and robust religion nourish civic and moral *virtù*. A multitude that is initially turned to anarchistic chaos can be molded into exemplifying a praiseworthy collective national character. Such change is possible only if human nature contains prospects for the good. While Guicciardini emphasizes the inherent inclination of human nature to seek the good, his considered view of the quality of the people's judgment is less sanguine than Machiavelli's. For Guicciardini, the initial turn toward the good does not issue in practical wisdom. To say that human nature includes possibilities for good and for evil is trivial, but true. Machiavelli's depiction of human nature is undoubtedly harsh, disproportionate, unfair, and unpersuasive. But Machiavelli's profound faith in the power of a strong state and its prospects for elevating the masses tempered these distortions. His drawing of human nature, then, is more of a prelude to the importance of strong leadership and sound government than a claim to metaphysical precision.

That Machiavelli's writings celebrate violent means and extraordinary measures is beyond dispute. Machiavelli is proudest when he venerates deeds that most people would find unspeakable: murdering a brother for political reasons; supervising the execution of counterrevolutionary sons; slaying 3,000 countrymen who falsely worship; eviscerating a governmental patsy in order to shock and awe townsfolk. Machiavelli does not seriously consider whether other means of resolving these situations might have been wiser nor does he explore explicitly the consequences for the interior life of those who commanded the killings. Ironically, despite his dark vision of human nature, Machiavelli is most appreciative that Romulus, Brutus, Moses, and Borgia acted in ways from which most leaders would shrink: they learned how not to be good when necessary.

More profoundly, Machiavelli's worldview lines up a relentless international zero-sum contest that morphs into a self-fulfilling prophesy. Once national leaders are convinced that the world is a battleground for survival, glory, and *virtù*, they have additional reason to act in ways that reinforce that conviction. Preemptive military strikes, aggressive expansionism, and doing-it-to-them-before-they-do-it-to-us calculations are muted only by the strength of a country's armed might, its current international commitments, and other prudential considerations. From Machiavelli's tragic vision of international relations, arises a vicious cycle: assuming that a virtual state of nature exists and acting on that assumption ensures that it will continue to exist.

Guicciardini neatly undermines Machiavelli's observation that the overall amount of *virtù* in the world remains constant. This thesis is important for Machiavelli's zero-sum worldview. On its face, the thesis is unconvincing for reasons beyond those Guicciardini advanced. Even if the overall results or comparative positions of, say, four nations remain the same, the quality of their participation in international affairs—one measure of *virtù*—may increase in all cases. As argued previously, the capabilities of participants in a competitive process may increase dramatically even though the results of the contests yield the same number of winners and losers. As Machiavelli otherwise reminds us, *virtù* cannot be judged by results alone. Once we abrogate the position that the overall amount of *virtù* in the world remains the same, we take the first step in mollifying Machiavelli's depiction of the world as a series of ruthless zero-sum events.

Still, even the relentless realist, Guicciardini, harbored some ideals. Although he doubted that they would be realized within his lifetime, Guicciardini reproduced three Machiavellian themes: "I want to see a well-ordered republic in our city, Italy liberated from all the barbarians, and the world delivered from the tyranny of these wicked priests" (R B 14). Moreover, he tempered competitive zeal and the relentless pursuit of glory with compassion: "There is nothing in life more desirable or more glorious than to see your enemy prostrate on the ground and at your mercy. And this glory is doubled if you use it well, that is, by showing mercy and being content to have won" (R C 72).

Guicciardini also agrees with Machiavelli that the pursuit of deserved, enduring glory marks the man of *grandezza d'animo* who resists his inevitable finitude and strives to transcend mortality: "the more men are honored, revered, and adored, the more they seem to approach and become similar to God. And what man would not want to resemble Him?" (R C 16). To recognize and act on the spark of the divine within each of us is to take the first step in living life robustly and passionately within vibrant military and political theaters. Those who "seek glory through honorable and honest means . . . produce great and excellent works" in contrast to "cold spirits, inclined more toward laziness than activity" (R C 32); "A man who esteems honor highly will succeed in everything, since he takes no account of toil, danger, or money . . . the actions of men who do not have this burning stimulus are dead and vain" (R C 118). But such men of honor must guard against losing their souls because "ambition is pernicious and detestable when it has as its sole end power, as is generally the case with princes" (R C 32). To lose sight of the common good and to amass power for its own sake are the stigmata of rampant ambition unleavened by normative insight.

To those ends, and in service of statesmen who must risk but should not lose their souls, Guicciardini notes, "I cannot praise those who always live by deception and wiles; but I can *excuse* those who use them occasionally (R B 46; emphasis added). He recognizes explicitly the phenomenon of dirty hands: "I do not say that a ruler is not sometimes forced to bloody his hands, but I do say that it ought never to be done except when absolutely necessary. And I will add that most of the time it brings more loss than gain" (R B 120). Guicciardini thereby cautions Machiavelli to soften his enthusiasm about viewing dirty hands situations as common and inevitable in political affairs. Again, Guicciardini advises that "the prince must take courage to use these extraordinary means when necessary, and should yet take care not to miss any chance which offers of establishing his cause with humanity, kindness, and rewards" (C I 26).

Accordingly, Guicciardini either echoes or to some extent softens Machiavelli's advice regarding statesmen and dirty hands. But, unlike Machiavelli, he leaves few clues as to the inner condition of his ideal statesmen and the process by which such leaders must risk their souls in service to their nations.

Despite their other theoretical differences, Machiavelli and Guicciardini were ardent patriots who loved their city more than their souls. Guicciardini echoes Machiavelli's deepest passion when he remarks that "the most praiseworthy thing to do is to put love of country before one's personal safety" (C I 10). However, he adds, such patriotism is uncommon.

Machiavelli's Legacy

Throughout the centuries since his death, interpreters of Machiavelli's work have portrayed the Florentine as anything from a purveyor of political evil to the precursor of *Realpolitik* to a patriarch of republicanism to a zealous Italian patriot, and everything in between. Contemporary authors follow and refine this tradition.

For example, in her spirited defense of Machiavelli as a humanistic moralist, Erica Benner argues persuasively that when Machiavelli seemingly declares that the ends justify the means he is typically describing a predominant view that requires critical scrutiny (D III 35; FH VIII 22).[13] According to Machiavelli, says Benner, judgments grounded in assessments of consequences are problematic for three reasons. First, they are indeterminate in that the effects of numerous actions are varied and intricate. Second, they are partial in that the perspective of different parties will yield different evaluations. Third, they are unstable in that, for example, short-term benefits can evolve into long-range detriments.[14] Benner concludes that "most of Machiavelli's overt, persuasive arguments have a consequentialist form, but the structure of his implicit, principled reasoning is, I submit, deontological."[15] She and I join hands on this issue.

Benner also cautions against interpreting Machiavelli's dictum "when the deed accuses, the effect excuses" (D I 9) too widely. She argues that the best interpretation of this slogan is to restrict its application to violent deeds that meet two conditions: a ruler who seizes power violently but who rules prudently and virtuously thereafter, and who transfers authority to the masses as soon as practicable instead of retaining authority and later bequeathing it to his heirs. On this view, Romulus is an exception to the general rule that statesmen should avoid gaining political power through violence.[16]

Although Benner correctly and acutely locates Machiavelli as a nonconsequentialist she does not define his deontology. To consider him a strict absolutist is implausible. But does Benner take him to be a flexible deontologist, one who prefigured the position of W. D. Ross? Does she view him as anticipating a version of threshold deontology? Or does she interpret Machiavelli's deontology differently? Moreover, Benner does not distinguish carefully between the moral significance of justifications and the moral significance of excuses. By conflating justifications and excuses, she obscures part of Machiavelli's deontological message.

She also restricts her analysis of Machiavelli's dictum about excuses to only one domain: whether statesmen should attempt to seize political power through violence. Although the slogan appears in that context in the section she analyzes, Machiavelli expresses similar sentiments throughout his work (P 15, 17, 18; D I 18; D III 3, 12, 34, 41). Although she argues that as a general rule Machiavelli held that seizing authority through violence should be avoided and that he advised that a person's imprudent choice of means can frustrate the good ends he or she seeks,[17] Benner does not present a general position on when, if ever, excuses (partially) exonerate a political agent from culpability when performing deeds that are typically evil. Her project avoids making sweeping claims about Machiavelli's views, but the alternative is a Machiavelli who patches together an olio of ad hoc musings that at times coalesce uneasily. Finally, Benner does not confront the problem of dirty hands and stained souls, perhaps because she believes that a proper statesman would rarely, if ever, encounter such situations given her radically humanistic reading of Machiavelli.

The most, perhaps the only, interesting aspect of Benner's Machiavelli—the only thing Machiavellian about him—is his alleged surreptitious writing style. According to Benner, he composes prose in the ancient manner of Thucydides and Xenophon in order to cleverly mask his intent. In this regard, Benner follows a line of thinkers such as Rousseau, Spinoza, Bayle, and Diderot who, in one fashion or another, concluded that Machiavelli concealed his true views, at least when writing *The Prince* and parts of *The Discourses*. Thus, Machiavelli employs "ironic dissimulation, deliberate ambiguities, dialectical ambivalence, metaphorical and allegorical writing"[18] to disseminate furtively his genuine views only to perspicacious readers who are able to pierce through literary appearances. In short, Benner's Machiavelli shocks readers with his explicit rhetoric in order to teach them the efficacy of conventional morality.

However, the motivation behind this alleged literary masquerade is difficult to fathom. First, the moral lessons that Benner's Machiavelli purportedly utters clandestinely were as old as air. Countless thinkers prior to Machiavelli had already argued that rulers should be virtuous ("until philosophers are kings or kings philosophers") and had exposed the immoralities that various tyrants had perpetrated to the detriment of their subjects. Second, Machiavelli's major works, *The Prince* and *The Discourses*, were first published almost twenty years after they were written and several years after Machiavelli died. Even at his death, Machiavelli could hardly have been assured that his writings would reach any significant audience, much less a readership discerning enough to decode his supposedly cryptic messages. Even if we assume that Machiavelli was writing for only a few potential rulers who might liberate Italy, to chance that they would keenly penetrate his literary subterfuges would be a dangerous, unnecessary gamble. Third, Machiavelli reiterates in his correspondence to friends and in his other literary works much of what he says explicitly in his major works. If Benner's interpretation is correct then Machiavelli *invariably* wrote esoterically: he was a serial literary trickster. How likely is this? Finally, Benner simply ignores or dismisses numerous passages in Machiavelli thought to be notorious that are seemingly impossible to reinterpret as secretly embodying a conventionally moral message.

Most important, Benner's stirring depiction of Machiavelli as a humanistic paragon contrasts sharply in some respects with the understanding of Guicciardini, Machiavelli's contemporary, political associate, and friend. If Benner's rendering is accurate, that implies that Guicciardini who knew Machiavelli well, corresponded with him, and to whom Machiavelli declared "love" in a letter to Francesco Vettori (Ltr. 331: 4/16/27) was radically mistaken in the most important respects of his analysis of Machiavelli's work. In my judgment, Guicciardini is a critical source for any interpreter of Machiavelli because of his special placement. If someone as close to Machiavelli and as politically astute as Guicciardini was unable to translate Machiavelli's supposedly covert moral messages accurately, what should we conclude about Benner's interpretation?

Ruth Grant takes a much different approach to Machiavelli. She invokes Machiavelli to support her thesis that hypocrisy and deception are crucial to political life. Grant argues that politics is an arena of human activity such that people depend on and need the cooperation of others who pursue unavoidably opposing interests. To obtain the required mutually beneficial cooperation, human beings mask or minimize their self-interested motives and the instrumental quality of their alliances; they amplify the congruence of the fulfillment of their interests and the advancement of the common good; they compromise or adjust their purported principles to facilitate the best results; and they obfuscate the methods they implement to maximize their own advancement. Accordingly, "politics is characterized by relationships of mutual need among parties with conflicting interests. To enlist the support of the other party requires flattery, manipulation, and a pretense of concern for his needs."[19] Moreover, human beings are subject to political passions such as vanity, pride, and ambition, forces "irreducible to calculations of interests."[20] Thus, politics, unlike economics, are not fully "negotiable in the manner of interests."[21] Matters such as political passions are inseparable from politics and their pursuit generates considerable hypocrisy and deception. Although society requires trust and morality, statesmen are too often untrustworthy and immoral—another reason why hypocrisy and deception are inevitable mechanisms for politicians of good will.[22] Thus, the structure of politics, the nature of human passions, and the conduct of political peers conspire to forge ineliminable vectors that necessitate the use of hypocrisy and deceit.

Most political relationships are neither friendships nor open enmities. Genuine friends are trustworthy and hypocrisy is typically unnecessary; overt enemies are openly untrustworthy and hypocrisy is typically ineffective. As most political relationships involve "relationships of dependence among people with conflicting interests,"[23] hypocrisy and deception are often required. Again, political relationships require hypocrisy and deceit because they are bonds of dependence among people with conflicting interests and significant passions. Those in such relationships must cooperate with others who remain competitors to one degree or another.

Typically, the social goods sought by people in political life cannot be achieved alone, but many such goods (for example, wealth, power, reputation, and honor) are diminished if widely shared. Thus, political agents must often conceal their real motives in order to nurture the cooperation required for success.

Also, politics cannot be conducted in an *openly* cynical way: public life must always include a "moral dimension of great political significance . . . a public doctrine that . . . encouraged people to act on the basis of interest alone would undermine the attachments necessary to sustain communal life."[24] Human beings aspire to be thought of as good and to think of themselves as good. Thus, the crucial role hypocrisy and deception play. A gap exists between the real and ideal: deceit is effective in situations where honesty and force are ineffective. Grant masterfully analyzes Machiavelli's play *Mandragola* to illustrate how hypocrisy and deceit can resolve conflicts among individuals and produce salutary outcomes that would not be possible to attain through honesty, reason, or force.

For Grant unyielding rationality in politics is not only an obstacle to a statesman's discharge of his or her duties, but it also promotes self-deception. Although Grant does not delve directly into the problem of dirty hands and the literature that surrounds it, she does address the interior life of the (necessarily) hypocritical statesman. The statesman's normative outlook and his or her invocation of moral principles are adjusted by understanding the character of politics and the responsibilities of office. The statesman confronts the Scylla of open cynicism and the Charybdis of a hypocrisy that rationalizes moral compromise too facilely. The statesman must maintain a personal integrity that permits him or her to discharge the duties of office, yet avoid both open cynicism and complacent faithlessness. Critical to this task is to avoid resorting to hypocrisy and deceit for purely selfish reasons; only the common good can trigger possibilities for permissible dishonesty. Following Grant's thesis, the ethical problem centers on defining what sorts of hypocrisy, deception, and manipulation are morally permissible under what circumstances, and identifying the degree of personal integrity that is compatible with robust political participation.

While Grant focuses on hypocrisy and deception, Machiavelli recognizes that coercion and force are also endemic to politics. At times, force and coercion are necessary to achieve results that are unattainable through honesty, reason, or deceit. The tension between the excused use of such methods and the political statesman's ability to preserve his or her integrity—the statesman's ability not to lose his or her soul—is a main theme of my book. Moreover, the need to avoid open cynicism, maintain communal life, yet hold statesmen accountable for their moral transgressions to the extent practicable constitutes a corollary theme.

John McCormick uses Machiavelli's ideas about economic class, political accountability, and popular empowerment as a point of departure for proposing his own changes in the structure of contemporary democracies. Animated by the convictions that economic power overwhelms popular will in determining public policy and that elections insufficiently make public officials accountable to constituents, McCormick analyzes Machiavelli's positive assessments of the institutions that ancient republics, especially the Roman republic, conjured to constrain the domination of wealthy citizens and public magistrates: "Commentators consistently ignore or acutely underplay Machiavelli's endorsement of class-specific offices, extra-electoral modes of appointing and punishing public officials, and assemblies where common citizens broadly discuss and directly decide public policy."[25] McCormick reimagines how such institutions might be reconfigured today and advances concrete policies that exclude economic and political elites from certain offices and that endow randomly selected citizens with significant veto, legislative, and censure authority within government and over public officials.

McCormick's Machiavelli seethes at the scornful treatment he has received from Florence's haughty political elites and responds by advancing a radical form of populism in his writings. McCormick stresses Machiavelli's respective evaluations of the motives of the *grandi* (the great or noble) and the *populo* (the people or plebeians), and his accompanying recommendation that the people must be able to "check the insolence of the *grandi* through accountability institutions such as Rome's tribunes of the plebes and popularly decided political trials (D I 5, 37; D III I)."[26] McCormick celebrates Machiavelli's appreciation for institutionalized class conflict and social discord, and his Machiavelli is the precursor of radical democracy: "Machiavelli's political theory was more popularly participatory and empowering than was republicanism, generally, and, for that matter, than is democracy as generally conceptualized and practiced today."[27]

Although I deeply appreciate McCormick's substantive policy recommendations that are designed to amplify popular participation in contemporary democracies, an analysis of those proposals is well beyond the scope of this work. Overall, though, McCormick's reading of Machiavelli is selective and suspicious. He ignores or underplays Machiavelli's ambivalence about popular judgment—for example, Machiavelli's convictions about how common citizens are easily deceived; how they are too often gulls for appearance; and how they invariably and unwisely judge actions only by outcomes.

Moreover, McCormick fails to account sufficiently for Machiavelli's profound appreciation of the Roman senate, a classic aristocratic institution that wielded significant political power in the republic for long periods of time.

Although McCormick is correct in identifying a host of popular mechanisms that Machiavelli advanced, concluding that the Florentine was a protodemocratic thinker is imprudent. Moreover, invoking Machiavelli as a populist is unnecessary to McCormick's paramount project: the reimagining of contemporary democracies on a more participatory basis. Why do we need McCormick's Machiavelli to provide a supposed imprimatur for policy proposals designed to rejuvenate democracies? Should those who are dubious about McCormick's substantive proposals be swayed by his summoning of Machiavelli as a precursor? Should those who are enthusiastic about McCormick's substantive proposals be further reinforced in conviction because Machiavelli would presumably bless them?

For my purposes, McCormick's contribution is the reminder that statesmen who must dirty their hands and risk their souls while faithfully discharging the duties of their public offices must remain publicly accountable for their actions. Grappling with the manner and extent to which public accountability for partially excused moral transgressions is practicable is, again, one of the corollary themes of my book.

These three contemporary writers, who depict Machiavelli as a consummate humanist, an insightful political realist, and a harbinger of radical democracy, respectively, brighten the Florentine's legacy and enhance his biographical life.

Rarely is Machiavelli interpreted as a man undergoing existential crisis. Yet that is precisely what he suffered. Embodying a *grandezza d'animo*, he was haunted by an obsession to resist the Grim Reaper; to carve out a piece of enduring glory; to realize a historical immortality bestowed only on those able to harness *ambizione*, attain military and political *virtù*, and transcend the natural depravity of mankind. Mortality, extinction, to evaporate from the historical record . . . these are the punishments meted out to the multitude who lead lives of tranquil desperation. Machiavelli understood keenly that nothingness and indifference are the cruelest cosmic responses to the deepest human yearnings.

Machiavelli severely doubted that an afterlife awaits human beings at their deaths. He was not deluded into thinking that leaving a rich legacy was a way of achieving immortality in a literal sense. We are finished at death if no afterlife awaits us. But Machiavelli accepted that generating a legacy is a way of enriching the meaning of our lives now. Some of our projects should reach beyond our lifetimes. Guiding the next generation, creating something that exudes vitality and identity outside of ourselves, transmitting a culture and heritage, attending to enduring yet finite projects, and influencing the future are not ways of halting Father Time, but they are paths to meaning. Although our biological lives expire, our biographical lives continue through such legacies. Again, this is not immortality as such, but it does mark a life well lived. Generating rich legacies energizes faith in life, binds us to something beyond ourselves, and nurtures meaning above narrow self-fulfillment. Machiavelli grasped this keenly.

However, the grand aspirations, profound patriotism, burning ambition, and relentless passion of Machiavelli's interior life coalesced uneasily with his worldly fortunes. As Barzini concludes:

> [Machiavelli] lived an irregular, almost bohemian life. He was a brilliant failure, never really managed to achieve his ends: he never made love to the women he wanted, satisfied his ambitions, reached the top in his political career and was never taken seriously as a thinker during his lifetime. He died penniless: he never even succeeded in persuading the republic of Florence to pay his arrears and to reimburse him for his expenses. He never managed to get his immortal works published. He was the permanent victim of political changes. . . . Such is the fate of very intelligent men who are, however, not intelligent enough to conceal their intelligence and lull other people's fears and suspicions to sleep. Machiavelli was, in reality, too much of a dreamer and an optimist to achieve practical results.[28]

Machiavelli, unlike Nietzsche, never envisioned the glory history would grant him. When discussing the types of men who merit praise, Machiavelli lists heads and founders of religion, founders of republics or principalities, commanders of armies who have expanded territorial holdings, and, finally, authors (D I 10). Although he burned to earn enduring glory in service to his country as a political *consigliere*, Machiavelli attained historical prominence as a writer. At his death, he could not have forecasted the literary distinction his work would reap. He never fully understood the teeming artistic *virtù* he exuded. Ironically, Machiavelli, during his lifetime, was never Machiavellian enough to realize his dreams or anticipate his enduring power.

Appendix A

Texts and Their Abbreviations

As is common practice in Machiavelli scholarship, where I have cited from Machiavelli's writings the references in all cases have been given immediately in the text and not in the endnotes. All references are to chapters or sections, not page numbers, unless otherwise stated.

References

AW II 45	*The Art of War*, book II, page 45 (Wood edition)
CC 34	*The Life of Castruccio Castracani*, page 34 (Brown ed.)
D I 55	*The Discourses*, book I, chap. 55
FH I 3	*Florentine Histories*, book I, sect. 3
Leg.13.18	*The Legations*, no. 13, sect. 18
Ltr. 247: 1/31/15	Letter 247: Jan. 31, 1515 (Atkinson and Sices ed.)
M 4:1	*Mandragola*, act 4, scene 1
P 18	*The Prince*, chap. 18

Abbreviations for Book Titles

AW	*The Art of War*. Edited and translated by Neal Wood. Cambridge, MA: De Capo Press, 1965.
CC	*The Life of Castruccio Castracani*. Translated by Andrew Brown. London: Hesperus Press Ltd., 2003.
D	*Discourses on the First Decade of Titus Livius ("The Discourses")*. In *The Chief Works and Others*, edited and translated by Allan H. Gilbert. Durham, NC: Duke University Press, 1989.

D   *Discourses on the First Decade of Titus Livius ("The Discourses")*. In *Selected Political Writings*, edited and translated by David Wootton. Indianapolis, IN: Hackett Publishing, 1994.

FH   *Florentine Histories*. Edited and translated by Laura F. Banfield and Harvey C. Mansfield. Princeton, NJ: Princeton University Press, 1988.

Leg.   *The Legations*. In *The Chief Works and Others*, edited and translated by Allan H. Gilbert. Durham, NC: Duke University Press, 1989.

Ltr.   *Machiavelli and His Friends: Their Personal Correspondence*, edited and translated by James B. Atkinson and David Sices. DeKalb, IL: Northern Illinois University Press, 1996.

Ltr.   *The Letters of Machiavelli*, edited and translated by Allan Gilbert. Chicago, IL: University of Chicago Press, 1961.

M   *Mandragola*. Translated by Mera J. Flaumenhaft. Prospect Heights, IL: Waveland Press, 1981.

P   *The Prince*. In *The Chief Works and Others*, edited and translated by Allan H. Gilbert. Durham, NC: Duke University Press, 1989.

P   *The Prince*. In *Selected Political Writings*, edited and translated by David Wootton. Indianapolis, IN: Hackett Publishing, 1994.

Citations to the Work of Francesco Guicciardini

C   "Considerations on the 'Discourses' of Machiavelli." In *Selected Writings*, edited by Cecil Grayson. Oxford, UK: Oxford University Press, 1965.

C I 29   "Considerations on the 'Discourses' of Machiavelli," book I, chap. 29.

R   *Maxims and Reflections* (Ricordi). Edited and translated by Mario Domandi. Philadelphia: University of Pennsylvania Press, 1972.

R C 110   Ricordi, series C, no. 110.

Citations to the Work of Plato

S 292e   Plato's *The Statesman*, Stephanus pagination 292e.
S   *The Statesman*, translated by J. B. Skemp. In *Plato: Collected Dialogues*, edited by Edith Hamilton and Huntington Cairns. Princeton, NJ: Princeton University Press, 1973.

Citations to the Work of Aristotle

NE II 1–2   *Nicomachean Ethics*, book II, chaps. 1–2.
NE   *Nicomachean Ethics*, translated by Martin Ostwald. Indianapolis, IN: Bobbs-Merrill, 1962.

Appendix B

Machiavelli's Life and Times

Niccolò Machiavelli was born in Florence in 1469, the year that Lorenzo ("the Magnificent") de'Medici rose to power in the city. His father, Bernardo, was a lawyer who had opposed the rule of the ruling hereditary Medici family and who had promoted republican governments—understood as political control by some of the city's most prominent citizens. The Machiavellis were well-respected but far from wealthy. They were not, however, as impoverished as Niccolò sometimes suggested. From what little information is available, Niccolò enjoyed an untroubled, secure, warm childhood. Bernardo had helped compile the index for an edition of Livy's history of the early Roman republic and the publisher rewarded him with a copy of the text. Niccolò enjoyed a solid education and, although unfamiliar with Greek, read the classical Greek and Roman authors in Latin. Niccolò would later extensively use his father's copy of Livy's history in his own writing. He was also enamored of modern authors such as Petrarch and Dante Alighieri.

In 1478, when Machiavelli was nine years old, the Pazzi, a wealthy family with an ancient Florentine lineage, plotted to oust Lorenzo the Magnificent and assume control of Florence. Part of the scheme was economic. The Medici bank was the most influential in Florence and much of the Medici family influence was grounded in its capability of controlling the purse strings. Most of the traditional Medici political power in Florence, in fact, was grounded in the family's economic advantage and shrewd manipulation of the electoral process. The Pazzi succeeded in having the papal bank account, the grandest in Italy, transferred from the Medici bank to its control. The Pazzi accomplished this by currying the favor of Pope Sixtus IV, who harbored dynastic ambitions. The Medici had earlier refused to finance one of the Pope's adventures. This hardened Sixtus's resolve to destroy the Medici. Pursuant to that aspiration, the Pope supported an enemy of the Medici as archbishop of Pisa, a port city Florence controlled.

The Pazzi hired assassins to murder Lorenzo and his brother, Giuliano, in the cathedral during a Holy Week mass. When the altar bells rang during the Eucharist, the assassins struck.

Giuliano was slain, but Lorenzo, wounded, escaped into the sacristy. The Pazzi, a case study in premature celebration, rode to the Palazzo della Signoria to seize power, while their minions rode through the streets of Florence shouting, "Liberty, liberty!"

Once the Florentine masses learned of the treachery, the brief reign of the Pazzi evaporated. The people admired Lorenzo and loved Giuliano. The Pazzi conspirators, enjoying the hospitality of the governmental palace, were arrested and their supporters were forcefully gathered. The Pazzi and the Archbishop of Pisa, who had a role in the plot, were executed and their corpses were untastefully displayed in the windows of the Palazzo della Signoria. The palaces of the schemers and their supporters were looted and burned. The people stormed through the streets shouting the anthem of the Medici.

Pope Sixtus, disappointed that the plot failed and stunned by the murder of the Archbishop, demanded that Lorenzo be turned over to Papal control. The Florentines refused and the Pope dispatched his minion, King Ferrante of Naples, to attack Florence and seize Lorenzo. Florence, as usual, was unprepared for war, and the Neapolitan army met no resistance. Lorenzo escaped, sailed to Naples, and convinced the King that the Pope's annexation of Florence to his territories would also disadvantage Naples. After protracted negotiations, the War of the Pazzi Conspiracy ended in 1480. Lorenzo returned to Florence, and the people greeted him as a conquering hero. The Pazzi conspiracy and its aftermath had profound effects on Machiavelli. He comments on this period of Florentine history frequently in his writings.

Lorenzo, understandably, was deeply affected by the Pazzi experience and his brother's murder. Feeling more insecure, he traveled only with armed bodyguards. He began to act more like a domineering prince instead of an avuncular *padrone*. He began to treat state revenues as personal resources in contrast to the Medici tradition of promoting Florence with Medici funds. Lorenzo constricted the city's constitution to increase his power and the authority of his confidants.

Every student knows that in 1492 "Columbus sailed the ocean blue." But fewer remember that Lorenzo the Magnificent died. His son Piero assumed political control. Two years later, the French, under

King Charles VIII, invaded Florence. Piero bungled the defense of the city. Piero was not merely less capable than his father; he was also immature and feckless. He had unwisely supported Naples in its dispute with Milan and France, virtually ensuring an invasion of Florence. When the attack occurred, Florence surrendered with almost no resistance, losing its control of Pisa as well. Piero was forced into exile and republican government was restored in Florence. Machiavelli was twenty-five years old.

The brief, brilliant, deranged influence of Girolamo Savonarola followed. Savonarola, a Dominican friar, was as austere as the rations at Auschwitz, as zealous as red ants at a picnic, and as driven as Silas Marner in sight of a dollar. Although inelegant and gloomy, Savonarola was a spellbinding orator who not only articulated his apocalyptic sermons but lived them. From 1490, working out of the monastery of San Marco, he spewed his fire and brimstone, criticizing the wicked ways of Florentines and the paganism of Lorenzo. Savonarola warned of an angry God whose imminent, final judgments would hurl terrible vengeance on the sordid Florentines.

The people, wracked by guilt and riddled with insecurities, listened and cowered.

The French invasions of 1494 presented opportunity. Savonarola revealed that God sent Charles VIII to punish Italy, purify the Church, and prepare the way for the second coming of Christ. Savonarola supported republicanism as a prelude to theocracy. He and his sanctimonious, puritanical disciples were able to outlaw horse races, dice and card games, dancing, carnivals, and brothels. Homosexuality became a capital offense. Torture and excessive punishment for moral offenses were instituted. Savonarola's main sources of entertainment were bonfires of the vanities in which everything from mirrors to the works of Boccaccio were immolated. Spiritual repression suffocated the city.

Isaac Newton's third law of motion assures us that for every action there is an equal, opposite reaction. Traditional Catholics, rival Franciscans, bankers, secular humanists, Medici holdouts, and miscellaneous others all had reasons to resent Savonarola's mercurial leap to power. Sectarian bitterness ensued between the *Arrabbiati* ("Hotheads") and the *Piagnoni* ("Sobbers"), the label that the Hotheads affixed to Savonarola's supporters who were renowned for weeping during the Dominican's sermons. Savonarola descended from power even more quickly than he had risen. As Machiavelli would later report, the friar was astonishingly inflexible and lacked an army. His defeat was inevitable. Eventually, the Franciscans challenged Savonarola to prove his status as a prophet. In a contest worthy of the World Wide Wrestling Federation, an ordeal by fire was proposed: a Franciscan and Savonarola would walk through flames and God would protect the favored son. Savonarola, unable to refuse precisely the type of zany challenge that was his stock in trade, accepted. But on "game day" he quibbled and nibbled over the terms and conditions of the ordeal for hours, while the entire city, including Machiavelli, waited anxiously for the advertised main event. Finally, God rendered His verdict: rained poured and the fires were extinguished. The people, finally recognizing Savonarola as a sincere but deluded fanatic, arrested him. He was soon tortured, hanged, and burned in 1498.

Machiavelli had a measure of admiration for Savonarola's ability to rouse a crowd and rally supporters, but also perceived his fatal flaws and doomed ideology. Merchant aristocrats regained political control of Florence at Savonarola's death. Machiavelli, at age twenty-nine, was appointed as secretary to the Second Chancery of the Republic of Florence and a member of the Council of Ten of Liberty and Peace. Specializing in foreign and military affairs, he was one of the more important administrators in the city. Machiavelli, though, was not an elected official. He was a state employee, not an independent politician.

From 1498 through 1512, Machiavelli made more than two dozen diplomatic missions to Italian city-states and European powers. This experience greatly influenced his conclusions about international military and political affairs. Machiavelli's conviction hardened that Italy was culturally superior to the barbaric, better-organized monarchies of northern Europe. Italy itself was divided into regional loyalties: Venice, Milan, Florence, the Papal States, and the Kingdom of Naples were the main players. Machiavelli understood that foreign armies too easily threatened the balance of power on the Italian peninsula. He looked to the glories of the ancient Roman republic for additional lessons on military and political matters. Those two sources—his experiences as a diplomat and his interpretations of Roman history—would animate his thinking and writing.

Pivotal to Machiavelli's political education was his diplomatic mission to Cesare Borgia, illegitimate son of Pope Alexander VI, who was consolidating his power in Northern Italy through force, fraud, and theatrical bluffs. Machiavelli was dispatched to ingratiate himself into Borgia's favor, and to advance and safeguard Florentine interests. He saw in Borgia a decisive, fearless, ruthless, often brutal commander. Backed by the power and influence of his father, Borgia had mastered the unforgiving techniques that had served foreigners so well in Italy. Machiavelli clearly admired Borgia's skills in foreign affairs—he was a conqueror—and in internal relations—he supposedly reformed Romagna (P 7; Leg 11.15: 7/26/02; Leg. 11.10: 10/13/02; Leg. 11.36: 11/3/02; Leg. 11.50: 11/20/02; Leg. 11.82: 12/26/02; Ltr. 247: 1/31/15; AW VII 194). Cesare advised Machiavelli that Florence was hamstrung by waffling, compromise, and delay. Florence, as with all cities in crisis, needed a strong man to lead resolutely. Machiavelli was greatly impressed by Borgia in his heyday, although he was ambivalent about the advice he rendered.

In 1502 Machiavelli married Marietta di Ludovico Corsini. His wife proved to be undemanding and uncommonly understanding. She bore six children, one of whom died soon after birth. Also in 1502 Piero Soderini was elected *gonfaloniere à vita*, chief magistrate of the Florentine republic. Machiavelli became one of his closest ministers. So close was Machiavelli to Soderini that he was known as *il mannerino di Soderini* [Soderini's puppet]. Machiavelli had genuine affection for Soderini, but later became disenchanted with the *gonfaloniere's* indecisiveness and squeamishness.

Soon thereafter, Machiavelli was sent again to Cesare Borgia. As Kenneth Bartlett reports:

> [Machiavelli] saw Cesare Borgia in action. He saw an Italian who appeared to be taking events into his own hands and directing them using the same techniques as the barbarians . . . here was an Italian who may, in fact, have been able to learn the lessons and to do something to protect Italy against those savages. . . . Machiavelli became entranced once more with Cesare. He was entranced by his energy, by his ruthlessness, and by his single-mindedness. Cesare would not let anything—not pity, not religion, not oaths or promises—interfere with what he saw as necessary policy. Machiavelli didn't particularly like this, but he also realized that perhaps it was the only solution to the situation of Italy.[1]

Machiavelli observed the unreliable nature of mercenary troops, which seemed to vacillate between treacherous and cowardly actions. He also noted the danger of auxiliary troops, which were loyal to their homeland not to the country that employed them. Machiavelli was enthralled by the accounts of the Roman historian Livy, who celebrated the citizen armies of volunteers that had energized Roman expansion. Such armies were not only militarily effective but they exuded patriotism, discipline, common identity, and civic virtue. Machiavelli petitioned Soderini. The *gonfaloniere* put Machiavelli in charge of military operations. The citizen army that was recruited, however, consisted mainly of politically disenfranchised rural peasants who lacked a strong stake in the Florentine republic. In 1508 Machiavelli was put in charge of the war against Pisa, which had been waged sporadically for over a decade. He directed the sea and land blockage that brought about Pisa's surrender in 1509. The citizen army, over 10,000 strong, appeared to be a success.

Soon thereafter, however, events spiraled uncontrollably and disastrously. In 1511 the Holy League of Mantua—led by the Papal States, Spain, some German regions, and some Italian city-states—was formed to oust the French from Italy. Florence, though, was allied closely with France. What should it do? Soderini fumbled, mumbled, and bumbled. He avoided serious participation in the dispute, eventually sending only a token force to France. As Machiavelli had predicted, both sides ended up despising Florence. Regardless of who won the war, Florence would suffer the sting of retribution.

Within a year, the Holy League had largely defeated the French. Just outside of Florence, an elite force of Spanish veterans attacked Prato. Machiavelli's large militia was ensconced within the thick walls of a fortress. Spanish artillery assaulted the fortress and penetrated its walls. Machiavelli's marauders threw down their weapons and ran helter-skelter into the countryside. Over 4,000 people were slaughtered in Prato. No obstacle to the Holy League's triumphant entry into Florence remained.

Soderini's prospects for remaining *gonfaloniere à vita* were zero. The "*vita*" turned out to be only a decade. He resigned and scampered into exile. Machiavelli resented the aristocratic political class he served. They often criticized him while failing to appreciate the sensitive diplomatic positions in which they placed him. All the while, he—more honest, capable, and patriotic than they—was dischargeable at their whim as he labored at their pleasure (Ltr. 176: 11/29/09). Moreover, the aristocrats generally hindered republican government with their amplified sense of entitlement, haughty skepticism, and deflated commitment to the common good. They were too weak to consolidate an alternate view of politics but pesky enough to swing the balance between republicanism and Medician principality. For Machiavelli, such aristocrats were the most annoying serpents in Florentine society. The aristocrats viewed Machiavelli similarly.

In his *Ricordo ai Palleshi* [Memorandum to Supporters of the Medici], written in late October or early November 1512, Machiavelli cautioned the Medici against publicizing the alleged misdeeds of Piero Soderini. Doing so, would only embolden the aristocrats who had long opposed Soderini. A wiser course of action was available: Expose aristocratic excesses to the people; invite the people to despise the aristocrats; and make the aristocrats dependent on the Medici rulers. In that missive, Machiavelli stigmatized the aristocrats as "those who play the whore between the people and the Medici." The diatribe backfired. The Medici were currying the favor of the aristocrats to buttress their return to power. Machiavelli's vitriol hastened his own fall from political grace. The aristocrats celebrated.

With Soderini's capitulation, Machiavelli would soon be between jobs. Giovanni de'Medici, the second son of Lorenzo the Magnificent, took control of Florence. Giovanni had strongly served the Holy League and was rewarded for his prescience. In 1513 Giovanni was elected Pope Leo X. The Florentine republic was no longer. Giuliano de'Medici, youngest son of Lorenzo the Magnificent, was governor of Florence.

Machiavelli was not only discharged, but he was soon implicated, apparently falsely, in a plot to overthrow the Medici. His name was included in a list in the possession of a Medici opponent. He was imprisoned and tortured with the *strappado*. Sebastian de Grazia gracefully describes the brutality: "Your wrists are tied behind your back and bound to a rope hanging from a pulley. The other end of the rope is pulled down and you are hoisted up to a ceiling, arms yanked up behind, your body turning almost horizontally, its weight borne by twisted arms and shoulders. Then the rope is released and you plunge almost to the floor, the halt virtually tearing your arms out of their sockets. The process is then repeated, four times being a rough average for interrogative purposes."[2]

The *strappado* was crude, but earned an impressive record: Almost everyone subjected to this torture confessed even though they knew that an admission of guilt was typically followed by an execution. For those with an unrefined sense of matching penalties to crimes, the *strappado* was an unmitigated success. Need a perpetrator? Subject the accused to the *strappado*.

Granted the notion of the "voluntariness" of the confession was stretched beyond recognition, but the *strappado* drastically reduced the need for investigative police work.

Machiavelli survived six yanks of the *strappado* and twenty-two days in manacles. He did not confess and from all accounts conducted himself honorably and courageously. Machiavelli later wrote that: "I should like you to get this pleasure from these troubles of mine, that I have borne them so straightforwardly that I am proud of myself for it and consider myself more of a man than I believed I was" (Ltr. 206: 3/18/13). Machiavelli was released as part of a general amnesty accompanying the election of Pope Leo X. With no prospects, few resources, and much to fear he left Florence and retired to a small family farm near San Casciano, about seven miles outside the city. When the weather cooperated, he could view the tower of the Palazzo della Signoria, the seat of Florentine political authority, now so far from his grasp. In 1513 Machiavelli was relegated to obscurity.

While in exile, Machiavelli hunted, farmed, squabbled with local merchants, hung out in taverns, played card and dice games, and wrote. The scholarly consensus is that Machiavelli wrote *The Prince* between July and December 1513, with the possibility that he added the dedication and final chapter as late as 1516. He wrote *The Discourses* between 1513 and 1517, although some historians argue it was composed mostly from 1515 to 1516, with late adjustments in 1517. A few scholars claim that *The Discourses* was not completed until 1519.[3] Machiavelli completed the *Art of War* in 1517 and published it in 1521—the only one of Machiavelli's major works issued during his lifetime. He wrote his first and best-received play, *La Mandragola*, from 1518 to 1519. He completed *The Life of Castruccio Castracani* by 1520 and *The Florentine Histories* in 1526. *The Prince* was not published until 1532 and *The Discourses* in 1531. Machiavelli also penned two sorts of letters: official correspondence, *The Legations*, when he was secretary of the Committee of Ten; and informal letters he wrote to his political associates and friends. Among the recipients of the latter were Francesco Vettori, ambassador of the Medici-controlled Florentine republic to Rome; Francesco Guicciardini; Biagio Buonaccorsi; Filippo Casavecchia; Agostino Vespucci; and Francesco del Nero. By far the most famous of these figures were Vettori and Guicciardini, the papal governor of Romagna. Machiavelli also participated in political discussions in the Rucellai Gardens, presided over by his republican friend, Cosimo Rucellai.

Many of the ideas compiled in *The Prince* were rehearsed in Machiavelli's correspondence with Vettori. In a December 10, 1513, letter, Machiavelli poignantly details a typical day in his life that culminates in the evening as he dons courtly garments and "converses" with great ancient writers. He also announces in that letter the completion of *The Prince* and his intention to dedicate the work to Giuliano de'Medici, who was briefly the governor of Florence prior to being named a cardinal when his brother was elected as Pope (Ltr. 224: 12/10/13). Machiavelli eventually dedicated *The Prince* to Lorenzo de'Medici, grandson of the Magnificent, who was the Duke of Urbino and the de facto ruler of Florence once Giuliano left for Rome. Throughout this period of exile, he longed to return to political office and implement the principles he had derived. Despite his maneuverings and his implorations to his friends Vettori and Guicciardini, Machiavelli's resume remained unsolicited.

Finally, Cardinal Giulio de'Medici commissioned Machiavelli to write *The Florentine Histories*. Machiavelli was eager to work and hoped it would lead to a return to politics, but he was anxious about describing the Florentine republic, 1494–1512. He assumed that he was expected to curry the favor of the Medici and sully the image of the republican era. Yet, he was an integral part of that republican government for fourteen years. Machiavelli solved the problem with characteristic aplomb: he ended the book at 1492, the year Lorenzo the Magnificent perished. Moreover, he finessed his account of Medici rule, honestly praising their foreign policy and paying less attention to the loss of liberty attending the Magnificent's final decade of rule. In 1525 Machiavelli traveled to Rome to present the work to Giulio, who had been elected Pope Clement VII two years earlier.

The Pope received Machiavelli's labors warmly and offered Machiavelli a return to Florence. By 1526 Machiavelli was given minor work related to the defensive structures in Florence. He thirsted for more critical assignments. Events conspired against him.

The following year, the Holy Roman Emperor, Charles V, sacked Rome, an event that eviscerated the power of the Medici. Machiavelli and others had implored the Pope to heavily fortify Rome in preparation for the emperor's unwelcomed arrival. Instead, Clement VII negotiated a series of truces with Charles V and released his own troops to save money. The result was completely predictable: The emperor, sensing an easy military victory, ignored his promises, broke the peace, and stormed into Rome. The imperial army included mostly undisciplined barbarians who savagely despoiled the city. For over a week, Charles's cutthroats murdered, raped, looted, ransacked, and kidnapped. Pope Clement VII retreated to safety. About 50,000 Romans either fled or were slaughtered. The foreigners left only decay, disease, and despair behind them.

As a direct result of the sack of Rome, the Medici were, once again, expelled from Florence in 1527. Machiavelli was convinced that the revitalized republic that emerged would thirst for his services. But Machiavelli was now associated with the Medici, whose benefits he had cadged. No job offer was forthcoming. He was fifty-eight years old, without hope or redemption. Machiavelli had not tasted the enduring glory he so relentlessly sought.

Niccolò Machiavelli died later that year and was buried in Santa Croce, a Franciscan church in Florence that also contains the bodies of Michelangelo and Galileo, and a memorial to Dante. By 1559 the Roman Catholic Church had placed Machiavelli's books, all allegedly contaminated by the evil ostensibly celebrated in *The Prince*, on its Index of Prohibited Books. Throughout the past centuries, thousands of tourists have strolled through Santa Croce every week. They take photos of Machiavelli's grave. The epitaph on his tombstone reads, "*Tanto nomini nullum par elogium*" [To such a name no eulogy is equal].

Appendix C

Case Studies—Heroes and Villains

Moses, ca. 1393 bce–ca. 1273 bce

After forty years as a shepherd, Moses drove the herd to Mount Horeb, where he was shocked to see a burning bush that was not destroyed. Having secured Moses' attention, God identified Himself and commanded Moses and his brother Aaron to travel to Egypt and demand that the Pharaoh free the Israelites. Moses reluctantly agreed (Exodus 3:1-4; 4:20-31).

The Pharaoh refused Moses' request; ten plagues befell Egypt; after which the 600,000 Hebrews escaped. A few months later, Moses ascended Mount Sinai and descended with the Ten Commandments (Exodus 5-18; 19:20-25). He then found the Israelites dancing naked, worshipping a golden calf. Moses called for supporters, the sons of Levi responded, and Moses ordered the murder of 3,000 men (Exodus 32:19-28).

Moses was confronted by an extreme emergency. His people were enslaved; their liberation depended on his military and political *virtù*; his concern for strictly personal glory vanished; force became necessary to maintain unity; and squeamishness was unwarranted. As Machiavelli concludes: "If you are discussing nothing less than the safety of the homeland, then you should pay no attention to what is just or what is unjust, or to what is kind or cruel, or to what is praiseworthy or shameful. You should put every other consideration aside, and you should adopt wholeheartedly the policy most likely to save your homeland's life and preserve her liberty" (D III 41).

The killings of the 3,000 idolaters resonate with familiar Machiavellian themes: how envy and ambition engender discontent that blossoms into conflicting sects that foster rebellion; the connections among ingratitude, fear, and hatred; the necessity of employing violence to establish or maintain the common good (D I 8; pref.; D III 30). While one might argue that Moses, unlike Romulus, required divine agency to accomplish his mission, that can be interpreted in Moses' favor: Even the omnibenevolent Judeo-Christian God understands that violence in the name of patriotism is sometimes recommended. Moreover, Moses, unlike Romulus, was a religious reformer. The importance for Machiavelli of religion, properly fashioned, in supporting good arms and good laws in setting the preconditions for security, order, and civic *virtù* cannot be overstated.

Moses crushed the bonds of slavery and demonstrated that religious commitment could animate heroic deeds. The Florentines of Machiavelli's time were also enslaved. Lured by economic security, they had squandered their civil liberties and were dominated by foreigners. They, too, needed a redeemer, a Moses who could wed military and political *virtù* to resoluteness, unsqueamishness, and prophetic vision. God would smile on such a man (P 26).

Numa Pompilius, CA. 750 BCE–CA. 673 BCE

After Romulus had died, probably slain by conspiratorial senators, Numa Pompilius was selected to be the next king of Rome. Numa, contemplative and philosophical by temperament, was reluctant to accept the post. Rome was an uncivilized mosaic of Sabines, Romans, runaway slaves, fugitives, and smaller tribes. Numerous disparate traditions and customs coalesced uneasily. Numa, although not a warrior by nature, had shrewd political insight. Rome needed a common culture to bind it more tightly. That culture would most easily be attained through strong religious rituals and institutions. Numa concluded that religion could best sustain the laws and customs that Romulus had initiated. Numa Pompilius prefigured the glorious Machiavellian union of strong arms and strong laws, underwritten by a vital religion that promoted military and political *virtù*. Civic *virtù*, territorial expansion, security, order, and prosperity were highly likely to follow.

For Machiavelli, religious worship is required for political greatness. Even the greatest human ruler leads a finite life. The power of religion endures. The crucial question is not whether to nurture religion in the polity. The critical question is what kind of religion to foster. The answer, for Machiavelli, is not an emasculated Christianity, with its eye on a transcendent world that rewards the meek, humble, and downtrodden. The solution is a robust religion that promotes the military and political *virtù* required to establish or invigorate the security, order, and civic *virtù* necessary for an expansionist republic. Ave, Numa Pompilius!

Gaius Julius Caesar, 100 BCE–44 BCE

As a young man, Julius Caesar was captured by pirates. Although not in a strong taunting position, he purportedly swore to his captors that he would track them down and crucify them once he was freed from their clutches. After being ransomed, Caesar fulfilled his oath. This tale better captures the character of Caesar than does any battlefield account of his destruction of the Gauls, any story of political maneuvering with Pompey and Crassus, or any rendition of his numerous stirring speeches.

Either the legend of Caesar's insolence in the face of his pirate captors is true or it is false. If true, we enjoy the vision of a relentless warrior, confident even when seemingly confronting hopeless odds and a resolute enemy. If false, we chuckle at the shameless self-promotion of a youth turning desperate adversity into practical, political advantage. In either case, Caesar did hunt and slay the offending pirates.

In a world where a small, gifted class of men smoldered with *ambizione,* Caesar was aflame. He served as aedile at age thirty-five and two years later wangled the post of pontifex maximus, probably through bribery. A year later, he became praetor. After serving as governor of Spain, he formed a political triumvirate with the wealthy Crassus and the great general Pompey. His older, more experienced partners assumed they could use Caesar for their own purposes then discard him when convenient. They were gravely mistaken.

With the help of the triumvirate, he was elected as a consul in 59 BCE. He proved to be a gifted politician who was able to enact the triumvirate's political program despite strong opposition in the senate. Within a year, Caesar launched a ten-year campaign in Gaul. He served as his own military propagandist, composing *The Conquest of Gaul* in a lean, crisp rhetorical style. Critics in the senate objected that the Gallic War was waged more to satisfy Caesar's boundless quest for glory and riches than for definable Roman purposes. This was Caesar's launching pad for his major aspiration: to become absolute ruler of the Roman republic. With added wealth, military reputation, and a loyal, expanding army, Caesar laid the foundations to attain that goal. He proved during the Gallic campaigns that he was Rome's greatest general.

His enemies in the senate, especially Cato the Younger (95 BCE–46 BCE), an uncompromising advocate of traditional Roman republican values, issued an ultimatum: Caesar must resign as proconsul of Gaul, yield his army, and return to Rome. Upon his return, his opponents would levy charges against him, destroy him politically, and call for his exile.

After failing in attempts to negotiate his way out of the impasse, Caesar and his army crossed the Rubicon River, the boundary of his province, and marched on Rome. Civil war ensued. Pompey led the forces of Caesar's senate enemies. Caesar marched through Italy into Rome, meeting weak resistance. At the Battle of Pharsalus in 48 BCE Caesar's forces, although badly outnumbered, routed Pompey's army. Caesar showed mercy at the end of the battle, insisting on no unnecessary killings or reprisals. Following Pompey to Egypt, he installed Cleopatra, who bore him a son, as queen.

After campaigns in Africa, Asia, and Spain, Caesar had eliminated all serious senate opposition and he had achieved his ultimate goal: he was absolute master of Rome. By 44 BCE Caesar was declared Dictator for Life. He dressed in the fashion of the ancient Roman kings, but rejected that title. Always restless, Caesar strategized a war against Parthia. Prior to his embarking, a conspiracy, led by Marcus Junius Brutus, Cassius Longinus, and a host of senators, was hatched. Although the plan was not a closely guarded secret, the assassins slew Caesar by brutally stabbing him repeatedly at the feet of a statue of Pompey. The Ides of March has never been the same.

Oliverotto Euffreducci (Oliverotto da Fermo), CA. 1475–1502

The short, colorful life of Oliverotto Euffreducci illustrates the limitations of pursuing *ambizione* only for personal gain. Oliverotto was raised by his maternal uncle Giovanni Fogliani, a leading figure in Fermo. As soon as practicable, Oliverotto joined the mercenary forces of Paolo Vitelli. He fought for Vitelli on behalf of the French at Pisa and Naples. In 1499 the Vitelli army was fighting for the Florentines against Pisa. Florence accused Paolo and Oliverotto of treason. Paolo was executed, but Oliverotto was freed due to the intervention of the political leaders of Fermo. Oliverotto then joined with Paolo's brother Vitellozzo Vitelli and served Cesare Borgia. Due to his boldness, developing military *virtù*, and passionate character, Oliverotto rose in the ranks to become second only to Vitellozzo. The Vitelli mercenaries were critical to Borgia's conquest of Piombino.

A man of Oliverotto's *ambizione*, ability, and self-image cannot remain a subordinate for long. He concocted a plan to seize control of Fermo, enlisting the support of Vitellozzo and of self-serving malcontents within Fermo. Oliverotto wrote to his uncle and asked for an invitation to return to Fermo and reacquaint himself with his childhood. He added that he had joined the military to gain honor and he would arrive at Fermo with 100 men—as a way of showing the citizens of Fermo that he had used his time away from home wisely. Oliverotto assured his uncle that his return would bring honor to everyone involved. In short, Oliverotto painted an appealing picture of local-boy-makes-good-and-returns-home-in gratitude-to-appreciative-homefolks (P 8).

Uncle Giovanni was easily lured by this ruse and saw to it that his nephew was accorded every honor and all due respect by the citizens of Fermo. He ensured that Oliverotto lodged at his home. Oliverotto, after transacting the required arrangements, invited his uncle and the most influential citizens of Fermo to an elaborate feast. After the meal and appropriate entertainment, Oliverotto began discussing serious political and religious matters. When the others began contributing to the discussion, he suggested they all retire to a more private room to continue the conversation. As soon as they all entered that room, Oliverotto's soldiers fell upon and murdered Giovanni and the others (P 8).

Oliverotto then mounted his steed, took possession of Fermo, and lay siege to the government building. The remaining authorities, sensing the political tide was swaying radically, pledged to obey Oliverotto and agreed to establish a new regime with Oliverotto at its head. Within a year, Oliverotto was securely entrenched at Fermo, having established new military and political structures (P 8).

Oliverotto conquered Camerino on behalf of Borgia and then played a role in the mounting conspiracy against Duke Valentino. Just as he was about to pursue the expansion of his authority to other towns, Oliverotto met his master. Poetic justice and, probably, political justice was served by Borgia's plot at Sinigallia, which climaxed with Oliverotto's strangulation. Fittingly, Borgia's attack bore striking resemblances to Oliverotto's treachery at Fermo.

Agathocles of Syracuse, 361 BCE–289 BCE

A potter's son, Agathocles raged with *ambizione*. He joined the military as soon as possible and rose step by step until he was supreme commander. Agathocles wanted more. Prefiguring Julius Caesar, he sought absolute power. Pursuant to that aspiration, he entered into a conspiracy with a Carthaginian general who was mounting a military campaign in Sicily.

One bright, sunny morning, Agathocles, under cover of discussing political issues, convened the senate of Syracuse and its wealthiest, most influential citizens. At a prearranged signal, soldiers murdered the entire lot of Syracuse's finest. With few obstacles remaining, Agathocles, after less than thorough consideration of alternatives, named himself absolute ruler of Syracuse. Later, the Carthaginians defeated his army twice and advanced to the walls of Syracuse. There Agathocles left part of his army to defend the city and transported the rest to Africa to attack Carthage. He proved an able commander, forcing Carthage to release its siege of Syracuse and seriously threatening to overrun the Carthaginians that stayed home. Carthage sued for peace, agreeing to leave Sicily in return for its security in Africa (P 8).

Machiavelli recognizes Agathocles's military *virtù*, his skill in working himself up through the ranks, the boldness of his tactics, his eagerness to confront danger and take risks, and his successful quest for power. Little, if any, of Agathocles's success could be attributed to *Fortuna*. Still, Machiavelli is critical of his later political actions: "One ought not, of course, to call it *virtù* to massacre one's fellow citizens, to betray one's friends, to break one's word, to be without mercy, and without religion. By such means one can acquire power but not glory" (P8).

Girolamo Savonarola, 1452–1498

Savonarola was a Dominican priest who relentlessly railed against Renaissance humanist values, the corruption of the papacy, and preoccupation with material goods. He first preached in Florence at age thirty without success. He left for Bologna where his apocalyptic style began to draw attention. He was recalled to Florence around 1489 and immediately drew a receptive audience. Claiming to communicate directly with God and unveiling his numerous prophetic visions, Savonarola targeted Pope Alexander VI and the Medici rulers of Florence. He preached energetically about the final days of the world and the need to cleanse souls in preparation for final judgment. Perhaps aided by a widely held superstition that the year 1500 would mark the end of the earth, the increasing economic disparity in Florence between the rich and the poor, and the rapidly expanding effects of a plague (probably caused by syphilis spread by returning seafarers), Savonarola's haunting message of impending gloom and doom leavened by the possibility of salvation resonated among the people.

In 1494 Charles VIII of France invaded Florence, as Savonarola had predicted, and ousted the Medici. Savonarola filled the political gap by serving as the spiritual leader of Florence. He struggled mightily to use his influence to create a Christian theocracy. He and his followers inaugurated bonfires of the vanities in which luxuries of all manner—fancy clothes, mirrors, cosmetics, secular art, musical instruments, dice, chess pieces, humanistic poetry, and the like—were immolated in the town square. Paintings by masters such as Michelangelo and Botticelli were among the treasures burnt. Savonarola placed no value on fun, recreation, and aesthetic pleasure.

Savonarola, emboldened by his success, ratcheted up the flames of his intensity. Demanding the regeneration of Christian spiritual values, veneration of asceticism, and repudiation of secular frivolity, he and his supporters organized a morality police. Through spying, rumor gathered from informants, speculation, and gossip, they passionately excoriated alleged wrongdoers, often publicly, and warned of impending retribution.

Our unworthy attributes, the ones that lead to our demise, are usually just our worthy features, the ones that led to our ascension, exaggerated. So, too, with the well-meaning, deluded, fanatical Dominican friar. Predictably he had gone too far. The world was not coming to an end, Savonarola's prescriptions had not enhanced the quality of life, and the people began to understand the dangers of his excesses. He was excommunicated by an increasingly irritated Alexander VI, outbreaks at his monastery occurred, and Savonarola was taken prisoner. Accused of heresy and schism (trying to split the union of the Church), Savonarola and two of his main associates were tortured, hanged, and burned. Their ashes were dumped eagerly into the Arno River.

While Machiavelli could admire the friar's verve, boldness, and, especially, keen awareness of the corruption in the Church, he anticipated Savonarola's fall: "He acts in accordance with the times and colors his lies accordingly" (Ltr. 3: 3/9/98). Savonarola's deceptions were too thin to endure, a textbook case of ineffective reform grounded on shaky rhetoric.

In addition, to give citizens added security, the friar had helped enact a right of appeal from sentences in political cases. Shortly thereafter, the government condemned five citizens to death. They lodged their right to appeal, but they were denied that right. Savonarola, who viewed the condemned men as his enemies, refused comment: "This took away more of the friar's influence than any other event . . . revealing his ambitious and partisan spirit. . . . [The event] brought him much censure" (D I 45). The rule of law can be a stern mistress.

Finally, Savonarola lacked the means—the strong arms and secular laws—required to harden the resolve of his remaining supporters or to persuade critics to obey his decrees (P 6). Moses and Romulus understood that in founding or reforming a state, enemies harboring envy had to be slain. Machiavelli credits Savonarola with that same knowledge. The friar, though, lacked a political or military position from which to launch the required assault. He had only the fire of his pulpit and the tenuous support of his followers (D III 30). Again, the message is that the unarmed prophet or the leader who cannot or will not take the horrifying steps required for political success must fail. Government is not run by prayers alone.

Piero Soderini, 1450–1513

Appointed to office three years before Soderini rose to power, Machiavelli, in his positions as secretary to the Second Chancery of the Republic of Florence and as a member of the Council of Ten of Liberty and Peace, flourished in Soderini's service. Piero descended from a distinguished Florentine family and was named prior of Florence and, later, ambassador to France under the Medici. After the French, under Charles VIII, ousted the Medici, the peculiar, fiery four-year influence of Savonarola held sway. Once the friar was slain, merchant aristocrats regained political control of Florence. Within four years, Piero Soderini was elected *gonfaloniere à vita*. The lifetime post lasted only a decade. Machiavelli had deep affection for Soderini, who proved to be a compassionate political centrist who greatly admired

Machiavelli. Under Soderini, Machiavelli embarked on more than two dozen diplomatic missions where he learned countless lessons about political intrigue. Soderini, in concert with Machiavelli's advice, instituted a Florentine militia to replace reliance on mercenary and auxiliary troops. In 1509 Pisa surrendered to Florence, bringing much honor to Soderini and to Machiavelli, who was in charge of military operations.

But by 1511 a chilling political wind was blowing in Europe. The Holy League of Mantua was formed. Led by Spain with the aid of some German and Italy city-states and the Vatican, the alliance was neither holy nor a league. Its expressed purpose was to drive the French out of Italy. Soderini was always sympathetic to the French, who had assisted him in several ways during his rise to and maintenance of political power. He straddled the fence, avoiding significant entanglement. His heart was with the French; his head concluded that the Holy League was too formidable a foe. So Soderini vacillated, sending only a token military force to France. As a result, both sides despised Florence, as Machiavelli had warned.

By 1512 the Holy League, with Swiss intervention, defeated the French. The Medici, who had allied with the League, ousted Soderini, dismissed Machiavelli, and regained political control of Florence. Soderini fled to Ragusa and was then called to Rome under Pope Leo X. He remained in Rome trying to advance the interest of Florence until he died in 1513.

Machiavelli was the envoy charged with explaining Soderini's flaccid policies to Louis XII of France. Despite Machiavelli's warnings, Soderini insisted on political neutrality to the detriment of the republic. Even after it was clear that the Holy League would triumph, Soderini was wrongly convinced that the Spanish would accept money in return for keeping the Medici out of Florence (Ltr. 203: 9/16/12; P 21).

Although retaining numerous fond memories of Soderini, Machiavelli summarized in an epigram his judgment of a politician unwilling to do what was necessary to save the Florentine republic, a leader who strove to retain his moral purity at the expense of his country:

> The night Pier Soderini passed away,
> His soul was halted on the brink of hell;
> And Pluto yelled: "No hell for you—you fool!
> In children's limbo you can only stay."[1]

Giovampagolo Baglioni, 1470–1520

Pope Julius II embarked on a mission in 1505 to depose all princes and tyrants who occupied the cities of the Church. Among his targets was Baglioni of Perugia. When the Pope, his bodyguard, and the College of Cardinals entered Perugia, Baglioni meekly surrendered even though he was accompanied by many soldiers. Machiavelli is stunned that Baglioni did not simply strike down his enemies and confiscate their riches. Machiavelli notes that we cannot attribute Baglioni's reluctance to act forcefully to his goodness because he was a "vicious man." Machiavelli adds that Baglioni "had a perfect opportunity to do a deed for which everybody would have admired his courage and for which he would have left an everlasting remembrance of himself, as being the first who had shown prelates what a low estimate was to be put on men who live and reign as they do" (D I 27).

Machiavelli's disparagement of Baglioni also underscores the Florentine's utter contempt for the role of the Church in Italian political affairs, the corruption infecting the leading religious figures of his day, and the need to undermine the Church's authority in service of patriotic concerns. Machiavelli considers the execution of the Pope and his Cardinals a deed "the greatness of which would have transcended every infamy, every peril that could have resulted from it" (D I 27).

Cesare Borgia ("Duke Valentino"), 1475–1507

Cunning grifter, colorful mountebank, ferocious warrior, charismatic opportunist, ruthless gangster, intellectual strategist, deceptive charlatan, cold-blooded murderer . . . Cesare Borgia was all of these and more. He was the illegitimate son of Cardinal Rodrigo Borgia. During the same year when Columbus sailed for the new world, the Cardinal became Pope Alexander VI. Cesare was immediately the beneficiary of the first of a recurring string of nepotistic acts: he was named Archbishop of Valencia and soon thereafter was anointed as a cardinal. At first, Cesare was content to enjoy *la dolce vita* in Rome. But, as Machiavelli would have anticipated, Cesare Borgia seethed with *ambizione*: "[Borgia was] a cold, relentless egotist, using men for his own ends, terrible and even treacherous in his reprisals, swift as a panther and as cruel when his anger was aroused, yet with certain elements of greatness: a splendid soldier, an unrivalled administrator, a man pre-eminently just, if merciless in that same justice . . . boundless in audacity, most swift to determine and to act, not impulsive. Cold reason, foresight, and calculation were the ministers of his indomitable will."[2]

The ecclesiastical life, although brimming with benefits and security, was too domesticated. He lusted after the political position of his older brother Giovanni, Duke of Gandia, who was the main architect of Pope Alexander VI's political stratagems. The Duke of Gandia was murdered, which insiders attributed to Cesare. In fairness to Borgia, numerous other suspects also had motive, opportunity, and means to dispose of the Duke.[3] With the death of his older brother, Cesare assumed the role of the Pope's political hatchet man. He traveled to Naples and crowned Frederick of Aragon king. After receiving permission from the Pope and the College of Cardinals, Borgia renounced the priesthood. God's loss was Treachery's gain. Borgia brought Louis XII a papal edict annulling Louis's marriage so the monarch could wed his latest favorite. Louis showed his gratitude by appointing Cesare the Duke of Valentinois and pledging military aid for Cesare's proposed military adventures.

The Pope dispatched Cesare to subdue the province of Romagna. With the aid of French auxiliaries, Swiss and Italian mercenaries, a dose of fraud, a measure of theater, an overpouring of ruthlessness, and recurring violence, Borgia was soon on the move: Imola, Forli, Pesaro, Rimini, Faenza, Piombino, Camerino, Urbino, and other regions soon fell under Cesare's heavy hands. A conspiracy against him, though, quickly ensued. Led by some of the princes Borgia ousted, such as the Orsinis and some of Cesare's own captains, such as Vitellozzo Vitelli and Oliverotto da Fermo, revolts at Urbino and elsewhere were temporarily successful. But Louis XII, presumably savoring his new marriage, pledged additional help. That, along with a rupture in the solidarity of the conspirators, swung the pendulum in Borgia's favor. For his part, Cesare managed, through fraud and savagery, at Senigallia to eliminate the captains who had betrayed him.

Early in 1503 Borgia went to Rome to track down the last of the Orsinis. He was amassing troops for a new offensive in central Italy, when both he and the Pope contracted a virulent fever. The Pope died. Cesare was incapacitated. Without his father's support, Borgia's power, especially his alliance with King Louis XII, softened. Pope Pius III replaced Alexander VI, but he was old and ill. Borgia's hold on conquered regions began to loosen, town by town. Pope Pius III died and was replaced by Pope Julius II, who had long opposed the

Borgias. The new Pope demanded all of Cesare's remaining territories be restored to the Church. Borgia was arrested, but was freed when he surrendered his territories. Borgia went to Naples and was there arrested under order of King Ferdinand of Spain. He was a prisoner in Spain for two years, but escaped and found refuge at the court of his brother-in-law, the king of Navarre. He died fighting on his behalf at Viana.

After Borgia had destroyed the power of the Colonnas in Romagna, he faced several obstacles. He doubted the reliability of his own military forces, he could not be certain of the continued support of Louis XII, and he doubted the allegiance of the Orsini troops. His reliance on the military forces and good will of others was bound to be his undoing (P 7).

Borgia responded resolutely. He moved against the Orsini and Colonna by luring nobles allied to them in Rome to his side through promises of pensions and power. After the Orsini and some of Cesare's own captains spawned the rebellion at Urbino, Borgia hatched the glorious stratagem that won Machiavelli's approval. Cleverly hiding his true intentions, Borgia arrived at a rapprochement with the Orsini. Their leaders, along with Borgia's formerly traitorous captains, arrived at Sinigallia to celebrate their supposed reunification (P 7, 8). Later that night, Vitelli and Oliverotto were strangled. The others were disposed of soon thereafter. Neither man showed moxie at the end. Vitelli begged that the Pope be petitioned to give him a plenary indulgence for his sins; Oliverotto sobbed and feebly tried to indict Vitelli as the true and only source of the injuries perpetrated upon Duke Valentino: "[Borgia] was a ruthless gangster and an expert confidence man, and the revolt of some of the smaller gangsters, his captains, gave him an opportunity to display his talents. Machiavelli watched, fascinated, while Cesare, all mildness and good will, lured his mutinous subordinates into a renewed friendship, and when they arrived unarmed and unescorted at a rendezvous where Cesare had hidden his bodyguards, had them seized and murdered. Machiavelli was delighted at the virtuosity of the performance."[4]

Borgia's telling of this incident differs. He claimed that the Orsini and Oliverotto, under the guise of reconciliation, had amassed a major military force at Sinigallia and were planning a full-scale attack. Borgia took them by surprise in a classic, justified preemptive strike.[5]

Another highlight of Borgia's reign, for Machiavelli, occurred in Romagna. Finding that ineffective nobles had exploited their subjects, and that internal corruption and destructive conflict—led by hordes of robbers, bandits, and criminals—were pervasive, Borgia acted decisively. He bestowed complete power over the region to the cruel, effective, Remiro d'Orco. Quickly, d'Orco established order through harsh and extralegal means. Then, fearing that the inhabitants were coming to hate d'Orco, Borgia named a civil court of justice to investigate complaints against him. The people received the message that Borgia could be tough (he had appointed d'Orco), and he could be just (he named a court to examine d'Orco excesses). To prevent the people from wrongly concluding that Borgia was not completely in charge, Cesare had d'Orco killed. For theatrical and symbolic effect, he had d'Orco sliced in two and the bodily halves placed in the corners of the town piazza, with a chopping board and a bloody knife beside them. The citizens of Romagna were at once pleased, awed, and shocked (P 7).

The conventional interpretation of this horrifying deed is that Borgia used d'Orco, then disposed of him when convenient and advantageous for Borgia: the autocratic governor was merely following Cesare's orders and murdered when he was no longer required for Borgia's purposes. The more charitable rendering is that d'Orco grossly exceeded what was necessary to pacify Romagna, expropriated and sold food for his own profit, and was also part of the conspiracy—involving Vitelli, the Orsini, and Oliverotto—against Borgia: the tyrant of Romagna was properly slain for offending Borgia's sense of justice and for plotting against him.[6]

Borgia used cruelty and deceit to unite and bring order and peace to Romagna. In order to accomplish his goals, Borgia coldly exploited d'Orco, apparently in premeditated fashion. Borgia also "established a civil court in the center of the province, placing an excellent judge in charge of it, and requiring every city to appoint a lawyer to represent it before the court" (P 7). In this manner, Borgia was able to exact his plan while avoiding the hatred of citizens ("better to be feared than loved, but avoid being hated"). Borgia had positioned himself to be viewed plausibly as forceful (he had d'Orco sliced in two) but fair (he established a legal system and short-circuited d'Orco's excesses).

But how could d'Orco have misread the situation so badly? How could he have not anticipated the treachery of his supposed patron? And should Borgia not have calculated the possibility of d'Orco anticipating that treachery and making provisions to thwart it? The simple answer is that those, such as d'Orco, who are elevated to positions of authority beyond their realistic hopes and demonstrated talents, are typically too concerned with exercising their privileges and power to question their apparent good fortune. Remiro d'Orco was too intent on proving himself an able executioner of his master's scheme to pacify Romagna to prepare for his eventual betrayal. As such, d'Orco was utterly devoid of the wiles of the fox: he could not recognize traps. As for Borgia, he understood keenly both d'Orco's penchant for cruelty and the unsubtle quality of his mind. Still, Borgia had undoubtedly concocted an alternate plan should d'Orco somehow have anticipated his destiny.

Prior to his father's death, Borgia had gained the friendship of Roman nobles, made allegiances in the College of Cardinals, and consolidated his power in conquered territories. Knowing his father was mortal, Borgia aspired to acquire so much force and influence that he would be able to independently resist any attack. Cesare, wisely, moved to distance himself from reliance on mercenary troops, the French, and the papacy (P 7).

Fortuna, though, turned against Cesare Borgia. He could not complete his master plan. He and his father were both seriously ill. His father died. Then, Cesare, his judgment weakened, made a huge mistake. He eventually allowed Julius II to be elected pope. Borgia apparently had enough influence to prevent this, but he agreed to throw his support to Julius. In return, Borgia was to retain control of conquered land and be placed in charge of the papal army. The great con man misread Julius's intentions. Predictably, the new Pope, who was a longtime enemy of the Borgias and who feared and hated Cesare, reneged on his promises and moved successfully against him (P 7; D III 4).

Regarding military matters, Machiavelli called Borgia "a model to be imitated" (P 13; Ltr. 247: 1/31/15). He had used French auxiliary troops to conquer Imola and Forli. Sensing these were unreliable, he switched to the mercenary troops of Orsini and Vitelli. Finding these dangerous and treacherous, he understood that he must form and train his own troops. At this point, Borgia's reputation soared as it was apparent that he was in total command of his own forces (P 13). Machiavelli also praised Borgia's military tactics (D II 24; AW VII 194): "A proof of the splendid discipline prevailing in Cesare's army is afforded during his brief sojourn in Pesaro. . . . Occupation by such an army was, naturally enough, cause for deep anxiety on the part of a people who were but too well acquainted with the ways of the fifteenth-century men at arms. But here was a general who knew how to curb and control his soldiers. Under the pain of death his men were forbidden from indulging any of the predations or violences usual to their kind."[7]

Machiavelli also uses Borgia indirectly to once again indict the use of power by the Church (P 11). For the most part, Cesare was the instrument of Pope Alexander VI. He was eventually defeated by the treachery of Pope Julius II. The church, yet again, had failed to act in the best interests of the country. It placed its own material interests ahead of the common good.

Romulus, CA. 770 BCE–CA. 716 BCE

The legend of the founding of Rome centers on the nearby city of Alba Longa, where Aeneas had settled much earlier after fleeing from Troy. Rhea Silvia, a vestal virgin of Alba Longa, became pregnant. She claimed that her suitor was the god Mars. Seduction by a god was one of the few available defenses against a sacrilege punishable by death. Rhea skirted capital punishment and bore twin boys. The twins were seized by the king's men and deposited into the Tiber River. Happily, the twins were tossed up on a river bank and nurtured by a she-wolf until they were discovered and adopted by a shepherd, Faustulus.

The twins, Romulus and Remus, grew up among shepherds and other coarse men. After allegations that Remus had stolen cattle, he was taken before a magistrate, a former king, in Alba Longa. Romulus rounded up enough men to march on the city and rescue Remus. The magistrate took the opportunity to regain the throne. Romulus and Remus decided to found their own city, but quarreled over which was the best hill upon which to build. Romulus killed Remus when Remus disdainfully leapt over Romulus's walls on the Palatine hill. As the first king of Rome, Romulus gained a reputation as a great warrior.

To what degree the rich narrative of Romulus, Remus, and the founding of Rome is legend and to what degree, if any, it is fact remains a matter of dispute.[8] This debate, though, should not directly concern students of Machiavelli. Nor should we quibble over the details of Machiavelli's historical rendering of Romulus. Was he truly motivated by the common good? Did Romulus really divest his power and welcome the authority of a senate? Did he not, according to legend, become increasing arrogant and arbitrary? Was he not assassinated by some senators because he abused his power?

Machiavelli focuses only on Romulus-as-founder. That Romulus had to kill his own brother and an elected officer adds to his luster from a Machiavellian perspective. Romulus demonstrated that he was willing to bloody his nose and dirty his hands in the face of necessity. The laws and strong military he introduced demonstrate the prerequisites for security, order, and civic *virtù* that define a healthy, expansionist republic. That he acted from a vision of the common good—at least in Machiavelli's telling—highlights his deserved claim to glory and immortality.

Lucius Junius Brutus, CA. 545 BCE–CA. 509 BCE

The early Romans bristled under the monarchy of Tarquin the Proud. The plebeians were forced into oppressive involuntary servitude; the aristocrats were subject to recurrent purges. The son of Tarquin, Sextus, ignited the flame of revolution. Sextus, smitten by the beauty of a married woman, Lucretia, made his intentions known to her. She refused his amorous overtures. Sextus raped her. Lucretia, upon being released from Sextus's custody, spewed the truth to her husband and father, and then committed suicide.

The masses of Rome, led by Lucius Junius Brutus, revolted and drove Tarquin, who quickly lost his pride, out of Rome. Brutus was especially instrumental in winning the military to his cause. A republic was instituted. Roman leaders would be elected by an assembly of the entire army; they would serve only one-year terms and share political power with a colleague. Brutus and Lucretia's husband were elected as the first consuls of Rome.

Brutus restored the power of the senate and the new Roman republic was on its way. Lucretia's husband, who was himself a Tarquin, drew suspicion and the people soon forced him into exile. Shortly thereafter, agents of Tarquin the Proud returned to Rome to discuss the return of the tyrant's personal property. They also took the opportunity to foment counterrevolution and found an unlikely audience in Brutus's wife and two sons. The young men joined the conspiracy against the republic. Happily, the traitors were exposed and brought to justice. Brutus had to choose between the rule of law and his family. He chose the rule of law and all conspirators, including his two sons, were executed under Brutus's supervision. Tarquin the Proud had not punished his son, Sextus, for Lucretia's rape. Brutus could not make the same mistake.

Within less than a year, Brutus, who now passionately despised all Tarquins, led the military defense when Tarquin the Proud's Etruscan allies marched on Rome. Legend has it that one of Tarquin's sons and Brutus clashed head-on, each dying at the hands of the other.

The English novelist E. M. Forster (1879–1970) famously intoned, "If I had to choose between betraying my country and betraying my friend, I hope I should have the guts to betray my country." The Roman historian Plutarch (ca. 45–ca. 120), as evidenced by his description of Lucius Brutus, would probably have agreed: "That ancient Brutus was of a severe and inflexible nature, like steel of too hard a temper, and having never had his character softened by study and thought, he let himself be so far transported with his rage and hatred against tyrants, that, for conspiring with them, he proceeded to the execution even of his own sons."[9]

Machiavelli, however, demurs. For him, "killing the sons of Brutus" becomes a rallying cry for all rulers who understand the requirements of their office and who accept the imperative to sometimes dirty their hands for patriotic purposes.

Hiero II of Syracuse, 308 BCE–216 BCE

Machiavelli praises Hiero for ascending to the monarchy of Syracuse from humble origins (P 6). For Machiavelli, Hiero is a paradigm of military and political *virtù*. His success did not arise from *fortuna*, but from his excellence. Prior to becoming king he was a military commander who defeated a group of Campanian mercenaries, the Mamertines, at Mylae. This military triumph was his springboard to the kingship. A decade later, the Mamertines reengaged in battle with Syracuse. The mercenaries called on Rome for support, while Hiero allied himself with Punic commander Hanno. The battle ended inconclusively, and Hiero negotiated a treaty with Rome to which he remained loyal throughout the rest of his life. He was an especially effective ally during the Punic wars.

Hannibal, CA. 247 BCE–183 BCE

This great military commander of Carthage distinguished himself in the Second Punic War. He won stunning victories at Trebia, Trasimene, and Cannae, earning accolades as a supreme military strategist. Hannibal's forces occupied a significant part of Italy for about fifteen years and lured several of Rome's allies to their side. Only when

Scipio Africanus invaded North Africa did the war swing Rome's way. Hannibal was recalled to defend Carthage, which had suffered devastating losses to the Roman military. Instead of recklessly attacking his enemy, Hannibal understood that a successful future for his country rested with a negotiated settlement and not with war. Thus, he sued for peace. The Romans calculated likewise and spurned Hannibal's overture. Hannibal then gathered for a last stand: either miraculous victory against all odds or a glorious defeat. Scipio defeated Hannibal at the Battle of Zuma. Machiavelli cautions those with less military skill than Hannibal to heed the lessons of his strategy: keep your military ventures realistic and calculate the odds of success carefully (D II 27).

Notes

Introduction

1. Michael Walzer, "Political Action: The Problem of Dirty Hands," *Philosophy and Public Affairs* 2 (1973): 176.

Chapter 1. The Value of Patriotism

1. Pasquale Villari, *The Life and Times of Niccolò Machiavelli*, translated by Linda Villari (London, UK: Ernest Benn Ltd., 1929), 516.
2. Francesco De Sanctis, "Long Live Italian Unity: Glory to Machiavelli," in *Machiavelli: Cynic, Patriot or Political Scientist?*, edited by De Lamar Jensen (Lexington, MA: Heath, 1960), 25–26.
3. Russell Price, "The Senses of *Virtù* in Machiavelli," *European Studies Review* 3 (1973): 315–345.
4. Harvey C. Mansfield, *Machiavelli's Virtue* (Chicago: University of Chicago Press, 1996), 6–7.
5. See, for example, Wayne A. Rebhorn, *Foxes and Lions: Machiavelli's Confidence Men* (Ithaca, NY: Cornell University Press, 1988), 18–19.
6. Although among the papers of Leonardo da Vinci, who recorded the Battle of Anghiari in a mural in the Signoria Palace, are notes in Machiavelli's handwriting that reflect a great number of casualties in that conflict. See Giuseppe Prezzolini, *Machiavelli* (New York: Farrar, Straus and Giroux, 1967), 41. Nevertheless, wars fought in Italy during this time "were not fought by large conscript armies in which tens of thousands of people died on the battlefield. They were fought by small professional mercenary armies led by professional mercenary captains, *condottiere* . . . there was not a huge amount of violence, and very often the wars fought by these professional *condottiere*

were more like ballets rather than actual armed conflicts in which thousands of people were killed." Kenneth R. Bartlett, *The Italians before Italy: Part Two* (Chantilly, VA: Teaching Company, 2007), 193–194.

7. Arthur Murphy, "The Common Good," *Proceedings and Addresses of the American Philosophical Association* 24 (1950): 12.

8. See, for example, Raymond Angelo Belliotti, *Seeking Identity: Individualism and Community in an Ethnic Context* (Lawrence: University Press of Kansas, 1995), ix-xiii, 191–193.

9. Raymond Angelo Belliotti, *Posthumous Harm: Why the Dead Are still Vulnerable* (Lanham, MD: Lexington Books, 2012), 101–134.

10. Russell Price, "The Theme of *Gloria* in Machiavelli," *Renaissance Quarterly* 30 (1977): 588–631.

11. Ibid., 621.

12. Belliotti, *Seeking Identity*, 13–14.

13. See, for example, F. W. Winterbotham, *The Ultra Secret* (London: Weidenfeld and Nicolson, 1974); William Stevenson, *A Man Called Intrepid* (New York: Harcourt, Brace, Jovanovich, 1976); Cave Brown, *Bodyguard of Lies* (New York: Harper and Row, 1974).

14. Christopher Hitchens, "The Medals of His Defeats," *Atlantic Monthly* 289, no. 4 (2002): 128.

15. See, for example, R. V. Jones, *Most Secret War* (London: Hamish Hamilton, 1978); Peter Calvocoressi, *Top Secret Ultra* (New York: Ballantine Books, 1981).

Chapter 2. Religion and Morality

1. Maurizio Viroli, *Machiavelli's God* (Princeton, NJ: Princeton University Press, 2010), 45–46.

2. See, for example, Raymond Angelo Belliotti, *Jesus or Nietzsche: How Should We Live Our Lives?* (Amsterdam, Netherlands: Rodopi Editions, 2013), 13–50, 115–125.

3. Francesco Guicciardini, *Dialogue on the Government of Florence*, edited and translated by Alison Brown (Cambridge, UK: Cambridge University Press, 1994), 159.

4. Isaiah Berlin, *Against the Current* (Princeton, NJ: Princeton University Press, 2001), 74–75.

5. Hannah Arendt, *Lectures on Kant's Political Philosophy*, edited by Ronald Beiner (Chicago: University of Chicago Press, 1989), 50.

6. Compare to Viroli, *Machiavelli's God*, 36.

7. Sebastian De Grazia, *Machiavelli in Hell* (Princeton, NJ: Princeton University Press, 1989), 341.

8. Raymond Angelo Belliotti, *Dante's Deadly Sins: Moral Philosophy in Hell* (Oxford, UK: Wiley-Blackwell, 2011), 157–165.

9. Benedetto Croce, "The Autonomy and Necessity of Politics," in *Machiavelli: Cynic, Patriot or Political Scientist?*, edited by De Lamar Jensen (Lexington, MA: Heath, 1960), 13.

10. Max Lerner, "Introduction," in Niccolò Machiavelli, *The Prince and The Discourses*, edited by Max Lerner (New York: Random House, 1950), xiv.

11. Giuseppe Prezzolini, "The Christian Roots of Machiavelli's Moral Pessimism." *Review of National Literatures* 1 (1970): 28.

12. Berlin, *Against the Current*, 74–75.

13. Ibid., 43–44.

14. Ibid., 44.

15. Tom Holland, *Rubicon* (New York: Doubleday, 2003), 5, 108–149.

16. Ibid., 33, 109, 113, 143.

17. Berlin, *Against the Current*, 71.

18. I have made that mistake more than once. See Raymond Angelo Belliotti, "Machiavelli and Machiavellianism," *Journal of Thought* 13 (1978): 293–300; Raymond Angelo Belliotti and William S. Jacobs, "Two Paradoxes for Machiavelli," *Terrorism, Justice, and Social Values*, edited by Creighton Pedan and Yeager Hudson (Lewiston, NY: Mellen Press, 1990): 1–14.

19. Leo Strauss, *Thoughts on Machiavelli* (Chicago: University of Chicago Press, 1958), 13–14.

20. Ibid., 67.

21. Ibid., 67–68.

22. Niccolò Machiavelli, *The Prince and The Discourses*, translated by Luigi Ricci and revised by E. R. P. Vincent (New York: Random House, 1950), 66.

23. Niccolò Machiavelli, *Selected Political Writings*. Edited and translated by David Wootton (Indianapolis, IN: Hackett Publishing Company, 1994), 55; Dante Germino, "Second Thoughts on Leo Strauss's Machiavelli," *Journal of Politics* 28 (1966): 803–807.

24. See, for example, John Austin, "A Plea for Excuses," *Proceedings of the Aristotelian Society* 57 (1956–1957): 1–5.

25. Germino, "Second Thoughts," 805.

26. Michael Walzer, *Just and Unjust Wars* (New York: Harper Collins, 1977), 254.

27. Russell Price, "The Theme of *Gloria* in Machiavelli," *Renaissance Quarterly* 30 (1977): 628.

Chapter 3. The Problem of Dirty Hands

1. Michael Walzer, "Political Action: The Problem of Dirty Hands," *Philosophy and Public Affairs* 2 (1973): 164.
2. Jean-Paul Sartre, *No Exit and Three Other Plays* (New York: Random House, 1976), Act V, p. 223–224.
3. Martin Hollis, "Dirty Hands," *British Journal of Political Science* 12 (1982): 390.
4. Bernard Williams, "Politics and Moral Character," in *Public and Private Morality*, edited by Stuart Hampshire, (Cambridge, UK: Cambridge University Press, 1978), 59.
5. S. L. Sutherland, "The Problem of Dirty Hands in Politics," *Canadian Journal of Political Science* 28 (1995): 482–483.
6. Thomas Nagel, *Mortal Questions* (Cambridge, UK: Cambridge University Press, 1979), 133.
7. Stuart Hampshire, "Public and Private Morality," in *Public and Private Morality*, edited by Stuart Hampshire, (Cambridge, UK: Cambridge University Press), 50.
8. See, for example, Larry Alexander, "Deontology at the Threshold," *San Diego Law Review*, 37 (2000): 893–912; Anthony Ellis, "Deontology, Incommensurability and the Arbitrary," *Philosophical and Phenomenological Research*, 52 (1992): 855–875.
9. Walzer, "Political Action," 171, 161.
10. Ibid., 168.
11. Ibid., 179.
12. See, for example, Gerald F. Gaus, "Dirty Hands," in *A Companion to Applied Ethics*, edited by R. G. Frey and Christopher Wellman (Oxford, UK: Blackwell Publishers, 2003): 167–79; H. Oberdiek, "Clean and Dirty Hands in Politics," *International Journal of Moral and Social Studies* 1 (1986): 41–61; R. M. Hare, *Essays in Political Morality* (Oxford, UK: Clarendon Press, 1989).
13. Oberdiek, "Clean and Dirty Hands," 53–54.
14. See, for example, Benedetto Croce, "The Autonomy and Necessity of Politics," in *Machiavelli: Cynic, Patriot or Political Scientist?*, edited by De Lamar Jensen (Lexington, MA: Heath, 1960), 13–16.
15. See, for example, Walzer, "Political Action," 175.
16. Sebastian De Grazia, *Machiavelli in Hell* (Princeton, NJ: Princeton University Press, 1989), 351.
17. Ibid., 323.
18. Niccolò Machiavelli, "An Exhortation to Penitence," in *The Chief Works and Others*, edited and translated by Allan H. Gilbert (Durham, NC: Duke University Press, 1989), 170–174.

19. Williams, "Politics and Moral Character," 64.
20. Walzer, *Just and Unjust Wars*, 264.
21. Ibid., 266–267.
22. Ibid., 267–268.
23. Michael Walzer, *Arguing about War* (New Haven, CT: Yale University Press, 2004), 46.
24. Walzer, "Political Action," 162–164.
25. See, for example, Walzer, *Arguing about War*, 46; *Just and Unjust War* (New York: Basic Books, 1977); "Terrorism and Just War," *Philosophia* 32 (2006): 3–12.
26. Henry A. Wallace, *The Price of Vision: The Diary of Henry A. Wallace, 1942–1946*, edited by John Blum (Boston: Houghton Mifflin, 1973), 473–474.
27. Alan H. Goldman, *The Moral Foundations of Professional Ethics* (Totowa, NJ: Rowman and Littlefield, 1980), 70–73.
28. Peter Digeser, "Forgiveness and Politics: Dirty Hands and Imperfect Procedures," *Political Theory* 26 (1998): 721 n.19.
29. Michael Stocker, *Plural and Conflicting Values* (Oxford, UK: Clarendon Press, 1990), 9–36.
30. Ibid., 18.
31. Harvey Mansfield, *Machiavelli's Virtue* (Chicago: University of Chicago Press, 1996), 27.
32. Raymond Angelo Belliotti, *Roman Philosophy and the Good Life* (Lanham, MD: Lexington Books, 2009), 107–109, 143–151, 158–177.
33. Rafael Sabatini, *The Life of Cesare Borgia* (Teddington, UK: Echo Library, 2006), 166–167.

Chapter 4. The Soul of the Statesman

1. Michael Walzer, "Political Action: The Problem of Dirty Hands," *Philosophy and Public Affairs* 2 (1973): 179.
2. Ibid.
3. Ibid.
4. Leo Strauss, *Thoughts on Machiavelli* (Chicago: University of Chicago Press, 1958), 190.
5. See, for example, Suzanne Dovi, "Guilt and the Problem of Dirty Hands," *Constellations* 12 (2005): 128–137.
6. Ibid., 137–143.
7. Walzer, "Political Action," 176.
8. Ibid., 177.

9. Raymond Angelo Belliotti, *Dante's Deadly Sins: Moral Philosophy in Hell* (Oxford, UK: Wiley-Blackwell, 2011), 84–87.

10. Raymond Angelo Belliotti, *Posthumous Harm: Why the Dead Are Still Vulnerable* (Lanham, MD: Lexington Books, 2012), 6–8, 10–16, 93–94, 110–114.

11. Luigi Barzini, *The Italians* (New York: Atheneum Publishers, 1964), 171.

12. Laurence Arthur Burd, "Introduction," in Niccolò Machiavelli, *Il Principe*, edited by Laurence Arthur Burd (Oxford, UK: Clarendon Press, 1891), 26.

13. Erica Benner, *Machiavelli's Ethics* (Princeton, NJ: Princeton University Press, 2009), 326.

14. Ibid., 348–349.

15. Ibid., 340.

16. Ibid., 358–360.

17. Ibid., 360, 343.

18. Ibid., 439–440.

19. Ruth W. Grant, *Hypocrisy and Integrity* (Chicago: University of Chicago Press, 1997), 13.

20. Ibid.

21. Ibid., 45.

22. Ibid., 52.

23. Ibid., 21.

24. Ibid., 49.

25. John P. McCormick, *Machiavellian Democracy* (New York: Cambridge University Press, 2011), viii.

26. Ibid., 6.

27. Ibid., 3.

28. Barzini, *The Italians*, 165–166.

Appendix B Machiavelli's Life and Times

1. Kenneth Bartlett. *The Italian Renaissance: Part Three* (Chantilly, VA: Teaching Company, 2005), 103–104, 105.

2. Sebastian De Grazia, *Machiavelli in Hell* (Princeton, NJ: Princeton University Press, 1989), 36.

3. See, for example, Eric W. Cochrane, "Machiavelli: 1940–1960," *Journal of Modern History* 33 (1961): 131–133; John H. Geerken, "Machiavelli Studies since 1969," *Journal of the History of Ideas* 37 (1976): 357–359.

Appendix C Case Studies—Heroes and Villains

1. Niccolò Machiavelli, *Lust and Liberty: The Poems of Machiavelli.* Translated and edited by Joseph Tisiani (New York: Ivan Obolensky, 1963), 47.

2. Rafael Sabatini, *The Life of Cesare Borgia* (Teddington, UK: Echo Library, 2006), preface, 162.

3. Ibid., 61–71.

4. Garrett Mattingly, "Machiavelli," in *Renaissance Profiles*, edited by J. H. Plumb (New York: Harper and Row, 1961), 26–27.

5. Sabatini, *Borgia*, 193.

6. Ibid., 187–188, 193–194.

7. Ibid., 125–126.

8. See, for example, John Noble Wilford, "More Clues in the Legend (or Is It Fact?) of Romulus," *New York Times*, June 12, 2007; Peter Kiefer, "Cave May Hold Secrets to Legend of Ancient Rome," *New York Times*, November 21, 2007.

9. Plutarch, *The Lives of the Noble Grecians and Romans*, translated by John Dryden, edited and revised by Arthur Hugh Clough, vol. 2 (New York: Modern Library, 1992), 572.

Bibliography

Books

Anglo, Sydney. *Machiavelli: A Dissection*. New York: Harcourt, Brace and World, 1969.
Arendt, Hannah. *Lectures on Kant's Political Philosophy*, edited by Ronald Beiner. Chicago: University of Chicago Press, 1989.
Aristotle. *Nicomachean Ethics*, translated by Martin Ostwald. Indianapolis, IN: Bobbs-Merrill, 1962.
Barincou, Edmond. *Machiavelli*. New York: Grove Press, 1961.
Baron, Hans. *The Crisis of the Early Italian Renaissance*. Rev. ed. Princeton, NJ: Princeton University Press, 1966.
Bartlett, Kenneth. *The Italian Renaissance: Part Three*. Chantilly, VA: Teaching Company, 2005.
———. *The Italians before Italy: Part Two*. Chantilly, VA: Teaching Company, 2007.
Barzini, Luigi. *The Italians*. New York: Atheneum Publishers, 1964.
Belliotti, Raymond Angelo. *Dante's Deadly Sins: Moral Philosophy in Hell*. Oxford, UK: Wiley-Blackwell, 2011.
———. *Happiness Is Overrated*. Lanham, MD: Rowman and Littlefield, 2004.
———. *Jesus or Nietzsche: How Should We Live Our Lives?* Amsterdam, Netherlands: Rodopi Editions, 2013.
———. *Justifying Law*. Philadelphia, PA: Temple University Press, 1992.
———. *The Philosophy of Baseball: How to Play the Game of Life*. Lewiston, NY: Mellen Press, 2006 (chap. 3).
———. *Posthumous Harm: Why the Dead Are still Vulnerable*. Lanham, MD: Lexington Books, 2012.
———. *Roman Philosophy and the Good Life*. Lanham, MD: Lexington Books, 2009.
———. *Seeking Identity: Individualism versus Community in an Ethnic Context*. Lawrence: University Press of Kansas, 1995.

———. *Stalking Nietzsche*. Westport, CT: Greenwood, 1998.
———. *What Is the Meaning of Human Life?* Amsterdam, Netherlands: Rodopi Editions, 2001.
Belliotti, Raymond Angelo, and William S. Jacobs. "Two Paradoxes for Machiavelli." In *Terrorism, Justice, and Social Values*, edited by Creighton Pedan and Yeager Hudson, 1–14. Lewiston, NY: Mellen Press, 1990.
Benner, Erica. *Machiavelli's Ethics*. Princeton, NJ: Princeton University Press, 2009.
Berlin, Isaiah. *Against the Current*. Princeton, NJ: Princeton University Press, 2001.
Boatwright, Mary T., Daniel Gargola, and Richard J. A. Talbert. *The Romans*. New York: Oxford University Press, 2004.
Bock, Gisela, Quentin Skinner, and Maurizio Viroli, eds. *Machiavelli and Republicanism*. Cambridge, UK: Cambridge University Press, 1990.
Brown, Cave. *Bodyguard of Lies*. New York: Harper and Row, 1974.
Burd, Laurence Arthur. "Introduction." In Niccolò Machiavelli, *Il Principe*, edited by Laurence Arthur Burd, 26. Oxford, UK: Clarendon Press, 1891.
Butterfield, Herbert. *The Statecraft of Machiavelli*. London, UK: Bell, 1940.
Calvocoressi, Peter. *Top Secret Ultra*. New York: Ballantine Books, 1981.
Caranta, Angelo. *Machiavelli Rethought: A Critique of Strauss' Machiavelli*. Washington, DC: University Press of America, 1978.
Cassirer, Ernst. *The Myth of the State*. Garden City, NY: Doubleday Anchor, 1955.
Chabod, Fredrico. *Machiavelli and the Renaissance*. London: Bowes and Bowes, 1958.
Coady, C. A. J. "Politics and the Problem of Dirty Hands." In *A Companion to Ethics*, edited by Peter Singer, 373–383. Malden, MA: Blackwell, 1993.
Croce, Benedetto. "The Autonomy and Necessity of Politics." In *Machiavelli: Cynic, Patriot or Political Scientist?*, edited by De Lamar Jensen. Lexington, MA: Heath, 1960.
De Grazia, Sebastian. *Machiavelli in Hell*. Princeton, NJ: Princeton University Press, 1989.
De Sanctis, Francesco. "Long Live Italian Unity: Glory to Machiavelli." In *Machiavelli: Cynic, Patriot or Political Scientist?*, edited by De Lamar Jensen, 25–26. Lexington, MA: Heath, 1960.
Falco, Maria J. *Feminist Interpretations of Niccolò Machiavelli*. University Park: Pennsylvania State University Press, 2004.
Fleisher, Martin, ed. *Machiavelli and the Nature of Political Thought*. New York: Atheneum Publishers, 1972.

Fontana, Benedetto. *Hegemony and Power.* Minneapolis, MN: University of Minnesota Press, 1993.
Fusero, Clemente. *Cesare Borgia.* London: Pall Mall Press, 1972.
Gaus, Gerald F. "Dirty Hands." In *A Companion to Applied Ethics,* edited by R. G. Frey and Christopher Wellman, 167–179. Oxford, UK: Blackwell, 2003.
Gibbon, Edward. *The Decline and Fall of the Roman Empire,* vols. 1–3. New York: Everyman's Library, 1993.
Gilbert, Felix. *Machiavelli and Guicciardini.* Princeton, NJ: Princeton University Press, 1965.
Goldman, Alan H. *The Moral Foundations of Professional Ethics.* Totowa, NJ: Rowman and Littlefield, 1980.
Grant, Ruth W. *Hypocrisy and Integrity.* Chicago: University of Chicago Press, 1997.
Guicciardini, Francesco. *Dialogue on the Government of Florence,* edited and translated by Alison Brown. Cambridge, UK: Cambridge University Press, 1994.
———. *Maxims and Reflections,* edited and translated by Mario Domandi. Philadelphia: University of Pennsylvania Press, 1972.
———. *Selected Writings.* Edited by Cecil Grayson. Oxford, UK: Oxford University Press, 1965.
Hadas, Moses, ed. *Essential Works of Stoicism.* New York: Bantam Books, 1960.
Hampshire, Stuart, ed. *Public and Private Morality.* Cambridge, UK: Cambridge University Press, 1978.
Hare, R. M. *Essays in Political Morality.* Oxford, UK: Clarendon Press, 1989.
Holland, Tom. *Rubicon.* New York: Doubleday, 2003.
Holy Bible. King James Version (1611). Nashville, TN: Nelson Publishers, 1990.
Hulliung, Mark. *Citizen Machiavelli.* Princeton, NJ: Princeton University Press, 1983.
Jensen, De Lamar, ed. *Machiavelli: Cynic, Patriot, or Political Scientist?* Lexington, MA: Heath, 1960.
Jones, R. V. *Most Secret War.* London: Hamish Hamilton, 1978.
Lerner, Max. "Introduction." In Niccolò Machiavelli, *The Prince and The Discourses,* edited by Max Lerner, xiv. New York: Random House, 1950.
Machiavelli, Niccolò. *The Art of War.* Edited and translated by Neal Wood. Cambridge, MA: De Capo Press, 1965.
———. *The Chief Works and Others.* Edited and translated by Allan H. Gilbert. Durham, NC: Duke University Press, 1989.
———. "An Exhortation to Penitence." In *The Chief Works and Others.* Edited and translated by Allan H. Gilbert, 179–174. Durham, NC: Duke University Press, 1989.

———. *Florentine Histories*. Edited and translated by Laura F. Banfield and Harvey C. Mansfield. Princeton, NJ: Princeton University Press, 1988.

———. *Il Principe*. Edited by Laurence Arthur Burd. Oxford, UK: Clarendon Press, 1891.

———. *The Letters of Machiavelli*. Edited and translated by Allan Gilbert. Chicago, IL: University of Chicago Press, 1961.

———. *The Life of Castruccio Castracani*. Translated by Andrew Brown. London: Hesperus Press, 2003.

———. *Lust and Liberty: The Poems of Machiavelli*. Edited and translated by Joseph Tusiani. New York: Ivan Obolensky, 1963.

———. *Machiavelli and His Friends: Their Personal Correspondence*. Edited and translated by James B. Atkinson and David Sices. DeKalb: Northern Illinois University Press, 1996.

———. *Mandragola*. Translated by Mera J. Flaumenhaft. Prospect Heights, IL: Waveland Press, 1981.

———. *The Prince and Selected Discourses*. Edited and translated by Daniel Donno. New York: Bantam Books, 1966.

———. *The Prince and The Discourses*. Translated by Luigi Ricci and revised by E. R. P. Vincent. New York: Random House, 1950.

———. *Selected Political Writings*. Edited and translated by David Wootton. Indianapolis, IN: Hackett Publishing, 1994.

Mansfield, Harvey C. *Machiavelli's Virtue*. Chicago: University of Chicago Press, 1996.

Mattingly, Garrett. "Machiavelli." In *Renaissance Profiles*, edited by J. H. Plumb, 26–27. New York: Harper and Row, 1961.

Matyszak, Philip. *Chronicle of the Roman Republic*. New York: Thames and Hudson, 2003.

McCormick, John P. *Machiavellian Democracy*. New York: Cambridge University Press, 2011.

Nagel, Thomas. *Mortal Questions*. Cambridge, UK: Cambridge University Press, 1979.

Najemy, John M. *Between Friends*. Princeton, NJ: Princeton University Press, 1993.

Nietzsche, Friedrich. *Beyond Good and Evil* (1886). Translated and edited by Walter Kaufmann. New York: Random House, 1966.

———. *Thus Spoke Zarathustra* (1883–1885). In *The Portable Nietzsche*. Translated by Walter Kaufmann. New York: Viking Press, 1954.

———. *The Will to Power* (from unpublished notebooks, 1883–1888). Edited by Walter Kaufmann, translated by Walter Kaufmann and R. J. Hollingdale. New York: Random House, 1967.

Olschki, Leonardo. *Machiavelli the Scientist*. Berkeley, CA: Gillick Press, 1945.

Parel, Anthony, J. *The Machiavellian Cosmos*. New Haven, CT: Yale University Press, 1992.
———, editor. *The Political Calculus*. Toronto, ON: University of Toronto Press, 1972.
Pitkin, Hanna. *Fortune Is a Woman*. Berkeley, CA: University of California Press, 1984.
Plato. *The Statesman*. Translated by J. B. Skemp. In *Plato: Collected Dialogues*, edited by Edith Hamilton and Huntington Cairns. Princeton, NJ: Princeton University Press, 1973.
Plumb, J. H., editor. *Renaissance Profiles*. New York: Harper and Row, 1961.
Plutarch. *The Lives of the Noble Grecians and Romans*. Translated by John Dryden, edited and revised by Arthur Hugh Clough, vols. 1 and 2. New York: Modern Library, 1992).
Pocock, J. A .G. *The Machiavellian Moment*. Princeton, NJ: Princeton University Press, 1975.
Prezzolini, Giuseppe. *Machiavelli*. New York: Farrar, Strauss and Giroux, 1967.
Rebhorn, Wayne A. *Foxes and Lions: Machiavelli's Confidence Men*. Ithaca, NY: Cornell University Press, 1988.
Ridolfi, Roberto. *The Life of Niccolò Machiavelli*. Translated by Cecil Grayson. Chicago: University of Chicago Press, 1963.
Sabatini, Rafael. *The Life of Cesare Borgia*. Teddington, UK: Echo Library, 2006.
Sacerdote, Gustavo. *Cesare Borgia*. Milan, IT: Mondadori-Medusa Publishers, 1950.
Sartre, Jean-Paul. *No Exit and Three Other Plays*. New York: Random House, 1976.
Skinner, Quentin. *Machiavelli*. Oxford, UK: Oxford University Press, 1981.
Stevenson, William. *A Man Called Intrepid*. New York: Harcourt, Brace, Jovanovich, 1976.
Stocker, Michael. *Plural and Conflicting Values*. Oxford, UK: Clarendon Press, 1990.
Strauss, Leo. *Thoughts on Machiavelli*. Chicago: University of Chicago Press, 1958.
Styron, William. *Sophie's Choice*. New York: Random House, 1979.
Villari, Pasquale. *The Life and Times of Niccolò Machiavelli*. Translated by Linda Villari. London: Ernest Benn, 1929.
Viroli, Maurizio. *Machiavelli*. New York: Oxford University Press, 1998.
———. *Machiavelli's God*. Princeton, NJ: Princeton University Press, 2010.
———. *Niccolò's Smile: A Biography of Machiavelli*. New York: Farrar, Straus and Giroux, 2000.
Wallace, Henry A. *The Price of Vision: The Diary of Henry A. Wallace, 1942–1946*. Edited by John Blum. Boston: Houghton Mifflin, 1973.

Walzer, Michael. *Arguing about War.* New Haven, CT: Yale University Press, 2004.
——. *Just and Unjust Wars.* New York: Harper Collins, 1977.
Whitfield, J. H. *Machiavelli.* Oxford, UK: Blackwell Publishers, 1947.
Williams, Bernard. "Politics and Moral Character." In *Public and Private Morality*, edited by Stuart Hampshire, 59. Cambridge, UK: Cambridge University Press, 1978.
Winterbotham, F. W. *The Ultra Secret.* London: Weidenfeld and Nicolson, 1974.
Zinn, Howard. *A People's History of the United States.* New York: Harper Collins, 1980.

Articles

Alexander, Larry. "Deontology at the Threshold." *San Diego Law Review*, 37 (2000): 893–912.
Austin, John. "A Plea for Excuses." *Proceedings of the Aristotelian Society* 57 (1956–1957): 1–5.
Belliotti, Raymond Angelo. "Machiavelli and Machiavellianism." *Journal of Thought* 13 (1978): 293–300.
Bertelli, Sergio. "Machiavelli and Soderini." *Renaissance Quarterly* 28 (1975): 1–16.
Bonadanella, Peter E. "Castruccio Castracani: Machiavelli's Archetypal Prince." *Italica* 49 (1972): 302–314.
Brudney, Kent M. "Machiavelli on Social Class and Class Conflict." *Political Theory* 12 (1984): 507–519.
Cochrane, Eric W. "Machiavelli: 1940–1960." *Journal of Modern History* 33(1961): 113–136.
Colish, Marcia L. "Machiavelli's *Art of War*: A Reconsideration." *Renaissance Quarterly* 51 (1998): 1151–1168.
D'Amico, Jack. "Three Forms of Character: *Virtù, Ordini* and *Materia* in Machiavelli's *Discorsi.*" *Italian Quarterly* 22 (1981): 5–13.
Dietz, Mary. "Trapping the Prince: Machiavelli and the Politics of Deception." *American Political Science Review* 80 (1986): 777–799.
Digeser, Peter. "Forgiveness and Politics: Dirty Hands and Imperfect Procedures." *Political Theory* 26 (1998): 700–724.
DiMaria, Salvatore. "Machiavelli's Ironic View of History." *Renaissance Quarterly* 45 (1992): 248–270.
Douglass, Bruce. "The Common Good and the Public Interest." *Political Theory* 8 (1980): 103–117.
Dovi, Suzanne. "Guilt and the Problem of Dirty Hands." *Constellations* 12 (2005): 128–146.

Ellis, Anthony. "Deontology, Incommensurability and the Arbitrary." *Philosophical and Phenomenological Research*, 52 (1992): 855–875.
Fallon, Stephen M. "Hunting the Fox: Equivocation and Authorial Duplicity in *The Prince*." *PMLA* 107 (1992): 1181–1195.
Ferrero, Guglielmo. "Machiavelli and Machiavellism." *Foreign Affairs* 17 (1939): 569–577.
Fontana, Benedetto. "Love of Country and Love of God: The Political Uses of Religion in Machiavelli." *Journal of the History of Ideas* 60 (1999): 639–658.
Geerken, John H. "Machiavelli Studies since 1969." *Journal of the History of Ideas* 37 (1976): 351–368.
———. "Machiavelli's Moses and Renaissance Politics." *Journal of the History of Ideas* 60 (1999): 579–595.
Germino, Dante. "Second Thoughts on Leo Strauss's Machiavelli." *Journal of Politics* 28 (1966): 794–817.
Gilbert, Felix. "On Machiavelli's Idea of *Virtù*." *Renaissance News* 4 (1951): 53–55.
Hitchens, Christopher. "The Medals of His Defeats." *Atlantic Monthly* 289, no. 4 (2002): 118–137.
Hollis, Martin. "Dirty Hands." *British Journal of Political Science* 12 (1982): 385–398.
Howard, W. Kenneth. "Must Public Hands Be Dirty?" *Journal of Value Inquiry* 11 (1977): 29–40.
Ingersoll, David E. "The Constant Prince: Private Interests and Public Goals in Machiavelli." *Western Political Quarterly* 21 (1968): 588–596.
Kahn, Victoria. "*Virtù* and the Example of Agathocles in Machiavelli's *Prince*." *Representations* 13 (1986): 63–83.
Kiefer, Peter, "Cave May Hold Secrets to Legend of Ancient Rome," *New York Times*, November 21, 2007.
Kraft, Joseph. "Truth and Poetry in Machiavelli." *Journal of Modern History* 23 (1951): 109–121.
Langton, John, and Mary Dietz. "Machiavelli's Paradox: Trapping or Teaching The Prince?" *American Political Science Review* 81 (1987): 1277–1288.
Lodge, Sir Richard. "Machiavelli's *Il Principe*." *Transactions of the Royal Historical Society* 13 (1930): 1–16.
Lukes, Timothy J. "Lionizing Machiavelli." *American Political Science Review* 95 (2001): 561–575.
Mansfield, Harvey C. "Strauss's Machiavelli." *Political Theory* 3 (1975): 372–384.
Maritain, Jacques. "The End of Machiavellianism," *Review of Politics* 4 (1942): 9–32.
Mattingly, Garrett. "Machiavelli's *Prince*: Political Science or Political Satire?" *American Scholar* 27 (1958): 482–491.

Moravia, Alberto. "Portrait of Machiavelli." *Partisan Review* 22 (1955): 357–371.
Murphy, Arthur E. "The Common Good." *Proceedings and Addresses of the American Philosophical Association* 24 (1950): 3–18.
Najemy, John M. "Machiavelli and the Medici: The Lessons of Florentine History." *Renaissance Quarterly* 35 (1982): 551–576.
Nicholls, Rod. "Ghosts, God and the Problem of Dirty Hands." *Ars Disputandi* 4 (2004): 1–21.
Oberdiek, H. "Clean and Dirty Hands in Politics." *International Journal of Moral and Social Studies* 1 (1986): 41–61.
Parkinson, G. H. R. "Ethics and Politics in Machiavelli." *Philosophical Quarterly* 5 (1955): 37–44.
Preus, J. Samuel. "Machiavelli's Functional Analysis of Religion: Context and Object." *Journal of the History of Ideas* 40 (1979): 171–190.
Prezzolini, Giuseppe. "The Christian Roots of Machiavelli's Moral Pessimism." *Review of National Literatures* 1 (1970): 26–37.
Price, Russell. "The Senses of *Virtù* in Machiavelli." *European Studies Review* 3 (1973): 315–345.
———. "The Theme of *Gloria* in Machiavelli. *Renaissance Quarterly* 30 (1977): 588–631.
Scott, John T., and Vickie B. Sullivan. "Patricide and the Plot of *The Prince*." *American Political Science Review* 88 (1994): 887–900.
Sutherland, S. L. "The Problem of Dirty Hands in Politics." *Canadian Journal of Political Science* 28 (1995): 479–507.
Thompson, Dennis F. "Moral Responsibility of Public Officials: The Problem of Many Hands." *American Political Science Review* 74 (1980): 905–916.
Voegelin, Eric." Machiavelli's Prince: Background and Formation." *Review of Politics* 13 (1951): 142–168.
Walzer, Michael. "Political Action: The Problem of Dirty Hands." *Philosophy and Public Affairs* 2 (1973): 160–180.
———. "Terrorism and Just War," *Philosophia* 32 (2006): 3–12.
Wilde, Norman. "Machiavelli." *International Journal of Ethics* 38 (1928): 212–225.
Wilford, John Noble. "More Clues in the Legend (or Is It Fact?) of Romulus." *New York Times*, June 12, 2007.
Wood, Neal. "Machiavelli's Concept of *Virtù* Reconsidered." *Political Studies* 15 (1967): 159–172.

About the Author

Raymond Angelo Belliotti is SUNY Distinguished Teaching Professor of Philosophy at the State University of New York at Fredonia. He received his undergraduate degree from Union College in 1970, after which he was conscripted into the U.S. Army where he served three years in military intelligence units during the Vietnam War. Upon his discharge, he enrolled at the University of Miami where he earned his Master of Arts in 1976 and his doctorate in 1977. After teaching at Florida International University and Virginia Commonwealth University, he entered Harvard University as a law student and teaching fellow. After receiving a juris doctorate from Harvard Law School, he practiced law in New York City with the firm of Barrett Smith Schapiro Simon and Armstrong. In 1984 he joined the faculty at Fredonia.

Belliotti is the author of fifteen other books: *Justifying Law* (1992); *Good Sex* (1993); *Seeking Identity* (1995); *Stalking Nietzsche* (1998); *What Is the Meaning of Human Life?* (2001); *Happiness Is Overrated* (2004); *The Philosophy of Baseball* (2006); *Watching Baseball Seeing Philosophy* (2008); *Niccolò Machiavelli* (2008); *Roman Philosophy and the Good Life* (2009); *Dante's Deadly Sins: Moral Philosophy in Hell* (2011); *Posthumous Harm: Why the Dead Are Still Vulnerable* (2011); *Shakespeare and Philosophy* (2012); *Jesus or Nietzsche: How Should We Live Our Lives?* (2013); and *Jesus the Radical: The Parables and Modern Morality* (2014). *Good Sex* was later translated into Korean and published in Asia. *What Is the Meaning of Human Life?* was nominated for the Society for Phenomenology and Existential Philosophy's Book of the Year Award. He has also published seventy articles and twenty-five reviews in the areas of ethics, jurisprudence, sexual morality, medicine, politics, education, feminism, sports, Marxism, and legal ethics. These essays have appeared in scholarly journals based in Australia, Canada, Great Britain, Italy, Mexico, South Africa, Sweden, and the United States. Belliotti has also made numerous presentations at philosophical conferences, including the

Eighteenth World Congress of Philosophy in England and has been a featured lecturer on the *Queen Elizabeth 2* ocean liner.

While at SUNY Fredonia Belliotti has served extensively on campus committees, including as the chairperson of the Department of Philosophy, as the chairperson of the University Senate, and as director of General Education. Belliotti also served as Vice President for Academics for the local United University Professions. For six years he was faculty advisor to two undergraduate student clubs: the Philosophical Society and *Il Circolo Italiano*. Belliotti has been the recipient of the SUNY Chancellor's Award for Excellence in Teaching, the William T. Hagan Young Scholar/Artist Award, the Kasling Lecture Award for Excellence in Research and Scholarship, and the SUNY Foundation Research & Scholarship Recognition Award. He was also a member of the New York State Speakers in the Humanities Program from 2006–2014.

Index

Absolutism, strict, 89
Agathocles of Syracuse, 20–22, 35, 125–126, 128, 136, 184
Alexander VI, Pope, 6, 172, 185, 188–190, 192, 193
Alighieri, Dante, ix, 64, 139, 141, 143
ambizione, 23, 25, 29, 52, 79, 163
Anghiari, Battle of, 27, 197n.6
animo effeminato, 20, 35, 37, 50
Aristotle, 147–148, 154
Arendt, Hannah, 58
Arnold, Benedict, 34
Augustine, St., 63, 66–67

Baglioni, Giovampagolo, 38–39, 127, 128, 140, 188
Bartlett, Kenneth, 173
Barzini, Luigi, 150, 164
Bayle, Pieree, 158
Benner, Erica, 157–159
Berlin, Isaiah, 56, 67–70, 79
Bluebeard, 34
Borgia, Cesare, 6, 57, 103, 116, 125, 127–128, 172–173, 182–183, 188–193
Botticelli, Sandro, 185
Brutus, Lucius Junius, 103, 128, 129, 194–195
Brutus, Marcus Junius, 182

Buonacorsi, Biagio, 176
Buonarroti, Michelangelo, 178, 185
Burd, Laurence, 153
Bush, George H. W., 46

Caesar, (Gaius) Julius, 21, 124–125, 128, 181–182
Callimaco, 104
Casavecchia, Filippo, 176
Cassius, Gaius, 182
Castracani, Castruccio, 176
Cato the Younger, 182
Charles V, King, 177
Charles VIII, King, 171, 185, 186
Christ, 34, 55–57, 67, 83–84
Christianity, 49–52, 57–59, 67–70
Church, Catholic, 10, 49–52, 53–59, 67–70
  and Guicciardini, 153
Church, Christian, 3, 55
Churchill, Winston, 2, 3, 42–44, 110–111
civic *virtù*, 8–9, 16–17, 18–24, 27
Clement VII, Pope, 177–178
clues, to Machiavelli's views, 3–4, 64–73, 78–81, 132–135
common good, 23, 29–32, 55–59, 68, 80–81
The Conquest of Gaul, 181

consequentialism, 92–97
  rule version, 93–95
  strong version, 92–93, 96
  tribal act version, 71–72
  weak version of, 93, 96–97
Corsini, Marietta di Ludovico, 173
Coventry, 2, 3, 42–44, 110–111
Crassus, Marcus Licinius, 181
Croce, Benedetto, 64–65
Cyrus (the Great), 6, 57

da Vinci, Leonardo, 34
del Nero, Francesco, 176
deontology, 90, 90–92, 94–95, 96–101
  flexible version, 90, 94, 95
  Machiavellian version, 96–101
  threshold version, 90–92
De Sanctis, Francesco, 7
Diderot, Denis, 158
D'Orco, Remiro, 191–192
Digeser, Peter, 115
dirty hands, 1–4, 78–81, 83–130, 134–135
  and case studies, 107–113
  and historical military leaders, 124–130
  and Guicciardini, 156–157
  and Machiavelli, 101–107, 122–124
  and moral theory, 89–101
  and partial excuses, 113–122
  and remorse, 144–145
  and ways they occur, 83–88
Discourses on the First Decade of Titus Livius, 8, 49–52
"Duke Valentino," *see* Cesare Borgia

Eight Saints, War of, 5
ends and means, 33, 73–74, 76–78
"ends justify the means," 33, 73–74, 76–78, 105–106

Euffreducci, Oliverotto (da Fermo), 125, 128, 182–183
evil, ill-/well-used, 8, 33, 40, 47, 77–78, 133, 148
excuses, 42–44, 74–78, 99–101, 106–107, 113–122
  partial, 113–122
  triggers for, 113–122
expansionism as goal of governments, 13, 23

Ferrante, King, 170
"a few ends excuse some means," 79–81, 103–107, 113–124
Florentine Histories, 27, 58, 176, 177
Fogliani, Giovanni, 182
Forster, E. M., 195
fortuna/Fortuna, 7, 14, 17, 19, 24, 35–39
Fortuna is a lady, 36–37
fox, qualities of, 20, 68
Freud, Sigmund, 59

Galileo, Galilei, 178
glory, 8, 13, 16, 21, 23, 33–39, 59–64, 139
"the good end justifies every means," 74–75, 79–81, 122
grandezza d'animo, 7, 13, 17, 24, 26–27, 35, 37, 163
  and Guicciardini, 156
Grant, Ruth, 160–161
deGrazia, Sebastian, 175
Gregory XI, Pope, 5
Guicciardini, Francesco, 3, 61, 149–157, 159, 176
guilt, 141–143, 144–145

Hampshire, Stuart, 88
Hannibal, 130, 195–196
Hiero II, 130, 195

human nature, 16–17, 29–32,
    41–42, 151
  and Guicciardini, 153–154
human temperaments, 37
Hurricane Katrina, 36
Hurricane Sandy, 36

Ideal Observer, 39, 86, 95, 97–99,
    101, 119, 131
immortality, quest for, 33–39, 59–64
Index of Prohibited Books, 178
Iran-Contra, affair of, 2, 45–47, 111

Jesus, 34, 55–57, 67, 83–84
Julius II, Pope, 6, 38, 189–190,
    192, 193
justifications, 42–44, 74–78, 99–101,
    116–118

Kantianism, 86
Kennedy, John F., 144

La dolce vita, 26, 188
The Legations, 176
Leo X, Pope, 176, 187
Life of Castruccio Castracani, 176
Lincoln, Abraham, 114
lion, qualities of, 20, 68
Livy, 61, 169, 173
Longfellow, Henry Wadsworth, 80
Lorenzo the Magnificent.
    See de'Medici, Lorenzo
Louis XII, King, 189
Lucretia, 194
Lycurgus, 101

Machiavelli, Niccolò
  and clues about the inner life of
    statesmen, 3–4, 132–135
  and corollary principle of
    morality, 78–81

and dirty hands, 101–107,
    122–124
and morality, 64–73
and power 134–135
legacy of, 157–164
life and times, 164–178
popular view of his position on
    morality, 73–74
public service of, 6
See also Statesman
Machiavelli and Nietzsche, 26–27
Mandragola, 61, 104, 161, 176
Mansfield, Harvey, 21–22, 122
Manson, Charles, 34
Marxism, 12, 59, 98
masses, 24, 151
  misled by appearances, 27, 33,
    74–75, 122
McCormick, John, 162–163
de'Medici, Giovanni, 175
de'Medici, Giuliano, 175, 177–178
de'Medici, Giulio, 169–170, 177
de'Medici, Lorenzo, 169–170,
    175, 177
de'Medici, Piero, 170–171
military strength, primacy of, 28–29
military *virtù*, 8, 17, 19–22, 125–126
morality:
  and dirty hands, 89–101
  and religion, 2–3, 48–81
  flexible deontology, 90, 94, 95
  Machiavellian deontology, 96–101
  rule consequentialism, 93–95
  strict absolutism, 89
  strong consequentialism, 92–93, 96
  tribal act consequentialism, 71–72
  threshold deontology, 90–92
  weak consequentialism, 93, 96–97
morality, conventional, 3
  and dirty hands, 83–88, 89–101
  and Machiavelli, 64–73

moral optimism/pessimism, 42–44, 99–101, 101–107, 111–113, 116–118
moral pessimist: Machiavelli as, 101–107
moral *virtù*, 8–9, 16–17, 18–24, 27, 31–32, 125–126
Moses, 6, 52–53, 56–57, 62, 75, 101, 103, 104, 116, 128, 179–180, 186
Murphy, Arthur, 30

Nagel, Thomas, 87–88
neutrality, avoidance of, 126–127, 173–175
Newton, Isaac, 171
Nietzsche, Friedrich, 26–27, 34, 50, 59, 164
North, Oliver, 45–47
Numa Pompilius, 52–53, 54, 129–130, 180–181
and Guicciardini, 152

Oliverotto da Fermo, 125, 128, 182–183
Orsini, family of, 190–191, 192
Ozio, 20, 24, 26, 50

partialism, case for, 40–42, 87–88, 97–98
patriotism, 2, 5–47, 133
and religion, 52–57, 67–70
and soul, 57–64
significance of its value, 39–42
Patton, 81
Pazzi, attempt to overthrow the Medici, 169–170, 171
Pazzi Conspiracy, War of the, 169–170
Personal identity, requirements of, 29–32

Personal security, importance of, 32–33
pessimism, moral, 42–44, 99–101, 101–107, 111–113, 116–118
Pius III, Pope, 189
Plato, ix, 11–12, 19, 61, 63, 65, 137, 139, 141, 143, 154
Plutarch, 61
political *virtù*, 8, 17, 19–22, 125–126
Pompey the Great, 181
Pontius Pilate, 67, 83–84
Prezzolini, Giuseppe, 66–67
Prezzolini-Berlin interpretation, 67–70
The Prince: final chapter of, 6–16, 57–58, 73–74, 75–76, 79–81
purposes of, 64–73

Reagan, Ronald, 2, 45–47
religion:
and morality, 2–3, 48–81
and patriotism and the soul, 57–64
refashioning in service of patriotism, 52–57
value and uses of, 49–52
remorse, 144–145
Remus, Romulus and, 53, 75, 116, 128–129, 193–194
Ricci, Luigi, 74–75
Ricordo ai Palleshi, 175
Risorgimento, 7, 51
Roman history, influence on Machiavelli, 12–14, 49–59, 67–73
Romulus, 9, 11, 21, 53, 54, 57, 75, 101, 103, 106, 116, 128–129, 136, 180, 186, 193–194
and Benner, 158
and Guicciardini, 152

Ross, W.D., 158
Rousseau, Jean Jacques, 158
Rucellai, Cosimo, 5, 59, 176
rule consequentialism, 93–95

Sartre, Jean-Paul, 84
Savonarola, Girolamo, 126, 128, 171–172, 184–186
Scipio Africanus, Publius Cornelius, 124, 196
seven deadly vices, 63–64
Sextus, 194
Sforza, Francesco, 6
Sherman, William T., 81
Sisyphus, Myth of, 28
Sixtus IV, Pope, 170
Socrates, 19, 26, 34
Soderini, Piero, 126–127, 128, 150, 173–175, 186–187
"Sons of Brutus" 72, 75, 84, 120, 129, 195
Soul, of Statesman, 1–4, 58–64, 71–73, 97–101, 101–107, 131–164
Spinoza, Baruch, 158
The Statesman, 11–12
Statesman, the Machiavellian
  and inner life, 1–4, 135–141
  and Machiavelli's clues, 132–135
  and relation of ruling and condition of the soul, 3–4, 58–64, 71–73, 97–101, 101–107, 131–164
  and state of mind, 146
  and worry about the condition of the soul, 141–143

strappado, 175–176
Strauss, Leo, 73–74, 75–76, 79–80, 137

Tacitus, 61
Tarquin the Proud, 194–195
Theseus, 6, 57, 101
Thucydides, 158
Titus Tatius, 128–129
tribal act consequentialism, 71–72
Truman, Harry S., 3, 107–110

values of Christianity, 49–52, 53–59, 67–70
Vettori, Francesco, 149, 150, 159, 176, 177
Villari, Pasquale, 7
Vincent, E. R. P., 74–75
virtù, 7–8, 8–9, 16–17, 18–24, 27, 31–32
Vitelli, Paolo, 182–183, 192
Vespucci, Agostino, 176

Walzer, Michael, 1–2, 83, 100–101, 108–109, 118, 135–136, 138
war, knowledge of, 28–29
War of the Pazzi Conspiracy, 169–170
Williams, Bernard, 85
Wooten, David, 74
world, nature of, 24–29

Xenophon, 158

zero-sum worldview, 24–29, 39, 41, 68, 71, 80
  and Guicciardini, 152, 155

www.ingramcontent.com/pod-product-compliance
Ingram Content Group UK Ltd.
Pitfield, Milton Keynes, MK11 3LW, UK
UKHW041950140426
5217IPUK00014B/725